For Rosemary —
with much
affection and
gratitude

Mercedes

Mc*[signature]*

"Sanest woman I've ever played."
The Madwomen of Chaillot, Dallas, 1975.
(Photo by Keith Nichols.)

The Quality of Mercy

AN AUTOBIOGRAPHY BY

Mercedes McCambridge

NYT
Times
BOOKS

Excerpt from Edna Ferber's previously unpublished correspondence and inscription, Copyright © Harriet F. Pilpel, Executrix and Trustee of the Estate of Edna Ferber; excerpt from *Who's Afraid of Virginia Woolf* by Edward Albee, Copyright © 1962 by Edward Albee, reprinted by permission of Atheneum Publishers; excerpt from "Blue Valentine" by Joyce Kilmer, Copyright © 1917 Harriet Monroe, from POEMS, ESSAYS AND LETTERS by Joyce Kilmer, reprinted by permission of Doubleday and Company, Inc.; article "Mercedes Takes a Case to Canine Review Board" by Bill Burrus, Copyright © 1967 *New York Post*, reprinted by permission of the *New York Post*.

Special thanks to: Lorimar Productions; Senator Adlai E. Stevenson Jr.; Walter J. Murphy; and Henry Kissinger.

Published by TIMES BOOKS, a division of Quadrangle/The New York Times Book Co., Inc. Three Park Avenue, New York, N.Y. 10016

Published simultaneously in Canada by Fitzhenry & Whiteside, Ltd., Toronto

Library of Congress Cataloging in Publication Data

McCambridge, Mercedes.
The quality of mercy.

1. McCambridge, Mercedes. 2. Actors—United States—Biography. I. Title.
PN2287.M12A297 1981 792'.028'0924 [B] 80-5780
ISBN 0-8129-0945-3

Designed by Sam Gantt

MANUFACTURED IN THE UNITED STATES OF AMERICA

If you can love me for what I am, we shall be happier. If you cannot, I will still seek to deserve that you should. I must be myself. I will not hide my tastes or aversions. I will so trust that what is deep is holy, that I will do strongly before the sun and moon whatever only rejoices me and the heart appoints. If you are noble, I will love you; if you are not, I will not hurt you and myself by hypocritical attentions.

Ralph Waldo Emerson, "Self-Reliance"

꙼

Doubt not, O poet, but persist. Say, "It is *in* me, and shall out." Stand there, balked and dumb, stuttering and stammering, hissed and hooted, stand and strive, until, at last, *rage* draw out of thee that *dream*-power which every night shows thee is thine own; a power transcending all limit and privacy, and by virtue of which a man is the conductor of the whole river of electricity.

Ralph Waldo Emerson, "The Poet"

꙼

PART One

1

࣫

*M*OST PEOPLE CALL ME Mercy. I like it. It's difficult to sound cross when you say that word. Shakespeare tells me that "The quality of mercy is not strain'd,/ it droppeth like the gentle rain from heaven/Upon the place beneath." But the quality of the Mercy that I am is *very* strained, and it droppeth like a ton of bricks onto everything into which it stumbleth.

The most amazing thing about me is that I am still here. Three-score years of bumps and bruises, and I am a slow healer. But I can still kick up a little dust from time to time, and in spite of the fumbles I've made, I keep tearing along, clutching the old beanbag!

People have always asked me if my name is real. It *is* a mismatch . . . Mercedes and McCambridge, but it *is* real! Obviously Doris Day is not real, Rock Hudson, Cary Grant, Pith Helmet, Sally Forth . . . these are not real, but if your name is what my name is, you would hardly have chosen it; it would surely have been thrust upon you. It is not a name which comes easily to mind. Once you get the hang of it, it "rolls trippingly on the tongue," particularly if you are adept at emphasizing middle syllables. Nevertheless, it is a weird name and has been somewhat of a nuisance.

One day in a New York taxi Jocelyn Brando and I were trying to talk about whatever it was that we were talking about. The driver wanted it his way. He kept butting in with little things like "Graffiti is native to Puerto Rico. There was no graffiti in Manhattan until Puerto Rico took it over." Jocelyn said, "Okay, driver. Thanks a lot." He jerked his head to look into the rearview mirror to see me. I guess he wanted me to say okay, too. Instead, he bellowed at me, "Hey, like what do you know? Back there, hey." So I said, "Hey!" He said, "I mean, like I know who you are! I seen you, haven't I? Sure I have, I seen *you!* Yeah, hey." So I said, "Hey," again. Jocelyn said, "Hey," too. Then the driver said, "You got a funny name, I mean, right?" I said, "Right." He said, "Don't tell me, I'll get it, okay? I'll get it, I know I'll get it." He slapped the steering wheel and yelled, "I got it! I knew I'd get it! It come to me right away! I got it." I had to say, "What is it?" And he said, warning me, "I told you it was funny, didn't I? You're Burgess Meredith!" I told him he was right, and that's how I signed his "little girl's" autograph book.

A lot of people call me Miss Sadie Cambric. I had a Hollywood agent from mittel-Europe named Kurt Frings, he never did get my name, the closest he came was Cheddahs Cameritz, which probably explains why I never became a superstar . . . how would that look in lights?

This name of mine has always called for explanation, but my post-adolescent parents would hardly have gazed on my wee newborn face and breathed, "Thou art Mercedes McCambridge," without having some idea of why they were doing such a thing!

It has long since become common knowledge—in press interviews, and in *Playbill* notes, and in obscure biographical summaries—that my paternal grandmother was Carlotta Mercedes Herrero, who was born in the Calesero district of Andalucía in Spain. The Calesero region was where all the colorful old gypsy wagons were built and painted. My grandmother's family transplanted the art to Mexico, to the city of Guadalajara, where my handsome Illinois dude of a grandfather went a-touring on horseback and met and married and carried off the beautiful Senrita Herrero, who grew old and died in Illinois and rests 'neath a stone that reads: "Carlotta Mercedes McCambridge."

All the people in my family run to the red-haired, fair-skin variety. I was born with black hair (and probably even a mustache), and everybody said I was the image of my Latin grandmother, so I was christened for her. I've always said to people when they compliment me on my accentless Spanish that my grandmother spoke true Castilian and I learned it from her. I, Carlotta Mercedes Mc-Cambridge!

Now, the problem with all of this about my Spanish grandmother is that not a word of it is true. It is all lies.

Back in Illinois, from the time I could remember, I was always embarrassed by my name . . . Mercedes McCambridge sounds like Tondelayo Rappaport. People have always wanted to know how I came by the strange name. I was never so dull, even as a child, as to say that my mother read the name in a magazine (the Mercedes part, I mean . . . she thought it sounded nice with McCambridge). My mother had an ear for that sort of thing.

So I merely invented a grandmother with a nationality to match my name. My actual grandmother was a splendid, a magnificent Irishwoman named Kate Weir McCambridge—and the irony of Fate is that while I never knew her (my first year of life was her last), people say I am very much like her; perhaps not so magnificent nor splendid, but older relatives say I'm the spit 'n' image. I'm sorry. It wasn't that I was denying her; it was that I was trying to justify my own incongruity.

I rather miss the Spanish grandmother. She got to be very glamorous. I could spend an entire evening describing the way she danced flamenco out on the Illinois farm, and how her valuable collection of tortoiseshell peacock combs and her lace mantillas and her rare eighteenth-century guitar were bequeathed unto me, and, weeping, I would tell about her only brother who was crucified upside down by Pancho Villa's men in the lobby of the Gran Hotel Ancira in Monterrey. I miss all that.

My brother's full name is John Valerian McCambridge because his father and mine, whilst a soldier in the Big One, was wounded at Château-Thierry. His sorrowing company had to press on without him (he was a PFC), and he was left in an old French abbey which had been converted into a field hospital. He was lovingly tended by an aged monk-nurse named Frère Valerian. My father vowed that his firstborn son would bear that revered name in honor of the Holy Man in faraway France.

And that, of course, is another lie. Valerian was just another of mother's fancy front-name preferences, and my brother got stuck with it. True, my father *was* shocked from the war, more from the hell of it than from the shell of it, but he never spent a single night in a French abbey, and he frowned on male nurses of whatever religious persuasion.

Perhaps I am making a mistake in revealing these truths. Until now my brother and I had a distinction. We had been romantically named in honor of noble and glamorous nonpersons. Now we are merely two more gaudily named middle westerners, like so many others in Wisconsin and Illinois and South Dakota . . . people called Callista and Olympe, Dania and Darlene, Veronique and Tiffany. I KNOW a Tiffany Goldberg, and I know just how she feels.

ે&

All my relatives knew that I was lying about how I came by my strange name, but all my relatives knew that I always lied about everything. When I was a little girl, they liked it. It had an appeal. They said it was a wonderful imagination! What happened? Nothing changed about me; I just got bigger. They were the ones who changed. One day, when I woke up as an old woman of six or seven, I found out I was no damned good. The night before, I had a wonderful imagination; I awoke a "nasty little liar." They all began to pray for my soul at that point, and they have never stopped!

I wish at least 50,000 Americans would stop trying to save me. I don't think there is another country in the world so hell-bent on "saving" as our country is. The land is overrun with them, and they're all after me. I am black and blue from being saved!

In a sense, I think it's regional. There are a lot of saviors in Ohio, for example; and Utah, of course, is noted for saving; and California is sticky with salvation—the occasional agnostic you run into out there thinks the stickiness is humidity, but it isn't, it's leftover salvation polluting the air. But the place were I am grabbed at most often is in the South. It's a shame because I like the South. I like to sit in the gazebo that William Faulkner built himself. Eudora Welty autographed a book for me. I have dangled my feet from the Tallahatchie Bridge where that terrible thing happened to Billy Joe. I have seen a star fall on Alabama. I have an Oscar because a no-good politician came from Louisiana. I have slept in Thomas Wolfe's bed in Asheville. A Texas university has given me an honorary doctorate. I've eaten hush puppies in Tennessee Williams's hometown in Mississippi, forty miles from where I observed sterile boll weevils being bred, and where I patted a cow whose side is made of glass so that students can observe her inner workings. I didn't look at *her*, but I will long remember the soft, bewildered eyes that looked at *me*. I do like the South, but I'm going to have to stay out of it. The Messiahs are multiplying like minks! Every time I go down there it gets worse.

A couple of months ago a benign lady in Little Rock touched my cheek and asked if I was ready to be "born again." I told her I thought I'd better die first and if she wanted to hang around for a while, I felt sure I could accommodate her and she could take it from there. She said I had to be washed in the blood of the Lamb, and since I had just ingested, with some effort, a typical ladies' club luncheon, I excused myself to stand closer to the air conditioner. They're persistent, these blood sisters. She gave me a tin medallion that looked like the top of a cat-food can. She said it was all I would ever need. The medallion was stamped with one word: "REPENT!"

In Fayetteville, North Carolina, it was suggested that a meeting be arranged for me with the town's most noted resident: President Jimmy Carter's sister . . . the one who arranged for poor "brief candle" Jimmy to be born again one day when they were walking together in a shady glen. I had seen her talking about it on TV. I declined the opportunity, none too diplomatically, I'm afraid. Bert Lance is one of that crowd, and he would have me believe, in his testimony before Congress, that God thinks it is okay to write bad checks. I'm not qualified to cope with such strange celestial bookkeeping.

In Monroe, Louisiana, in a motel, for God's sake, there was a knock on my door one morning. A sallow young man with a stack of *Watchtower* magazines wanted to know if everything was all right between me and Jesus, so I said everything was just swell; but before I could close the door in his sanctified face, he had turned cranberry color. I had been on my way into the shower just before his intrusion, and all I had in front of me was a bath towel. I presented to him a covered anterior, but there was a mirror on the wall behind me. He's probably telling about me in some gospel meeting, and they are all probably praying for me.

In Dallas, Texas, there is a powerful all-night radio station beamed from south of the border. On my way home from the theater I used to hear a commercial that was positively spooky. If you sent the station a dollar bill, you would get an autographed picture of CHRIST!

Most of the automobiles in the South have bumper stickers which read: "HONK IF YOU LOVE JESUS!" I have to fight against running them right into the ditch. Beaten-up broken-down campers proudly proclaim, "I FOUND IT." I can't stand those people. They've all got God in the back seat, and they're trying to get me back there, too. They all think of me as synonymous with sin. Sin never touched the South, and I've lived with it all my life. But so have a lot of marvelous people with whom I'd rather spend my time, and I have a feeling that in their company is where God and/or Jesus would rather be.

I have dinner with some remarkable men from time to time. I meet with them individually because I want all of their attention. I don't want to mix them up.

All of them have been dead for a long time, some of them for more than 2,000 years, but they come to life when they are with me, and my legacy from them, in their writings, is my private property. One of them, little old Seneca, whose words on the turned-down pages are smudged with mayonnaise and pizza droppings, puts all those southern go-to-glory folks in their proper place for sure. He said there is a great difference between a man who does not *want* to sin and one who doesn't know *how* to! I've laughed with Seneca about that many a night; sometimes in the middle of a McDonald's hamburger joint, where the other patrons wonder why I'm sitting there all by myself, slapping my thigh in glee at a book! Seneca and I know that it takes imagination to sin, it takes talent. I've never understood all the ranting about praying for forgiveness. In order to be forgiven . . . first, you've got to sin! The move to damnation must be made by the sinner. Unless, like all those desperate people in Dixieland, you are praying to be forgiven for that nonsense back in the Garden with the apple and the snake!

I just don't want to be saved anymore. I'm all worn out from it. The threat of salvation damn near killed me! I know I have thought about dying ever since I was old enough to realize I was living. I planned my own funeral when I was five. It continued to be one of my most elaborate and enchanting childhood fantasies. I am, by nature, a brooder. At best I am what Freud said *he* was—"a cheerful pessimist."

I remember one night in Arizona . . . Carefree, Arizona, which is ridiculous . . . Orson Welles was very angry with me. There is so much of Orson, and when he gets angry, it is formidable.

He was wearing his purple-towelling, circus-tent-size bathrobe. He wore it from early morning until late at night, when he never went to bed. Orson has never understood why some of us need to sleep. He doesn't. Once for five days he didn't. I did, and he'll never forgive me.

There he was in that ghastly robe, which in itself was something I found difficult. He obviously was wearing nothing else, except for his gigantic alligator slippers. I'm certain that the inner flap of the robe was secured by a tie cord somewhere in the region of his equator, but the robe's great outer flap kept doing just that—flapping. Nothing indelicate ever loomed, but I had the uneasy feeling that it could happen any minute. Not a pretty sight, I thought.

Anyhow, Orson was striding and snorting because a scene in the film was not going well. I wasn't even in the scene. I was huddled in a chair, off camera, probably trying to sneak a little sleep. Suddenly Orson boomed, "Look at you, look at you sitting there now!" I turned to see who was behind me who was catching this hell, and he bellowed, "No, you, Mercy, I mean *you.*" I asked him what the matter was *now.* With Orson something is always the matter. The terrible thing is, Orson is usually right. Even his mistakes are more right than they are wrong. So he was zeroed in on me, pouncing back and forth. I waited until the flapping robe stopped waving in front of me. Then he said, "You are three things sitting there. You are gloomy, you are intense, and you are thoughtful. Now stop all three!" I felt almost benevolent as I said, "Orson, I am one hundred percent Irish. I was born to be gloomy, intense, and thoughtful. Where would Eugene O'Neill have been—"

He didn't let me finish. He said, "It comes to this, doesn't it? We have Damien the Leper, Jude the Obscure, and now Mercy the Morbid . . . three sorry saints." Then he turned and addressed the camera crew and John Huston and the other assembled actors as he prated, as only Orson can, "Teresa of Ávila has written that a sad saint is a sorry saint," and in full flap, a gargantuan purple tornado, he stormed out into the desert night. But once again, Orson was right. "Mercy the Morbid," that's me.

꒰ꙸ

One September afternoon in London I lingered longer than the rest of the tourists in a particularly dark corner of Westminster Abbey. I had come on private business to this chapel called St. Andrew, and so I waited until I was alone except for a few weary and apathetic stragglers, and then, head bowed, I approached to pay my solitary homage to the greatest actress who had ever lived.

The yellowing, mellowing statue of Sarah Siddons is set atop a great marble block which must be almost five feet tall because her broad stone feet that rest upon it were of a height comfortable enough for me to rub my nose between her toes.

I read from a pamphlet: "This is Sarah Siddons, the most intellectual actress who ever interpreted Shakespeare. . . . She has never had an equal, nor will she ever have a superior." . . . Lord Byron said, "I refuse to see other actresses perform, having made and kept a resolution to see nothing that will disturb or divide my recollections of Siddons." . . . Coleridge wrote, "Thou, Siddons, meltest my sad heart." . . . Washington Irving said, "I scarcely breathe when she is on the stage. She works up my feeling until I am like a mere child." . . . King George III proclaimed, "She is the foremost example of genius in woman that England has so far produced . . . the noble sentiment of the public mind!" Of herself, she wrote, "I was an honest actress." I was weeping. I placed my hands on the stone folds of her skirt, and I prayed. To Sarah Siddons.

I asked that she intercede for me; that she beseech the Almighty that some semblance of her wisdom, her wit, her dedication, her energy, her compassion, her power and style, and, please God, her talent be bequeathed unto me, one bruised and disenchanted American thespian. And with that *de profundis* spent, I brushed my wet cheek against the cold stone feet of the Tragic Muse and "walked back to the hotel in the rain."

The damp twilight of late summer felt soft and muzzy. It was benevolent to me, an alien actress of no renown, weeping her way across London town.

I was weeping for the same reasons I have wept my life through. As much as I was grieving for my dead dreams, my lost hopes, I was grieving because of the certain knowledge that I would continue to dream, continue to hope. That awareness, for me, is monumentally sad. And as I wept in the London evening, I knew, as well, that under the quiet tears there lay a terrible rage.

I knew that I wasn't Sarah Siddons. There never was a chance that I could be Sarah Siddons, but I broke my back trying to be Sarah Siddons, and (the more fool I) I will go on dreaming of being Sarah Siddons until I die . . . at which time my tombstone will hardly read: "I was an honest actress." I deserve that epitaph, but I am not Sarah Siddons.

Never in a million years will I accept the lame excuse that Sarah Siddons worked harder than I have. Nor was she any less unbeautiful than I am. Gainsborough said while painting her, "Damn it, Madame, there is no end to your nose." Her eyes were too deep-set, dark-circled. So are mine. Her brow was low. Mine is nice and high. God knows what shape her teeth were in in her late-eighteenth-century time.

The claim that she "was the most intellectual actress who ever interpreted Shakespeare" is not all that marvelous. When I was eighteen and a sophomore in college, the critic of the Chicago *Tribune* wrote of my Viola in *Twelfth Night*, "the finest intellectual reading of Shakespeare I have heard by any amateur player." As for the critics and poets who wrote of her so glowingly, theirs was an era of gentility and sentiment. They weren't playing Christians and Lions in the theater the way our critics play. I blame Alexander Woollcott and Robert Benchley and Dorothy Parker for parenting the cutesy and cruel critics who carve up the theater we know now. These vicious ones are as lustful to be another member of the Algonquin Round Table as I am to be another Sarah Siddons.

However, I cannot believe that Sarah Siddons was any more gifted than Simone Signoret, Glenda Jackson, Kim Stanley, me, or Patty Duke. I DO believe that the way the cookie crumbles is a dirty rotten trick, and I am mad, hopping mad; hidden way down deep inside *I am* mad!

It turns out life is a bitch. I was not taught after this fashion, however. I was taught that God "counted every hair" on my head! Try that on as a *modus vivendi* and rush right out into life's busy highway and you are going to end up with no hair . . . no head! All the time I thought God was counting my every hair, He was probably working on the potholes on Jupiter.

During our one-to-one sessions, in our private vis-à-vis, when I confront God with His unfortunate oversight in not making me Sarah Siddons, I grant him that my name was better than hers at the start. She was born Sarah Kemble, a name in which there is no music, but then she married William Siddons. When you have said "Sarah Siddons," you realize you have made a commitment. Probably the most important contribution lazy, old, gouty William Siddons ever brought into Sarah's life was sharing with her the use of his name. Both my leftover husbands had nice enough names, but like the gentlemen themselves, they were not for me over the long haul. Yes, I give God full marks for not calling me Kemble, because if I had had to marry and live with William Siddons in order to call myself by his name, I think I likely would have had to drop a little something in his ale. From what I know of Sarah I'm sure she thought of it from time to time.

So my name is fine. I could become the greatest actress in the world with a name like that. I think names have a lot to do with it. I'll never know why Joan Crawford didn't keep her real name. Joan Crawford WAS a Lucille le Sueur; she certainly was never a Joan Crawford. You could believe that a Lucille le Sueur would strap her adopted children to the bedpost, but a Joan Crawford would have to be sitting in the solarium sipping Pepsi with Cesar Romero.

Poor old rotten-egg Joan. I kept my mouth shut about her for nearly a quarter of a century, but she was a mean, tipsy, powerful, rotten-egg lady. I'm still not gong to tell what she did to me. Other people have written some of it, but they don't know it all, and they never will because I am a very nice person and I don't like to talk about the dead even if they were rotten eggs.

2

HERE WAS NO POINT IN spending an entire afternoon of "color tests" with Joan Crawford staring me in the face. It was a farce, and a cruel one, because she had already decided that I would wear nothing but a heavy black, slightly modified nun's habit throughout the whole film. She knew that she would be costumed in finest gabardine jodhpurs, silken shirts, and, best of all (and most unbelievable), a diaphanous white chiffon gown which she would wear in the scenes on her horse and in the sequence where I was supposed to hang her. She had also already decided that my hair had to be dyed jet-black to contrast with her warm russet-brown, also a dye job.

The film was a western, *Johnny Guitar,* shot in Oak Creek Canyon

p 12

wind that ground the
Margo in *Lost Horizon*
what passed for Miss
appeared on the giant
n . . . Saint Joan with
while I looked like the
e explained by revealing
e as big a star as Joan
anybody to photograph
ong, long, long shots. If
e going to get any closer
ctures of people like Miss
ed interior light, you had
of them had to!
don't remember whether
off the balcony, tumbling
the canyon) my fall was
. He looked so funny in a
digo wig. Sterling Hayden
drag. However, until the
lcony is me. It is even me
ailing. I did the fall onto a
down. Then the camera
death way down there in the
of that sequence—i.e., Miss
Crawford's footage—w.. , back at the studio, in the
San Fernando Valley. The lighting crew painted the lustrously soft
light and shadows on the constructed indoor balcony against a canvas
sky, and when all was set, Miss Crawford was escorted from her
lavishly decorated dressing-room trailer, retinue surrounding her . . .
director, assistant director, second assistant director, script man,
secretary, costumer, wardrobe woman, makeup man, hairdresser, and
propman with sweat spray and spirits-of-ammonia ampules . . . the
spray for the skin's glow, the ampules for the eyes' tears because it was
a very emotional scene and noble leading ladies like Miss Crawford
don't kill people easily, even bad guys like me. You could tell on the
screen she was obviously very upset, but it was simply a question of
her or me, one of us had to go. She looked absolutely dazzling,
squeaky-clean and velvet-skinned, moisty-eyed. It was a dirty rotten
trick, it was.

But, back to the day of the color tests before the filming started. It was pure charade because Joan knew what she wanted and Joan knew she was going to get it. I'd never met her until that day. I felt I had a certain edge because a gentleman with whom she had, not long before, had some association, to the degree that she had given him gold cuff links, was now my husband. He isn't anymore, but he was when Miss Crawford and I met, and he had picked *me*. So there, Miss Crawford, so there! We stood facing each other in a state of social smirk . . . she the great star, and I the one in whose bedroom could be found a rather attractive pair of gold cuff links *and* a most attractive man to whom they had been given.

Of course we had little to say to each other, and color tests are long and tiring. You stand there while they drape bolts of material on you, and you endure the conferences between the costume and camera crews, and it's a drag.

To fill in the empty space, I guess, Miss Crawford suddenly extended one of her slack-covered legs and placed her foot against my middle. I couldn't believe it. She had kicked off her shoe, and there was her stockinged foot flat against my not-altogether-flat tummy!

She smiled at me. Joan Crawford had a truly sensational smile. Everybody in Hollywood has such gorgeous teeth, not a crooked fang among them. My dentist said capping my teeth would be a waste of his time and my money. He said it wouldn't make that much difference. I've had to live with variations of that theme all my life. My mother always recited the pathetic tale of my birth. Dr. Lennon wrenched me from her womb and said, "Mrs. McCambridge, this is the most beautiful baby I have ever delivered." At this point in the story my mother's voice began to quaver. She peered at me, trying to gauge what went wrong. That story always caused my mother great pain.

When I first went to Hollywood, MGM said my chief problem was flaring nostrils. They felt if we could get rid of that flare, I might stand a chance. Several hours were set aside in the makeup department to experiment on my nose. While I was waiting for them to begin, Ava Gardner walked in. She was so beautiful I wanted to die. I looked very closely, and I swear her nostrils flared, maybe not as much as mine, but there was a flare, I swear it. Then Elizabeth Taylor came in (this was way back when Michael Wilding was Mr. Elizabeth Taylor), and I had to face it. There was no point in trying to improve your appearance in a world where there was an Elizabeth Taylor. I thought about running all the way from Culver City to throw myself off the Santa Monica pier. I really should have, because the nose experiment was straight out of *Frankenstein*. I'm not a person who has nightmares, but that's because all of mine take place when I am awake.

They put me in a chair, in an almost-prone position. Two white-jacketed makeup men muttered over me. They were a team. One patted my face with talcum powder, the other man inserted two wide-tunneled paper straws in my nose, and they taped them to my cheeks. I was a walrus. Then together they applied the warm wax, having placed pads on my eyes for protection. It felt like having puddles poured on me. I could feel fingers mushing around in it. They spoke seductively to me . . . telling me to breathe normally. You bet! They nudged and pushed the goo as it began to cool and harden. By this time the molten wax was cement. I lay there, breathing through the straws. My lips seemed to have permanently sealed. Then they said they were going to take it all off. Oh, my God! I made a firm Act of Contrition. Tiny metal blades were sneaked under the wax, next to my skin, and zippz! it came off as easily as bubble gum does when you press a wad of it against itself. They said the talcum made it painlessly possible. Then they told me I could wash my face back in the ladies' makeup room.

I have yet to see the mask they made of my flaring nostrils. They told me to go home, and they would let me know what they decided. They never did. I never heard from them again. It's always been like that. Experts are only slightly interested in the way I look, and not for very long.

Anyhow, there was perfectly toothed Joan Crawford smiling at me with her foot braced against my navel. She said, "Look at my funny little feet." There's not a hell of a lot you can say at a time like that. I must have said, "Well, well, you're right. They sure are funny little feet." I was glad that she was losing her balance in that stupid position . . . she looked like a flamingo in a splint. She put her foot back on the floor, but she continued to look at it. She obviously expected me to concentrate on it, too. So I did. It was just a foot. I didn't think it was particularly funny, nor did I think it was particularly little. She went on and on about what happened to her feet from the time she came to Hollywood. She said as a young girl she wore size 4½B. Perfect model size. She waited for me to react. I think I said, "My, my, my!" Now she was quite serious. She said that "*all* that dancing in *all* those films" had spread her feet to their present size of 5½ and, sometimes, even 6! "Good heavens!" I cried. I almost cried, this was so silly. But she said that even now, at their most spread out, her funny little feet were too small for a woman of her stature. I don't know what I said to that, and I was glad when the whole nutty afternoon was over. It was easy for me to forget all about Miss Crawford's funny little feet until one night after we had been several weeks into the film.

I have great regard for stunt persons, and Helen Griffith was one of the best there ever was. She could make a horse do anything, and for me she rode (in a duplicate of my costume and in a black wig) a splendidly spirited mare, upon which she crossed a rock-bedded swirling stream straight into and through a waterfall which fell before the mouth of a cavern. The horse had to be blinded because it refused the headlong plunge through the cascading water. Helen Griffith brought it off with great style. I think it's the best shot in the film. Watching her, we were all terribly excited at the magnificence, and so was Helen. She was high for hours, and neither she nor any of the rest of us realized what was happening.

Helen's own riding boots were the taffy-colored, well-worn, suitably scuffed, modern cowboy kind. But they weren't right for the film, which takes place back in prerailroad days (which was what all the shooting was about . . . Miss Crawford was *for* the railroad, and I was *agin* it). Helen couldn't wear her own boots because I had already been photographed wearing proper old-fashioned black ones and her feet would have to match mine on the giant silver screen. So it was agreed that Helen would have to wear my boots for the waterfall stunt. She said they were a little tight around her calves, but she could stand it.

Naturally during the stunt Helen was drenched, and so were my boots on her feet. The boots had dried, Helen's legs had swollen, and she was in considerable pain. There was nothing to do but cut the boots away from her! That was done. BUT I had to wear those boots the next day, and that couldn't be done!

When a movie company panics, particularly out in the desert, it's like a raid on a whorehouse (I imagine!). Everybody flees, nobody was there when it happened, and nobody saw anybody do anything!

We could hardly hold up production for the time it would take to have another pair made back in Hollywood and then flown up to us. There were lots of boots in the cowboy store in town, in Sedona, but none that were old-fashioned. Someone suggested we drive into Phoenix and wake the curator of the Old West Museum; maybe there were proper boots on exhibit.

Then from out of the gloom, dashing toward us over the red sand from the supply-trucks area, came the most mincing member of our wardrobe crew. Being gay, he shouted gaily, "I've saved the day, dear hearts. Fear not, the problem is solved. I mean it's actually solved!" He flung a laundry bag down on the ground before us, and he did a little dance. He was very happy. Then he opened the drawstring of the bag and shook out a lovely pair of proper riding boots from it. Exactly like mine except they were mahogany brown. He said he could dye them black and they would be dry by morning, and he pinched both my cheeks and rubbed his nose against mine as he cooed at me, "You can just put them right on, sweetie. I mean *right on!*" Everybody was ecstatic. The cowards came out from behind the boulders, and we were a team again. Someone asked our happy little rescuer how he had managed to come up with the magic slippers, and he pushed at me playfully as he said, "They are one of several pair that were made for Miss Crawford, but she rejected them because they were a bit pinchy!"

Instinctively I willed every inch of my lower extremities to shrivel, shrink, diminish, but I knew I had to say it, and the sooner, the better. I told them, sorrowfully, about Miss Crawford's funny little feet that had spread from a perfect model size 4½B because of *"all* that dancing in *all* those films" to their present still-funny little size of 5½B. My companions were struck dumb, but not the wardrobe man. He roared! "Sweetie, please, I can't stand it! I mean I *really can't stand it!* It's too much! Just tuck one of your size seven tootsies in one of those glorious boots! Please, do it for me, sweetie!"

I did. Not only did the boots slip on easily, but even after they had been dyed (which causes shrinking), I found them more comfortable when I wore them over heavy white socks! My feet are neither funny nor little. They are size 7, and I will not lie about them in order to impress people. I lie about a lot of things in order to impress people, but I have not yet been reduced to telling tall tales about my long feet!

I really can't be bothered thinking anymore about Joan Crawford or Lucille le Sueur or whoever she was; I never wanted to be what she was, but I *did* and *do* want to be Sarah Kemble, or Siddons, and it doesn't matter about her feet.

3

ESPITE HER NONLYRICAL name, little Sarah Kemble had a professional edge on me. Her family, the Kembles, were a traveling theatrical troupe who performed in order to eat. My family, the McCambridges, never traveled anyplace, but they were certainly a theatrical troop, and they performed in such volatile fashion that they were usually too upset to eat!

I wish that I could take first grade over again. I should like to be able to select my own school and choose my own courses of curriculum. I should rule out reading and writing (my father taught me those things at home). I'd like to hang onto recess, but mainly I'd like to be inundated with exhaustive studies covering "The Situation of the Child [namely, me] in Connection with the Parent [namely, my mother]." Maybe my mother could have taken a course, too, a course corresponding to mine, from the parent's view.

Two such women, with their built-in diligence and determination, having been exposed at the outset to the proper education, surely would have united to form an alliance that would have altered history! If we had been taught, each of us, to run for the nearest empty furnace each time our tempers flared; if we had kept at constant availability our own vomitoria into which we could have spewn those molten tempers, there might well have been produced enough heat to warm a fair-sized city until doomsday! And we, the stokers, might well have understood each other; might well have sung a gentler song instead of flailing and fanning the flames that were already uncontrolled.

Mother's flame was brighter, I know that now. I can remember marveling at the woman's might as she read me still another riot act! If I had been watching such a display in a theater, I would have been star-struck at such raw serpentine majesty!

I think God miscalculated a generation. He was ahead of Himself in reincarnating Mrs. Sarah Siddons. He undoubtedly should have saved her for me, but He jumped the gun and gave her to my mother.

And my mother, blessed with the equipment, was not fated to use it except to her own detriment . . . and mine. Mrs. Siddons herself admitted that she was a "difficult" mother, particularly to her daughters Maria and Cecilia, both of whom were dead by the time they were twenty. Their situation was rather more involved than my mother's and mine. Mrs. Siddons and the two girls were having an affair with Sir Thomas Lawrence . . . all at the same time!

The nearest approximation to that sort of arithmetic in the relationship of my mother and me had to do with Sir Shane Leslie, the author and poet and dearly foppish fellow who had come to lecture at our college my freshman year. He watched me work as Rosalind and said he thought I should go to the Royal Academy to train. I brought him home to talk to my folks about it. My father was in Kansas City, but Mother was there . . . all there!

That night my mother was Mrs. Sarah Siddons—not the reincarnated, but the one and only original.

I am not sure to this day how much of it she planned, but it was dastardly effective. Mother's hair was, by God's grace and unfair prejudice, auburn gone bronze, and she had eyes to match. For Sir Shane Leslie's evening in our cluttered nest, my mother chose to function in an early-hypnotic state that would make the Mona Lisa look like a certifiable hysteric! She floated in and out of our little living room, into our little dining room, and into our little kitchen to fetch little cakes and little glasses of punch to our titled guest. She wore an amber-colored dress and her "really good" strands of amber beads. Just a lovely topaz wisp of a woman piteously misplaced on this crass planet of harsh realities.

The evening had been designated to discuss my future. It was startlingly clear from the goings-on that I wasn't about to have a future; I was lucky enough to have had a past. Who could have survived in a house with such staggering beauty? Sir Shane may have mentioned the business of my going to the Royal Academy, but it wasn't paid much notice. Mother drew Sir Shane out very lengthily and very flatteringly on the subject of Irish lakes. Mother sang "Galway Bay" to Sir Shane. Mother said she had studied with a star of the Chicago Opera Company until she had to give it all up for her family's sake. Sir Shane, now smitten, told her what a great loss it was. I might as well have gone to the movies. I really should have left the room at one point. Sir Shane Leslie said my mother had the most delicately beautiful ankles he had ever seen. That was true. He actually reached across the chair and held my mother's slippered foot in his hand, examining it as if it had just been discovered in King Tut's tomb!

No wonder Mrs. Siddons's daughters died in the flower of their youth. It was said that they died of pneumonia. Another opinion held that they each died of a broken heart because mama was lying in Sir Thomas's arms, but I believe the young ladies died from dazzle . . . sheer dazzle. It is most difficult to breathe in that kind of atmosphere. Thine own mother is using up all the oxygen; thou art left bereft in a vacuum. It is probably just as well that Garbo never had a little girl.

The unrelenting ache in my soul comes from knowing that if I had really wanted to go to the Royal Academy, my mother would have moved the earth to get me there. She might never have let me forget it, but she would have done it. And Mrs. Siddons would have, too, I'm sure. Mother had to steal the show. How can you be less than all your glow when an opportunity presents itself? Should you douse your own skyrocket because somebody else in the room is twirling a sparkler? My mother shone for Sir Shane!

I have seen my young mother play everything from Rosalind to Lady Macbeth. Iambic pentameter was not her meter. Shakespeare was not her source. Mother was never much for dialogue. She played in soliloquy, monologue, uninterrupted, inexhaustible, and mad as a hornet. Very impressive—cunning, vicious, pitiable, dangerous, and despairing—this woman ran the gamut from A to Z and back again, stooping to pick up a stray cat, lashing out at all who differed with her, giving everybody the shirt off her back, banishing all Protestants to hell, and praying all Catholics out of purgatory. (Mother believed that Christ and Mary were the only ones who had a direct nonstop flight to heaven. ALL other humans had to sweat it out in purgatory, IF they were lucky!)

Mother erased me from her life when I married the second time. This time, of course, outside the Church. I was dead to her. But when the first fruit from that union which she had deemed damned was born without life, I awoke from a drugged sleep and saw in the half-light of the hospital room a tired woman mouthing her prayers, fingering her rosary, praying for me and my dead babe. She had flown to Los Angeles from Miami. She had never flown. She dreaded airplanes, but she had to fill an empty space next to her daughter who was damned. In her eyes I was still damned. Had I been in a state of grace, in a matrimony that was holy, it would have been understandable that she would have risked her life in a flying ship to be at my side, but to have done it for one of hell's angels was true Christian endeavor.

In spite of my scars, inside and out . . . some still unsightly . . . the price I have paid and still pay because of my mother's "fury" is probably worth it, because mother had the nerve to be open about it. She, being the kind of woman she was, had no choice. Chekhov was surely writing about my mother when he told us that the "kitchen of life" is a narrow little room from which we must escape if we are to keep from doing harm to ourselves and everyone around us. My mother didn't spend very much time at the sink or stove, but the kitchen of life was her prison. There was no room for her passion. In the crises somebody always got hurt; never mortally but always deeply.

Sarah Siddons wrote near the end of her forty-year reign as undisputed queen of the London theater: "So often in my career I have got credit for the truth in my acting when I was doing nothing more than relieving my heart's own grief."

If my mother could have had a script into which she could have poured her rage, her fears and tears, I truly don't think I would ever have become an alcoholic, an attempted suicide, and latterly an emotionally adolescent senior citizen! I do not *blame* my mother, or her mother, or the Virgin mother of us all! BLAME is a meaningless jumble of letters forming a word that has no legitimacy. Everybody is at *fault*, but nobody is to *blame*. My mother did whatever she did whenever she did it because she had to.

Picasso told my first leftover husband the same thing. Bill, dear husband number one and father of our son, is a splendid writer (his latest book is *Modigliani*, and he is the most civilized but least earth-acclimated man I have ever known. His name is William Fifield (and Mercedes Fifield is nearly as dull as Sarah Kemble). This great Tolstoyan terror, to whom I was wed too soon, asked Picasso why he painted canvases that he himself did not understand, and Picasso said, "Simple! Why does anyone do anything? Because one cannot help oneself!"

Makes sense to me. How could my mother be reasonable about her emotions? It's mixing apples and kumquats, I think. In sheer self-defense I had to learn early on to hide behind a chair or run for the bathroom and lock myself in until Mother had finished her matinee or evening performance, or both.

It was lucky for me that I was such a good liar, even as a little girl. I was able to fool my mother . . . often. But not often enough. I know

now there were times when if she hadn't caught up with me, I would deliberately set things up so that she *would!* What's the use of executing a diabolical plot if nobody knows you do it? I don't remember my mother's ever catching me in the truth! Those times can hardly have been memorable. I remember well the lies! I lie so easily, so often, so well.

ટ્રે

I have always had a lot more trouble with my truths than with my deceits. It's always been hard for me to make people believe I am telling the truth. It has never been a problem with lies.

Robert Penn Warren, great man who wrote *All the King's Men,* for which I won an Oscar long years ago, said that "imagination is only the lie we learn to live by, if we are going to live at all." I'm very good at it . . . I lied to the Pope! I looked tiny Pius XII right in his sky blue eyes and lied. The Pope asked me what I was doing in Rome, and I couldn't say, in that gloriously ornate chamber with about fifty of the faithful . . . men and women all in black . . . with my hands full of religious articles to be papally blessed, I couldn't look at Christ's representative on earth and say, "I'm here with David Selznick, Jennifer Jones, and Rock Hudson to do a remake of *A Farewell to Arms.*" It was the wrong line in the wrong scene in the wrong drama. I told the Pope I was a tourist. I was just passing through.

My passionately Papist mother, had she known I'd lied to His Holiness, would have had a major stroke, and I feel certain that the last wave of her operative arm would have been spent in a wild whap upside my head! BUT, if I could have told my mother *why* I had lied to the Pope, she would have understood. The point is, I couldn't ever tell my mother anything. She couldn't wait for that. The fuse needed to be no more than warmed and the explosion hit the air. God, what a Medea she could have played!

Almost all the significant changes in our family life seemed to have something to do with the lies I told. But in looking back over this great distance, I don't know how I could have done differently . . . and lived! Mother needed my lies to protect her from killing me!

My closest friend when I was five was a sex maniac who was six. His name was Donald, and my mother thought he was cute. He was a sex maniac who thought all I wanted to do in life was play with his equipment in my grandmother's outhouse. I didn't mind a few minutes of this carrying-on from time to time, but Donald never wanted to do anything else. I told my mother I didn't want to play with Donald anymore, and she said I was just jealous because he was so good and I was so bad. I knew I had to let it go at that. To tell my mother that Donald had a lot of trouble to keep from taking his pants off every time he set eyes on me would have been inviting a spanking; isolation in the back bedroom; and hours of carping about how sharper than a serpent's tooth is a loose-living five-year-old daughter.

I tried to avoid Donald, but he was the only other kid around, and once we finished the outhouse foolishness, he might play other games with me and not act like a sex maniac at all.

Donald was adept at lying, too. Donald was actually every bit as mean and horrible as I was. Nobody believed it because he was cute, but I believed it. I knew it for a fact!

Our little town of Kinsman, Illinois (pop. 164), leaned itself against the main line of the Santa Fe Railroad. Oh, the glory of the *Santa Fe Chief* blowing through town like a tornado each evening! I'd already had my supper back at our kitchen table, but these people in that beautiful *Chief* were eating their supper while they sped along like lightning. You could catch glimpses of the white-coated waiters moving among the diners, and there were fancy little lamps on each table . . . every night I tried to see something more, something I hadn't been able to see the night before because the *Santa Fe Chief* went by my life so fast.

The Santa Fe Railroad allowed a few of its trains to stop in our town, but not often and always briefly. Sometimes they stopped only if they were flagged down by the stationmaster, Mr. Farrar. Mr. Farrar was the single most awesome figure of my early years, precisely because he had the power to bring a gigantic railroad train to a stop. Of course, the *Chief* and the other fancy trains wouldn't be caught dead stopping in our chintzy little town. Mr. Farrar was effective only with lesser locomotives. I really believed he did it all by himself. I was desolate when somebody told me, years later, that Mr. Farrar's magnificence was purely window dressing. It was company policy for him to get out there and wave his flag like that, but with his telegraph key in the station, he had already notified the previous station stop that there would be a passenger pickup in our town. The train was going to stop anyhow, Mr. Farrar was just out there making a fool of himself; but I didn't know that, and I'm glad. I should have preferred never knowing the shoddy truth . . . a child *needs* to see a little man with a warty nose step right up and wave a tattered red flag and thereby bring to a steaming halt the whole Industrial Revolution. I've had to do with a couple of matadors in my time . . . and theirs . . .

one in Mexico, one in Spain. I have always thought of them in kinship with Mr. Farrar! *Olé*, Mr. Farrar. ¡*Olé!* Stop that fuming monster in its tracks and strut away like a king! ¡*Olé!*

At the time of our crime my sexy partner was seven and I had become six! One of our favorite mischiefs was to climb one of the old fruit trees on the far end of Mrs. Heffley's garden to see if we could watch her being crazy. Mrs. Heffley was our town's crazy lady. Every little town has to have one. Ours was a widow lady who lived in a falling-down house smothered by bushes and shrubs, who kept herself from starving to death by raising chickens. I think now it is safe to speculate that she drank a little. And of course, why not? Anyhow, with or without alcohol, she DID carry on a bit. Always at night, always in pitch-blackness, not a glimmer of light from her house, she wailed, is what she did; she wailed long and loudly. I could hear her from my bed, and her house was halfway down the road from ours. It wasn't every night; sometimes weeks went by, but sooner or later it was cuckoo time again. My nasty little boyfriend and I loved it. We had a witch, a crazy lady, and Halloween was something we could count on as an ongoing feast! It always came as a surprise. Neither he nor I was allowed out at night, but on "mornings after," as soon after the crack of dawn as we could make it, we would be hunched on a branch of one of Mrs. Heffley's big old crab apple trees, trying to see what lunacy was left from the night before. We might see her standing over a washtub full of blood; we might see the bones of all the dead people she had dug up from our cemetery; we might see the two old cows she had skinned alive to make a cowhide blanket for her bed. We might see all that stuff. We never did, but we might! It was fun to sit in the tree and make up more stuff we might see.

And then the day came when we could finally get even with her. There was nothing about which we had reason to "get even" with Mrs. Heffley. We were just determined to do it, and when we saw our chance, we grabbed it.

Mr. Farrar had "spilled the beans" when we dropped by the railroad station to "chew the fat" (as he called it and as I never understood it). Mr. Farrar said that Mrs. Heffley had bought a ticket for the afternoon train to Coal City and "would not be coming home until tomorrow." He said she had to attend a wake that night and the funeral in the morning.

It still astounds me that two little people whose aggregate years of life were thirteen (barely) could latch onto such an innocent circumstance and, within a few hours, successfuly destroy an old woman's livelihood, shock an entire town, and still show up at church on Sunday, sweet and clean and full of grace! Amazing! My cohort-in-crime apparently had no trouble dismissing it from his conscience because he later purchased the very property on which his little-boy feet had jumped up and down in glee at the scene of collected gore. He must have forgotten completely. I still shudder over my part in it.

We decided the best thing to do was to lie around in the grass next to the road outside Mrs. Heffley's house. We would wait there for her to come out. She would lock her front gate and proceed to the railroad station. At first we had planned to sneak along behind her, but then we thought it would be better if we actually escorted her to the station. Kids who walk along with you and make nice conversation, even carry your suitcase, would hardly be kids who would shortly ruin your year's profit.

We actually stood alongside the train, grinning little hypocrites, waving good-bye to Mrs. Heffley as the train eased her out of sight. Then we casually ambled over the tracks and down the road to Mrs. Heffley's house. We made certain we were not seen as we shinnied ourselves over her backyard fence. We had broken into the vault. The clusters of Rhode Island Reds and white Leghorns were pecking away at the feeding tins, in constant scolding cluckings . . . doing best what all good henpeckers do. Over at the water trough some roosters were met in horny conclave. Mrs. Heffley's worldly goods seemed unaware of our intrusion. I think few forms of life hold humans in greater scorn than chickens do. Mrs. Heffley's chickens didn't even bother to look up. My friend and I had a short spell of indecision. We didn't want to open the gates and turn them loose . . . they probably wouldn't want to leave . . . they were probably satisfied to stay right where they were. All they really had to do was eat, make love, and lay eggs. What could the outside world have to offer that was a better deal? Granted their end was inevitable, death by wringing of the neck, but good heavens, they might slip in the bathtub and end up the same way. No, we wouldn't turn them loose, and we surely weren't going to carry any of them away with us. We really didn't want *them* any more than they wanted *us*. But we were determined to "get even" with crazy Mrs. Heffley while she was out of town, so we would have to do something.

I will accept the blame for our ultimate action. I was the one who spotted the chicken coop with the setting hens lined up like tea cozies drowsing on their nests. Beneath their fluffed-out feathers, all warm and browning in the straw, were the thin-shelled eggs full of nearly born chicks. A rough estimate of that entire generation of baby fowls would be, say, almost 200. We killed them. We killed them all.

It wasn't easy to chase the mother hens off the nests. We did it with sticks, but mother hens are vicious when their chicks are being stolen. One mama flew right at my face and attacked me. I still have a hole in my chin from her sharp beak. They all made wild and terrible noises, and feathers flew as we tumbled nest after nestful of warm brown eggs into pails and then ran out into the open chicken yard and flung them against the side of the old gray barn-shed. We were maniacal and frightened and crying and dangerous. A terrifying juvenile orgy. Eggs were spattered all over; the wee, wet-with-albumin, miserably ugly fetuses, naked and veined and scrawny and dead, covered the dirty wooden planking around the barn. The barn walls were frescoed with dried deep-yellowed yolk and stringy gluelike white stuff. I began to throw up, and we got too scared to stay there, and we ran to the fence, vaulted it, and took off for the railroad tracks and ran out of town—on the 1am, forever—crying and mortally afraid. A few months later my family and I moved to Chicago.

❧

If one were a small-town chicken killer, the old South Side of Chicago was not a bad place to hang out. Those were the days when whole gangs of criminals were next-door neighbors and pew renters at mass. I seemed to fit right in. I assumed an air of decency. I became known as a nice little girl at the candy store and delicatessen. For a few months there was a good chance that my ill-spent youth was behind me, but when I was seven, it happened again.

A holy Bride of Christ was the motive for my first South Side Chicago crime. Her name was Sister Rita, and she taught third grade. She didn't want me in her class because I was only seven. She said, "Sevens belong in second, not in third." Thanks to my father, I had learned to read and write when I was five. I entered first grade down in the country, zoomed right along into second grade when I was six and a chicken killer, and now I was in third grade. I was seven, and Sister Rita didn't like it, but her mother superior had plunked me into an empty desk in Sister Rita's room and that settled that.

Sister Rita had a neurotic aversion to left-handed people. I happen to belong to that group. Sister Rita was determined to deactivate my left hand. She expected me to let it dangle uselessly at the end of my arm. I, of course, refused. One of my mother's more interfering sisters insisted that a left-handed child stammers for life if forced to "change." She said that one's eyesight was also severely lessened. This nun wanted to turn me into a gibbering myopic idiot. Never, Sister Rita, never in a trillion years!

I would arrive in the mornings with the other third graders, all of us in proper uniform dress. Immediately after the nine o'clock bell, which sounded like a prison-break alarm in a Jimmy Cagney movie, we all rose for the prayer invoking the everlasting watchful eye of our celestial tattletales, our Guardian angels, "Oh, Angel of God, my Guardian dear, To whom God's love committest me here. Ever this day be at my side; to light and guard, to rule and guide. Amen." Then my Guardian Angel and I would squeeze into my seat, and Sister Rita would march toward me while she twisted a man-sized white handkerchief into a long kind of rope. I would have to hold out my left arm so that she could circle my wrist with the freshly laundered lasso. She would tie a single knot on the top side of my wrist, always saying she *trusted* it wasn't too tight. From somewhere in the folds of her endless black skirts she would bring forth two diaper-sized safety pins, open them, then stick them between her teeth and hiss at me while she told the rest of the class to stop their giggling . . . that it wasn't my fault I was left-handed and she was certain that the grace of God and her patience would soon make me right. Handed, that is. They all laughed at her stale old hissing joke, during the telling of which she was pinning each end of the white rope to a section of my pleated skirt with the gigantic safety pins.

She appointed the two students flanking me as her spies. If they saw me so much as attempt to use my left hand, they were under orders to snitch! And they loved it . . . never missed a trick! I felt like a one-armed witch in Salem, publicly ridiculed, about to stutter and go blind.

My right hand flopped like a dying fish when I tried to write with it. Day after day my writing tablet was wrinkled by tears of deep humiliation. I stood it as long as I could, and then I quit. I had come to the end of my formal education, never to go further than the first month of the third grade.

Our apartment was within sight of the school playground. Each morning, having cheerily left my mother on the third floor, I would crouch unseen down in the vestibule of the building and peer out at the playground until it was clear. That meant the prison-break bell had sounded and Sister Rita and my classmates were closeted in room 16.

The next few minutes were dangerous because my mother might be looking out of our windows upstairs and she would see me sneaking down the street in the wrong direction. I walked sideways up against the walls of the other houses in the hope that she wouldn't be able to see me. Once around the corner all was well. I was sucked up into the limbo world of Sixty-third Street . . . a fine place for a seven-year-old left-handed exile to lose herself. From 9:00 A.M. until five minutes to noon, I would wander the length of the lightless tunnel under the el from Cottage Grove to Stony Island Avenue. This academic hiatus of mine lasted for two full weeks, and in that time I memorized every shopwindow and its contents all along Sixty-third Street on both sides. It was only late September, and the usually disastrous Chicago weather was pleasant, and I sang to myself and languidly observed all the urban squalor and hubbub.

At about eleven-thirty every morning my feet were usually tired, but there was a narrow brick ledge rimming the lower edges of Walgreen's drugstore windows. It wasn't a wide enough ledge to sit on, but I could hunch my bottom against it, and by bracing my heels against the pavement, I could at least give my toes a rest. Besides, Walgreen's had a big clock that was always right. It gave me a signal at four minutes to twelve to beat it like hell for home.

Once inside the vestibule door of our apartment house, I would crouch and peer again at the schoolyard down the street. The first pupils to drift out into the playground were my all-clear sign. I would hum a happy little tune, skip upstairs, and bounce brightly into our apartment, calling out, "What's for lunch?" Mother would ask me how school went that morning, and I would tell lies until it was time to put my sweater back on and go back down into the vestibule to crouch and peer until the schoolyard was again empty. Then I sneaked out for my afternoon of vagrancy and dereliction.

From one o'clock until five minutes of three I went to the University of Chicago. It was only a few blocks away, on the other side of the Midway Park area. It was very beautiful there. Pretty bells in the carillon played for me. Sometimes I did dances to their music on the forecourt of Mitchell Tower. There was never anybody there but me. It made a wonderful dance floor. Sometimes people asked me why I wasn't in school. They were nice, but they were curious. I told them that I had been sick with an ear infection and the doctor said I shouldn't go back to school until it stopped draining . . . maybe next week. I wasn't sick enough to stay in the house, but I was sick enough not to go to school . . . until next week. Maybe . . . If the draining stopped.

I was having a splendid time altogether. I didn't care if I never wrote another word . . . left- or right-handed. Sister Rita could find herself some other handicapped child to pick on . . . I was free! Until five minutes to three, when the hightailing for home and mother began again. My mother would ask me if I didn't want to go out to play, and I would tell her that I would rather not because the neighborhood kids all talked dirty and stole stuff from the dime store and I would rather stay in my room and play my flute or say my rosary.

But the day came, as the day had to come!

Nosy old Sister Rita telephoned my mother one afternoon. Where was I? she wanted to know. Was I sick, had I been in an accident? (She didn't give a damn if I died; she just had to call as part of her job.)

Mother told Sister Rita she obviously had me mixed up with another little girl because, my mother told her, I had been at school every single day and I always came home with all the funny little stories about what had taken place in class!

I admire my mother's ability to maneuver battle scenes. She could always save up enough ammunition to wipe out an entire legion. I could never do that! I take aim and fire with all the force of a cork in a popgun!

Mother said nothing that afternoon when I breezed in. I told her all about what happened in assembly and how many nickels we had in our fishbowl for the starving children in India. Mother let me rattle on . . . and on! Oh, boy!

Next morning my father didn't go off to work. I DID go off to what *I* thought that *they* thought was school. It was raining . . . hard. I wore my Red-Riding-Hooded rain cape, but I found it more comfortable over on Sixty-third Street to stand in a doorway of a shop until I thought I looked suspicious, and then I would have to flit to the next overhead shelter. I kept fairly dry that way. I had just settled into a cozy corner under Corbett's shoe store canopy when I saw him! I merely turned my head, and there he was . . . in his brown raincoat . . . with his black umbrella . . . *my father* . . . my one-and-only father . . . handsome Irish dog that he was . . . *there he was!* And for me, the Irish jig was up! My father took me home; my mother whipped me; I locked myself in the bathroom and dabbed iodine around my mouth and ran out into the parlor, shouting that I had gulped the whole bottle. My mother started to call the ambulance and the police, and I got scared and told the truth, and soon after that we moved to another parish, where I wrote with my left hand.

Every time, without fail, that I play Amanda Wingfield, the mother in *The Glass Menagerie*, I replay so much of my mother's life with me. The scenes between Amanda and her daughter, Laura, are nearly identical with those my mother and I performed in "real life." Act One, Scene Two, is, in its entirety, a scene between those two women. The mother, psychotically angry, has found out that her daughter has been DITCHING school and has been lying about it! I fly around that stage as my mother, as Tennessee Williams's mother, maybe as everybody's mother; and I *drain those lines dry*. There is always a fine catharsis for me in that scene. I can be just as enraged about *my* ungrateful, humiliating little snip of a daughter with her lying tongue as my mother was with *me*, and somehow, it's a way of getting even. That's what Sarah Siddons meant about truth in acting being the relief of a hurting heart. I can holler just as loud as you can, Mother, and my stage daughter has to take it just as I did. Hooray for both of us, Mother! We both know how to grab hold of an emotion and shake it until it screams for Mercy! Mercy. That's me.

4

à▪

I WON'T LET MYSELF THINK WE had to move again merely because I was a liar. That may have been a contributing factor, but we moved a lot anyway. Mother enjoyed moving, and my father didn't care. I move quite a bit myself. A Freudian friend of mine says it's insecurity, but Billy Rose said that was a lot of eyewash. Billy said only a tree has roots; a man has legs and is supposed to use them, not dig them into the ground in one spot. Man should move. Billy lied a lot, too. He had a house on

Ninety-third Street with fifty-four rooms! That's a lot of digging in one spot.

I reformed after the school ditching, and it lasted for almost four years. After Sister Rita, all my other Sister-teachers left my left hand alone, and I found my law-abiding place among my peers, more or less. I'm sure there were misdemeanors of minor importance, but nothing really rotten. I even strove in those behaving years from seven to eleven for a wistful sort of sanctity. At my confirmation I chose the name of Agnes because that child-saint was burned at the stake for her religion. I didn't really want to grow up as a nun and have to be like them all my life, but if the nuns all got together with the Pope and decided to burn me when I was twelve, it had a certain appeal for me. I knew my place in history would be assured and I would be relieved from sixty-or-something more years of getting up and going to bed and putting food in one end of me and out the other, and washing hair and peeling carrots and seeing dead cats on the highway, and knowing my sins had driven the nails into the five wounds of Our Lord and I went right on sinning anyway. There have been no more than a few times when I have really believed that life is worth all that . . . day after day.

I have, for years, had the privilege of playing in Lillian Hellman's *The Little Foxes;* naturally I play Regina because everybody thinks of Regina as being a mean bitch . . . and therefore, of course, they think of me! I don't think Regina is a bitch. I think she is a wondrously vital and gifted woman, clever and quick and impatient with fools. I think audiences feel threatened by characters like Regina, and that's why they call them bitchy. In a great scene in this great play, dear drooping drunken Birdie, wilting little southern flower, says, in her long beautiful speech, that she has never known a full day of happiness, "never a single whole day." Dear tipsy Birdie, nobody EVER has a single whole day of happiness. Happiness is never a whole day's worth, Birdie. Happiness is a flutter-by.

Anyway, we didn't have to move again until my unborn sister died. My mother felt we had to get out of that apartment because it would always remind her of the dead baby. I argued with Mother about that. I didn't see how an apartment could remind her of a baby who had never lived there. I really didn't want to leave the neighborhood; I liked it. I'd stopped running for a little while, and it felt good. But my mother cried so much about the baby that she was getting mean anyhow, so we packed up and left . . . again.

When *I* cried about the dead baby, my mother told me to stop. She said I was a big girl now, I was eleven. Mother didn't know why I was crying, and I couldn't tell her. It was another one of those things "I could never tell anybody . . . ever."

When I was ten, Angela McGuigan, who shared a cloakroom hanger with me at school, and who knew everything there was to know long before anybody else ever knew it . . . Angela told me where babies come from. I never hung my coat on her hanger again, and I began, from that time, to think of myself as adopted. What Angela said had to take place between a mother and father before they could *become* a mother and father could never have happened to the two people who said they were my parents. No! No, it had to be two *other* people, who were killed in an accident, who gave me, their child, to two people who really didn't know each other well enough to do what was necessary to have a child of their own. That's the only way it could have happened for me to be living with these two people, who were only trying to give me a good home, but who never did what Angela McGuigan said! These two people, every morning during Lent, went to Mass and Holy Communion! These two people never even kissed each other!

Feeling that way about what Angela McGuigan said, I could hardly handle well what happened a year later. One night, when I was sleeping, my aunt Noonie, who had been staying with us because my mother had bad pains, woke me up. She seemed very nervous. She was shaking me, and her breath, on my face, smelled that way people's breaths smell when they have been asleep . . . sour and spoiled, brown-smelling breath. She said my mother was sick and had to go to the hospital right away.

My father had been in St. Louis for a week. Aunt Noonie and Mother and I were the only ones at home. I asked what was wrong with Mother, and my aunt said she had cramps . . . bad cramps! I told Aunt Noonie Mother often had bad cramps but she didn't have to go to the hospital. All we had to do was put a hot-water bottle at her back. My aunt Noonie told me to shut up and go get a suitcase! I told her that the suitcases were all locked up in a room down in the basement. I didn't know where the key was. My aunt dragged her own suitcase out of my closet and dumped what was left in it onto my bed and threw the suitcase at me, yelling, "Pack the damn thing, will you? Just pack it, for God's sake."

She ran from my room because we could hear my mother crying: "Hurry, Noonie, hurry, for God's sake." They were both yelling "for

God's sake," and I didn't know what they wanted me to pack in the suitcase, so I started taking Noonie's clothes out of my closet and folding them. Noonie came running in with Mother's good bathrobe and her old slippers and three of her nightgowns. Noonie said she would be back with cold cream and a toothbrush.

It was about one-thirty in the morning . . . cold . . . hard . . . hard Chicago snow stuck to the ground outside . . . bad, nasty night.

I wanted to see my mother, but Aunt Noonie told me to *"stay out of that room!"* She was getting very angry . . . about everything. We had a piercingly loud doorbell, and just then it rang . . . several short harsh jabs. Noonie said it must be the cabman she had called, and she told me to push the buzzer which would release the door downstairs so that the cabman could come upstairs to carry my mother down! Carry my mother down! What was wrong with my mother? Why did she have to be carried? I was following Noonie around, trying to stay out of her way (because by this time her frenzy was such that she was physically threatening to anything in her path). I just wanted to know what was wrong with my mother. At one point Aunt Noonie stopped, wheeled around, and snorted at me: *"Your mother is losing the baby!"* Meanwhile, the strange taxicab man had wrapped my mother in a blanket from her bed and was carrying her down the stairs. She was moaning horribly and saying the Hail Mary. Aunt Noonie followed the cabman, holding up the dragging blanket. She had thrown the suitcase at me to carry downstairs. I had only my nightgown on; no shoes, no robe, no nothing. There was ice on the sidewalk going out to the taxi. My bare feet felt as if they were stuck to the ice. I was crying so hard I didn't even know I was freezing. The cabman got Mother into the front seat with him, and Aunt Noonie got in the back and took the suitcase from me. My mother saw me standing there and shouted through her moans, "Oh, my God, she'll catch her death," and the taxi drove off. The street was black-night dark. Our regular streetlamp had been busted for weeks. It was cold, so cold. I thought my tears must be icicles. I ran for the door of our apartment building, and it was locked! I was locked out! I could be dead in ten minutes, and they would find me here in my nightgown! Oh, God! I couldn't seem to get enough breath inside me! The air was so sharp and cold that it seemed to enter my lungs in little bits and pieces!

It was the middle of the night. The only other doorbell was the Sandefers, and they were in South Carolina at her sister's house. I was alone in front of a locked, empty building, and my mother was being taken to a hospital to lose a baby I didn't even know she was having! There wasn't a single light in any of the other houses on either side of our street. There was only one thing I could do, if I didn't freeze to death before I could get it done.

I started to pick my way across the snow-packed ground to the tiny basement window on the far side of the building. I might be able to squeeze through if I could break it open. Of course, it would be locked . . . but it wasn't! It opened easily, and I slipped through, out of the Arctic into the hot blast from the furnace. When I was closing the window, I saw some dark marks on the white snow . . . dark red. My foot was bleeding. I must have torn it out there on something. There was no pain, but it was bleeding hard. Uncontrollable crying is truly blinding, and I groped my way across the filthy basement floor, touching only the heel of the bleeding foot to the ground as I hobbled up the wooden steps to the first floor, and that damned damned door was locked! I pounded against it. I cried for help for a very long time. My foot was now hurting terribly. I was so frightened. I couldn't see where the wound was on my foot because it was all dirty. The blood had stopped, but maybe that meant blood poisoning had set in and the foot would presently fall off. There was a filthy old toilet that hadn't been used for God-knew-how-long. I held my foot suspended in the grimy bowl and pulled the rusty old chain. I flushed it several times and then realized I hadn't anything to bandage the foot with. I tried to tear my nightgown with my teeth. I couldn't. I took the whole gown off and tied it in a big bulgy mess around my whole foot. I was now naked. It made everything much worse. My nightgown was a kind of shield. Now I was exposed to the dank walls of this cellar.

The great flatulent furnace in the corner with all its asbestos-wrapped pipes seemed to be staring at me. I limped up the stairway and huddled against the damned damned locked door. I banged my head against it for a long, long time. It hurt to do that, but I felt it kept me from flying out of my skin. I called out to God. "God," I cried, "if you can hear me, I promise if you get me out of here, I'll take my final vows! I promise I'll enter the convent on my sixteenth birthday." In no more than a few minutes, from above, I heard the voice! It was calling me by name. "Mercy," it called, "Mercy, where are you, kiddo?" I was surprised that God would call me kiddo . . . only my uncle Alf called me kiddo.

When I heard him calling me, I called back, and we met, face to face, at the little basement window, my uncle Alf and his naked niece! My aunt Noonie had phoned him from the hospital and told him to get over to our place as fast as he could and to bring a blanket. He saw the blood in the snow, and when he saw me, all of me, he was convinced I had been molested. I showed him my nightgowned foot and explained the blood . . . all of this from within the modesty of the nubby blanket he had brought for me. He took me home with him in his new blue Buick. I still didn't have anything on my feet but the nightgown bandage so Uncle Alf carried me into the house. I told him it had been a horrible night. My mother had been carried out of a bed in a blanket and placed in a car, and I had been carried out of a car in a blanket and placed in a bed!

Uncle Alf spent what was left of the night at his kitchen table drinking beer. I slept in a pair of his pajamas on the pullout bed in the parlor. Before I fell asleep, I called out to him to wake me if he heard anything about what was happening to my mother. He said we wouldn't know anything until Aunt Noonie got home, and then she would tell us everything. Uncle Alf never answered anything on his own. People used to ask him things, but he would always refer them to Aunt Noonie. People spoke of them as one entity. "Alf 'n' Noonie," people would say . . . and the emphasis was always on the Noonie; Alf was never more than a preliminary. So he spent most of what was left of most of his nights sitting at his kitchen table, drinking beer. But if ever I am again naked and locked out in the snow with a bleeding foot, I will call for God, and Uncle Alf will come. I can count on it.

I was awakened by Aunt Noonie's harsh voice giving Uncle Alf holy hell for having found me with no clothes on. He was trying to tell her that all the clothes I had were on my injured foot. Aunt Noonie was not noted for listening.

I rolled up the arms and legs of Uncle Alf's pajamas and went out into the kitchen. Aunt Noonie began to cry when she saw me. "Oh, your poor mother," she wailed. I was ready for her to say that Mother was dead. Aunt Noonie said the baby was dead. Mother was okay, but "it" was dead. The doctor said "it" couldn't possibly have lived because "it" weighed less than two pounds and was too premature to survive, so "it" died. I had to ask if "it" was a boy or girl. Aunt Noonie said "it" WOULD have been a girl. Would have been? I didn't know how much or how little that meant. Did it mean that if a baby weighed only two pounds, you couldn't really tell yet if "it" was a boy or a girl? Did it take longer to tell if "it" was a boy? Aunt Noonie said that she had a splitting headache and was going to sleep right through Mass, even if it was Sunday, and that Uncle Alf should call her at eleven o'clock because the body had to be taken to the funeral home. The body . . . the two-pound body? I whispered my questions to Uncle Alf, but he said I would have to ask Aunt Noonie when she woke up. He wanted to make me french toast, but they were out of syrup. I went back to the pullout bed and wept for my dead two-pound sister who would have to be taken to a funeral home. My geography book weighed three pounds!

My father phoned from St. Louis to tell me to be a good girl. He would be home in two days, and in the meantime, I should take good care of Mother for him. I said yes, but it was long distance, and I'd have had to explain to him how I couldn't take care of Mother while she was in the hospital because children weren't allowed to visit in the hospital. I just said yes to my father. There have always been those times when I have just decided to say yes about everything—to everybody. The decision usually comes at the times when my whole world seems stupid. When I can't make sense out of what people are saying to me, when things that are happening around me are in direct opposition to the things that were supposed to happen, it has been my pattern to sit down and start saying yes, to everybody, about everything!

At eleven o'clock Aunt Noonie called the funeral home and was told that the "remains" were already there. "They" were being held. Two pounds of "remains"? Where was the *rest* if there were only "remains"? How much of "her" was left for them to "hold" there?

Aunt Noonie chose to go into a serious emotional decline right there in the middle of her own kitchen. I'll never know how the whole thing turned out to be Uncle Alf's fault, but it did. Uncle Alf, in conjunction with all men everywhere, had really loused up the whole wide world. They had all the fun, and women had all the pain. Watching Uncle Alf as she stormed over him, I couldn't believe that he had had any fun of any kind for a long, long time. Once in a while during her lengthy tirade he would look up at me and nod as though he had just seen me passing him on the street. But through most of it, his shoulders drooped, his head was bent in penitential despair, and I prayed he wouldn't fall asleep because if he did, Aunt Noonie would kill him! Every time she got mad, he nearly got killed or something terrible happened to him. Once she stole his upper plate and hid it on him for three days. He couldn't go to work or anything. He just stayed in the house and hunted for his teeth. Aunt Noonie had cut a hole in the bottom of a loaf of rye bread and had stuffed the upper plate in there and then wrapped the loaf in wax paper and put it in the icebox. Uncle Alf swore that it was harder for him to "talk straight" after that. I myself thought he whistled more.

e to call my mother. She said it idn't want to believe that, but I'd to everybody, about everything, giving me fair warning . . . if e for a while, I would be sorry, to the hospital to be with my ld have to go through with the knew that he knew we had both out everything.

land Avenue in a depressing dark s looked as if they were sweating. aneled reception hall, where we Boston fern suspended from the ought, exactly above the only oom. If that thing ever fell on lace could it happen? We sat in two silent acquiescents to Fate. rtaker, at Mass on Sundays. His le, second from the front, right atron of lost causes. Birds of a red for the Mr. Burke I now saw ite coat like a doctor in a movie. ven o'clock Mass to meet us and ood clothes, so he had just put on users! He said we'd be surprised if was called on to do. Uncle Alf d pleased. Mr. Burke seemed so e wanted to stay there with us in

that dingy, dark room with its dangerous fern; he must have felt it was a nice place to have a little visit. I thought it might be that he was glad to see bodies sitting up rather than "remains" lying down.

He told us that he had made all the arrangements. The cemetery out on 111th Street, out on the far west side, was "all set" for us. The grave would be ready by one o'clock, and we could get right on out there and be back home before the heavy Sunday afternoon traffic got really bad. Then Mr. Burke turned to me and said, "Did you bring any clothes?" I didn't understand and said so. He told me that the "little angel" was lying on a slab down in the basement, but he could hardly place her in the casket without clothing!

[Handwritten marginal note:] p. 38 — describes funeral of premature infant - dressed in clothes taken from a toy doll bought on the way to the cemetery. = I have never been able to hold a toy doll since that day. My small granddaughter brings her dolls to me

Oh . . . oh . . . oh! Underneath my feet was a rug, underneath which there was a floor, underneath which there was a ceiling, underneath which there was a slab on top of which lay a two-pound little dead person with no clothes on who was my baby sister. That just could never happen to a person, could it? It was one of those things that just could never happen. Not in real life.

Uncle Alf said that he and I would go and get some clothing and be back as soon as we could.

We drove back down Fifty-fifth Street in Uncle Alf's new blue Buick and looked for some kind of store that sold clothing for "remains" of two-pound babies. Mr. and Mrs. Baer were Orthodox Jews. They closed on Saturday and opened on Sunday, and they ran a "Newsstand, Stationery Supplies, Notary Public, and Toy Store." Everything in there was piled on top of everything else. It was a tiny space, and it smelled tiny, and more than two customers at a time was impossible. Uncle Alf said at least it was open. He parked the car in front of Baer's and told me to wait. I knew he would never find clothing of any kind in there, but I waited. He emerged from the store with a sweet little smile on his face and an unwrapped sweet little toy doll in his arms. It was a baby doll in baptismal-type finery . . . phony-organdy gown with pink sleazy ribbons, a bonnet sewn on a crooked machine, cardboard shoes, and even a diaper.

On the trip back to Burke's Funeral Home I held the doll on my lap. Uncle Alf wanted me to undress it. I told him I couldn't do it. I couldn't. He said all right, Mr. Burke could do it. I have never been able to hold a toy doll since that day. My small granddaughter brings her dolls to me and I usually sit on my hands or pick up a book.

Mr. Burke was delighted with the doll. He started to undress it before he'd left the room. With every minute that passed this was becoming more of the worst day of my life. I really wanted to go to the bathroom, but I wasn't going to go in that place. I'd wait until we got out on the road, and then I'd have Uncle Alf stop at a Shell station.

When Mr. Burke returned to us, his white doctor coat had been discarded in favor of a black suit jacket with a pink carnation in the lapel. He looked like a completely different person. He didn't smile; he spoke very softly and asked us to step this way, please.

Across the hall, he held back a purple-red velvet drapery and bade us enter a totally purple-red draperied room where the only illumination was from two standards supporting phony candles made from light bulbs! These illuminati flanked a small purple-red velvet-drapery-covered table on top of which was a white plaster chest a little larger than a bread box. There was a gold-tin plate on the side of the casket that read: "Our Angel." I didn't want to see what it contained. I wish with all my heart I never had.

The doll's clothes were too big for the tiny graying body. The face was Goya-grotesque, and I had never seen Goya. I only saw horror in a foolish bonnet, a small slate-colored face, one lip malformed, a flattened nose, and a shockingly furrowed brow; all of it adding up to less substance than my geography book. Mr. Burke said the Lord's Prayer, Uncle Alf and I said amen, and Mr. Burke closed the lid of the cheap box which boasted another "Our Angel" plate on its topside. Mr. Burke carried the casket in front of him, out of the gloomy inside into the glary outside and down the steps to Uncle Alf's new blue Buick. Uncle Alf started to open the trunk, and I cried, "No," so Mr. Burke said he thought "IT" would slip right into the back seat and ride along quite safely on the floor there.

When we pulled away from the curb, I began praying that we would be hit by a truck and killed . . . at least me to be killed! Please, God, let a truck come and kill me! Just me, not Uncle Alf. He can live if he wants to, but I can't, God, honestly, I just can't! I should have gone to the bathroom back there. I couldn't have my dead little gray baby sister wait outside in a gas station while I went to the toilet. I'd have to wait. Maybe my kidneys would burst and it would kill me. Maybe I'd be that lucky.

It was long way to the cemetery. Uncle Alf was my closest ally in many things, but he was not very good at things like stop signs and lights. He always stopped, but it took him a long time to get going again. Somebody behind him was always honking a horn to get him moving. It took us a long time, and we were both heavily sad.

I hope it is not still true that Catholic cemeteries still have quarantine sections for babies who are unfortunate enough to die before the convenience of a priest can be arranged.

That's where the gatekeeper of the cemetery out on 111th Street directed Uncle Alf and me to go. It was called Angel's Corner, a small picket-fence-enclosed area where we found a small rectangular hole ready to receive our unbaptized alien, who (because of that lack of ceremony, performed by an ordained representative of Christ on Earth) would never see the face of Almighty God. Frigidly rigid theologians hasten to add that limbo, which is where such babies go, is a place of pure bliss . . . no pain, no joy, no anything at all, forever and ever, amen! That's a kind of Divine Love that takes a bit of understanding for some of us. I have a great deal of trouble with it because my too-soon-born, too-soon-dead baby sister has since been joined in Eternal Exile by two sons of my own . . . each of them more than six pounds, but each of them too-soon-born, too-soon-dead. Three little losers in the cruel celestial version of Russian roulette. Somewhere there is supposed to be a heaven where baptized babies see God every day, and somewhere else there is a limbo where my sister and my sons exist in Everlasting Nothing.

I stayed in the car and watched Uncle Alf carry the white plaster box to the open hole. He got down on his knees and set it in place and came back to the car.

And that's why I always cried when my mother cried about losing the baby. I cried because I could no longer love a God who refused to see babies because they died too soon.

5

THERE WAS ONE THING about the next life that nearly drove me crazy every time my people talked about it . . . that part about the LAST DAY, the Day of Judgment, when all the people who ever lived are going to ascend into heaven for a meeting! Only a few are going to get to stay there *after* the meeting—soldiers killed in battle . . . mothers who died in childbirth . . . the Pope . . . people like that—but the rest of us have to leave that same night and go back where we came from: to purgatory (if we haven't suffered enough yet) or to hell (if there isn't ever going to be any chance for us at all). And this time our souls have to take our bodies with them, wherever they are going. Before the Day of Judgment our bodies stayed in our graves in our lead vaults, and only our souls went to purgatory or hell, but after the big meeting on the Last Day (which is the last time anybody's going to meet anybody anywhere), our souls pick up our bodies at the exact point they left off when they ascended into heaven for the meeting. The way it is going to work is as follows:

First, there is going to be a terrible thunderstorm and the earth will quake and all the graves in all of the cemeteries all over the world are going to break open and pop right out of the ground. At the same time all of the dead souls will have left purgatory and hell, and even heaven itself, because they have to move back into the bodies they left at the hour of death. Every soul will know its own body, no matter how decayed it is. Next, the soul has to get its body out of its grave and fly its body up to heaven for the meeting. Every soul that ever *was* has to get there before the day is over! I used to think about that until my hair hurt! How could everybody make it in one day? What time would be left for the judging? Every person has to be judged, one by one. Every person has to answer to God for his sins. I thought of just the people in our own cemetery. I thought they would take up a whole day themselves.

I used to go into St. Hilary's Church in the afternoons when nobody was there. I would sit and think about it. I didn't know what I'd do on Judgment Day. I knew I didn't want to come face to face with everybody up there.

There was a stained glass window in St. Hilary's donated by the Fitzgerald family. The glass was all purples and reds and orange colors. It was a picture of Saint John the Baptist holding his own head in his hand! What if I met him like that? There was another stained glass window that was a picture of Saint Rita with many little swords in her heart. It was a messy picture. I thought her hands were very beautiful, but one of them was holding her robe back, and the other was pointing to her heart, which was splashing blood all over her.

When I looked at the main altar, it was worse! The crucifix was huge and ugly; the boards were heavy lumber. Poor suffering Jesus, hanging up there with blood dripping from the thorns in His head and from the wounds in His side and hands and feet! His head was drooped so sadly, as if they had broken His neck. There were large pink tears on His sunken face! All of His bones showed under His skin. One of His feet was on top of the other, and a single spike like the ones on railroad ties was driven through both His feet, close to His toes. Most of the time during Mass on Sundays I kept my eyes on the wooden part beneath His feet, and nobody could tell I wasn't looking at all of Him. But when I was alone in the church, I couldn't help looking at Him! I wanted to ask Him *why*? Why He had to let them crucify Him, all those years ago, to pay for the sins that I hadn't even committed yet. Did He know I was going to be so sinful that He had to let them crucify Him before I was born? If only He could have waited to find out if I *could* be good, because I could have been a saint if I thought it would have saved Him from dying on the cross! Anybody would be a saint to save Him. If He knew He had to give up His life for my sins, why did He let me be born? Why didn't He send me to limbo with my sister? Why does He make me live now, if all I do is make Him suffer and make His Blessed Mother weep?

Then I would look over at Her Altar. I never looked My Blessed Mother straight in the face in my whole life! She was immaculately conceived. Her mother and father never did anything bad to have her. All she did here on earth was cry because of our sins. I could never be good enough to make her stop crying. I couldn't blame her if she *did* hate me. I couldn't help it. I would not look at her. I would not!

Then I would look on the other side of the main altar at Saint Joseph. I could look at Saint Joseph. I loved Saint Joseph. He was old and soft and had a long beard and held a flower in one hand and the Infant Jesus in the other. Jesus was holding a ball, which was the world. He was smiling like a happy baby because He was too young to know what was going to happen to Him. Saint Joseph was the only saint who didn't look unhappy or hungry. He always made me feel better, enough so that I could get up from my knees and out of the yellow oaken pew and genuflect and go out into the air again. Judgment Day wouldn't be 100 percent horror if Saint Joseph was there. I always saved Saint Joseph until last! The rest of them could stay in that dark old church weeping and bleeding all night if they wanted to so much.

૨ૐ

I used to think it would be a good idea if I would wake up one day and keep count of all the sins I would commit until it was time to go to bed that night. Thoughts as well as deeds were sins. Even things I didn't do were sins. I could commit a sin just sitting in the depot. Just sitting there with nothing going on but the clicking of the telegraph key in the manager's office. The tack-tack-tack was tapping, and I was sitting on one long bench, not thinking of anything at all, and I was committing a sin. My grandmother had a sign in the kitchen that said the devil finds work for idle hands, and I hadn't done anything all day. Just got up and ate breakfast, and that's all. They said I had a nasty habit of staring into space with my mouth hanging open. I would sit in the depot and try doing that for as long as I could, until my mouth went to sleep the way my leg did if I sat on it. I thought about how I knew it was a sin to sit there and think about how much I didn't like living very much, not really much at all, when I stopped to think about it. There were too many things about me that weren't right. My mother used to make me sit and pull my nose down because she said it was pugged. I didn't make my nose, and I didn't make my bronchitis either. And from where I sat, things could only get worse.

I knew that the longer I lived, the closer I was getting to being a grown-up woman, and they all said they had such a hard time of it. They had pains everywhere, because they had some kind of curse, and went to bed with hot-water bottles and nerve medicine, and I had to keep out of their way and get out from under their feet, they said. And I would have to do that and have children and get torn, and that's all the thanks I would get, they said, and they told me it was a crying shame that I had to grow up, and I should enjoy myself while I could because life's hard knocks were all ahead of me. They said everybody has a cross to carry, and on days when my cross wasn't bothering me I was supposed to help Jesus carry His!

They told me about a saint that came along when Jesus was on His way to Calvary to be crucified. Jesus was walking along very slowly, carrying His cross, and it was a long way to the top of the hill of Calvary. They had already stuck a crown of thorns in His head, and His hair was bloody. People were lined up along the roadside sneering at Him, and He fell down in the dirt a couple of times because He was getting so weak from the thorns and His cross was so heavy. Then this saint came along and moved up next to Jesus and lifted the weight of the cross onto his shoulder so that Jesus could have a little rest!

I thought about how that was the most wonderful thing that anybody ever did! When they sent me to the store for groceries, I used to carry the sack on my shoulder to feel the way that saint must have felt! Sitting in the depot with my mouth open, staring into space, I would wonder how I could get my shoulder next to Jesus' shoulder. I wasn't tall enough. What I would have to do is get behind Jesus and kneel down in the dirt and get my shoulder under the part of the cross that was dragging on the ground. I could lift the back end of the cross up onto my shoulder and then stand up and walk behind Jesus, and that would make it easier for Him. I had watched them build a new part of the grain elevator and the workmen carried boards that way, one shoulder at one end and another shoulder at the other end. And then I got sad! That was the trouble. Every time I sat down to think I got sad. Even when I was thinking about not committing sins, I got sad, because everybody had to bear a cross or help poor Jesus with His, and everybody had to work too hard to make ends meet and keep two steps out of the poorhouse, and everybody got old and had serious operations and died and went to purgatory or hell, and everything we do down here on earth is marked up against us in heaven, and we will all be counted on the Last Day at the big meeting! The whole thing was sad! It was just too hard to live all your life.

If only it wasn't a mortal sin to kill yourself! It wouldn't be hard to get hit by a train. I could walk out of the depot and pretend I was walking down the rail, balancing myself, to pass the time of day, and I could keep walking until I was out of sight, and then I could lie down and pound my head on the rail until I got unconscious, and then I could just lie there unconscious until a train hit me and carried my body back into town on the cowcatcher. But it was a sin! Only God has the right to take a life, and He will let me know when it is time for Him to strike. Before I learned the Pledge of Allegiance, I learned from a chorus of aunts and my mother, "You'd better be good, for you never know when God will strike."

So many people have told me that I am a funny person, that I say and do funny things. They say I have a zest for life. They are so wrong. I don't know much about life, but from my earliest years until today all my relatives have been more concerned with my knowing what is likely to happen to me after death than with pointing out any of the guideposts by which I might travel through life. Everybody in my grandmother's house sat around the oilcloth-covered kitchen table with a cup of tea and talked about death. Particularly the women. They all were in agreement with one another, but they managed to waste away evening after evening, proving the same point. People are no damned good. All bad. God gives us our cross to bear, and He always is the hardest on the ones He loves the best! The man the world considers most unfortunate is the favorite of God. In His gracious mercy, He sends us our afflictions until He decides it is time for us to go, and all He asks in return is that we be ready. My entire family spent their entire lives getting ready to die! They drew great comfort from knowing that we had an undertaker, by marriage, right in the family group!

Cousin Matt and his family lived about thirty-five miles to the west of us in a town that was the county seat. People came from "all over" to our cousin Matt for their furniture and funeral arrangements. He had a double storefront on the main street. On one side of the store he sold strictly class home furnishings, and behind the wall partition on the other side of the building was his funeral home and waking parlor. Cousin Matt had added a second floor to the structure, and that's where his family lived with him. Right on top of dead people! Eating breakfast right on top of dead people! Lying in bed, knowing that underneath you was a dead person lying in a coffin!

Cousin Matt had had the entire front of the building faced with red brick and added four white fluted pillars. He said it looked like a fine old southern mansion. There was a low-lying shed connected to the rear of the funeral side. That's where Cousin Matt "fixed them up for viewing." The shed was kept locked at all times, and nobody but Cousin Matt was ever allowed in there. There was a large room at the back of the furniture store that was also kept locked. Everybody said there was a "big bundle of investment in there, all right." It was where Cousin Matt had his "display": a half dozen assorted metal and wooden coffins with choices of satin linings and pillows. If you wanted velvet, you could choose either oyster white or dove gray.

Cousin Matt was a small man. His wife, Adele, bought his shirts and shoes in the boy's department. I wasn't altogether captivated by Cousin Matt. I thought he had a mean streak. When his twin sons would reach for something at the supper table, Cousin Matt rapped their knuckles with his knife. Hard! He said all of his words SHORT! Every word stopped suddenly, like water dripping from a wide-mouthed spigot! "Don't! reach! for! things! at! the! table!"

There was a vegetable garden out behind the embalming shed, and at sunset, after monkeying with dead bodies all day, Cousin Matt would pick rhubarb stalks and wash them off under the lawn hose, and he would sit on the back porch reading his newspaper chewing on the rhubarb! Raw rhubarb! In my memory that's how I best remember him. My cousin Matt was, more than anything else, raw rhubarb. He looked and acted the way raw rhubarb tastes.

He always carried a spool of dental floss in his pocket, and he would draw the long string through his teeth and then hold the string up to the light to see if he had caught anything on it. I don't even think there was dental floss back then. He probably just used an old spool of thread left over from sewing up the dead people after he'd drained all the leftover life out of them.

One time Cousin Matt came to my grandmother's house and put two tin strongboxes on the kitchen table. He opened them as if they contained the original Treasure of the Sierra Madre. The first box was full of different kinds of eyeglasses, all piled in there together. The other box was only half filled, but with false teeth! Cousin Matt told my grandmother that he had been meaning to bring those boxes and their spooky contents for a long time, but he kept forgetting it. He said she could pass them out to her friends if anybody could get good use out of them. He said some of the teeth were like new. I ran out of the house and over to the railroad tracks and sat on them until I saw Cousin Matt's big old black sedan going down the road. Then I went home and got a spanking because I wasn't nice to good-hearted Cousin Matt. My grandmother said I ought to be ashamed because I didn't know what a lucky girl I was to have a wonderful undertaker for my own cousin. She said, "You can't count on any of your fancy friends to help you when it's time to be laid out for all the whole world to gape at. Little Cousin Matt will be the one to curl your hair and color up your cheeks and fill in your wrinkles and place the rosary in your hands."

My grandfather bought our lot when the cemetery was built. Not exactly built—they just put an iron fence around part of a cornfield and waited for people to die and fill it up. My grandfather got a big plot for a cheap price because most of it was on a slant. The more expensive lots are on the level ground, where there is less likelihood of slipping or seepage during rains or spring thaws. My grandfather put in ivy plants and dwarf evergreens to hold the ground, but most of the family are on tilt, a little. Still, there is room enough for everybody. Our monument is not as flashy as some of the others in the cemetery, but it preserves a beautiful sentiment. Standing on a simple granite block is a carving of Our Lord as a little boy, holding a seashell to His ear to listen to the waves. The inscription reads: "Suffer the Little children." Our plot is always well kept because not only did we pay for perpetual care, but somebody in the family was always working around the graves, keeping them neat. My family said it was a crying shame the way some people neglected the resting places of their own flesh and blood and that the poor forgotten souls would remember the way they were treated when we all come face to face on Judgment Day.

So much of my girlhood was ghoulish. All the death-and-hell preoccupation didn't seem to bother my cousins and older relatives. They didn't think it was strange to pack a lunch of a Saturday and drive over to weed the graves in the family plot. Sit right there in the nice warm sun and eat the meat-loaf sandwiches and tollhouse cookies. The luncheon conversation usually dealt with those who lay beneath the sod on which we sat. If I do say it myself, our family tombstone *is* rather grand. Pearl gray granite with raised block letters . . . imposing . . . simply grand! Except for an Italian family's tombstone, on the other side of the oak tree, ours is the largest stone, but ours is simply grand; the Italian one is "a dirty shame," my people said. They said, "It spoils the look of the whole place." It was a big brown rock with a lying-down statue of a dead angel on top of it. The broken wings of the angel drooped over the sides of the immense stone. The granite face expressed real joy; big smile. Stupid!

One of the pastimes at our Memorial Park picnics was "picking out the spaces." There is still plenty of room in my family plot. There was even more room when I was a little girl at the happy graveyard picnics, listening to my munching relatives trying to decide where they would like to lie in the plot. Nobody wanted to be on the slant because of the seepage. Uncle Alf said it wouldn't matter if you had a really good vault. That was the thing, he said; never mind the fancy coffin, just do yourself a favor and get yourself the best vault money can buy!

Once in a while I get a twinge, realizing that I won't be lain to my rest with the rest of them. I, like my dead sons and my sister, cannot be buried in consecrated ground. Not unless my first husband dies and I confess that my second marriage was "a life of sin and adultery in the eyes of God." Then I could be placed there, in a really good vault, and one day my grandchildren could come and have picnics on me.

&

My mother kept, on the back of her stove, a pot of saints. An aluminum pot, full of saints! The pot was maybe ten inches round and four inches deep with a bent metal handle. It was a well-worn dimpled and scorched old pot full of little plaster saints. I hated it! As a small child I'd pull a chair over to the stove and climb on it to see the unholy sight.

My mother prayed to these things for answers to her "special intentions." The circle within the pot was composed of seven small statues. Every Sunday after Mass my mother bought from Father Harty a fresh, week-long vigil candle for a dollar. My mother had promised our Lord that she would keep an eternal vigil light burning in gratitude for her tumor's being nonmalignant. The candle was placed in the center of the pot. She said the reason she kept it and the saints on the stove was that if, for some reason, the vigil light got tipped over some night, the house wouldn't burn to the ground and we wouldn't all be burned to a crisp while we slept without even a chance to make a last Act of Contrition.

The vigil candle was in a tall dark red glass, taller than the saints, who were only about eight inches high. The sanctified potted people were gathered in eerie assembly around the ugly red glow of the candle in their silent communion for my mother's "special intentions." Some nights I used to sleep in my mother's bed. She never woke up unless I shook her. I would sneak out to the kitchen to watch the pot of saints. There was no other light than the dancing red candle glow. I'm sure I didn't know what the word "fiendish" meant, but that is how I felt, watching them in their pot. It was a wild kind of feeling, very uncomfortable. Shakespeare's "evil sisters."

The mouse-brown little statue of Saint Anthony, patron of lost articles, was the oldest statue in the pot. Time had not been good to him. His nose was completely gone, he had only one eye, and his white underwear showed through the nicks in his brown robe. Part of his little stone loaf of bread had been broken off . . . the exposed plaster looked like real bread! Saint Rose of Lima, a great favorite of my mother's, lay in a somewhat slovenly manner against the side of the pot . . . the bottom part of her was uneven, and she couldn't stand up by herself. Saint Jude, patron of lost causes, was supposed to have a tongue of flame coming out of the center of his head, but he had been knocked over, and in gluing the tongue of flame back on, my mother got it enough off center that it looked like a little red pointed horn! The once cerulean blue mantle of Our Lady of Perpetual Help was faded to a murky gray. Saint Francis of Assisi had lost the birds from his shoulders, and his right arm had been amputated at the elbow. These were our saints. They were interceding for us before the throne of Almighty God.

Sometimes Mother carefully bathed the saints in warm soapy water. She let me dry them in a coarse towel. I could feel their imperfections beneath the cloth. They were in awful shape, our saints.

I don't look at stoves any oftener than I can help, but when I do, even today, I feel less than secure in a house that has no pot of saints to call its own, gleaming on the back part of the stove in the bloody red light of eternal vigil.

6

❧

I NEVER DISCUSSED SEX WITH A living soul. I just never did. Superficially, sure, everybody does that. Lots of experts running around. I've heard too many of them, but I'll be damned if I want to sit down and talk the whole thing over with them. Anyhow, "them as can, do. Them as can't, preach." The self-styled experts who have inflicted their sexual narratives on me have never been what you might call outstanding examples of what they are talking about.

There was a girl in high school who nearly destroyed me with her knowledge of things lustful. We were sixteen. Her name was Marianna. She was rich. I wasn't. I was a student at the neighborhood parochial school; she was a boarder at a ritzy academy in Evanston that was run by French nuns in starched white bonnets, the ones who always teach the rich girls, the status of the sisterhood.

Marianna had her own horse in the academy stable, and she won prizes for jumping. She jumped a lot, in many ways as it turned out. Her father lived in England, and her mother was in New York half the time. On weekends the chauffeur would bring her home from the academy to her big stone house. Usually she was alone there with the chauffeur and his housekeeper wife. Sometimes I spent Friday or Saturday night at Marianna's house. My mother would never let me stay both nights. It had to be either/or. Often Marianna and I were alone until the chauffeur and his wife got home, very late and slightly tipsy. They lived in two rooms on the top floor, and we could tell which nights they made love. On the no-love nights the toilet only flushed twice . . . once for him, once for her. On the make-love nights, the toilet flushed four times . . . two before and two after. Right after the last flush we could hear the housekeeper start to snore. Almost as soon as the water stopped filling up in the tank, she was snoring away. We heard her right through the walls. I wondered how it made the chauffeur feel. So soon after love . . . the snore!

Whenever I stayed at Marianna's, we talked most of the night. Most of it was lies; about boys and where we went with them, and how we felt with them. Mostly lies.

The beds in Marianna's room were too big to be twin beds, but her mother had bought them at an auction, and there was no other place to put them. My bed at home was a plain old bed. At Marianna's the headboard was covered with tufted gray velvet. Like pussywillows. I loved to rub my face against it in the dark. So soft. I enjoyed it, spending the night there.

But one night all hell broke loose. It was right after Christmas vacation. Marianna had spent the holidays in Virginia with her grandparents who raised horses. Marianna was telling me about all the parties she went to . . . 150,000 parties on a two-week vacation. She said all the boys in Virginia were much more exciting than any boys I ever knew. She said every boy in Virginia was very good at French kissing. I said I didn't like to kiss like that. I didn't either! I didn't want to hear any more, so I rolled over and pretended to be falling asleep.

Marianna got out of her bed and came over to mine and began hitting me with her pillow. Hitting me hard. She said I was a dummy. She got back into her bed and said it again. She said she was going to tell me a few things I ought to know and I had better listen if I had any sense in my prize dummy head. She got up and turned the light on in the bathroom. She came back and got into her own bed. Then she started. She said the whole thing as if she were reading a composition in English class.

The first thing I had to learn, she said, was that boys need to have girls teach them how to do it. Boys don't know what to do, and boys don't know how to do it. She said a girl always has to know more than a boy. Besides, she said, boys want you to. They like it better when girls make it easier for them. She said they had to concentrate on their erections! I started to recite the Act of Contrition to myself . . . the prayer to remember just after an automobile runs over you. Marianna was telling me I'd never get anyplace with a boy if I didn't know how to make it easier for him. She said that's why so many people get divorced or "have adultery" with other people. She said that was why she never bought a dress or a sweater that couldn't be opened from the top. Because boys hate it if they can't get their hands on your bare breasts. She said she hated the word "breasts," that old woman had breasts, but girls had "titties." She said whenever she bought a new dress, even when her mother was with her, she would find a way to be alone in the trying-on room so that she could see if she could get her hand in there and take a titty out.

OH MY GOD, I AM HEARTILY SORRY FOR HAVING OFFENDED THEE AND I DETEST ALL MY SINS BECAUSE I DREAD THE LOSS OF HEAVEN AND THE PAINS OF HELL!

Marianna said that when she parked in a car with a boy, that was almost her favorite part of the whole thing . . . when a boy puts his head down and she holds it and it's easy for him to take her titty out and tickle it with his tongue. She said she liked a boy to do it for hours and hours. She said she would take a little spit from her mouth on her fingers and rub the inside of the boy's ear with it while he was wetting her titties with his spit. I was getting a pain in my back from lying so still. Marianna was telling me that boys loved to be touched all over with wet fingers. She said sometimes she put her finger up inside herself and rubbed it on a boy's mouth and told him it was honey; that once at the beach she rubbed it on a boy's little titty and licked it off herself and it made his little titty stand up just like hers, all pink and hard. I was pushing down so hard on the mattress, I wanted it to break and fall in and smother me to death. I was afraid to ask her to stop. She sounded very nervous. If I said anything, she might hit me with the lamp or something. I knew she was sitting up in her bed. She threw something at me. It was her nightgown. She was sitting there, naked, in her bed, and saying all that stuff. That she liked a boy to suck her titties until they were sore and hard and red and sticking straight out of her. Then she got out of her bed, and I could see her in the light from the bathroom. She went over to the door, and I thought she was going to open it and maybe run out on the street like that and get arrested. But when she got to the door, she put her whole naked body against the long mirror on the back of it. Flat against the door, against the glass! I closed my eyes. I was beginning to cry. I heard her making little noises. I thought she didn't even know I was there any longer. She was making sounds the way I talked to a cat once when I was trying to coax it out of a tree.

Marianna was talking to a boy she was imagining. She was telling a boy she had made up all the things she was going to do to him. I knew names of things. I knew words; she wasn't saying any words I didn't know, but she was saying them in a funny way. She must have had her mouth pressed against the mirror because the things she was saying came out of her as if her mouth were full of Novocain. She sounded horrible, filthy, terrible-sounding! She was bumping her whole body against the mirror and the door was making noise, and I was afraid the housekeeper and her husband might wake up and think a burglar was trying to break in. Then I heard her throw herself back on the bed. I thought she must have hurt herself, but when I opened my eyes, she was under the covers and she was moaning and swearing and saying dirty words over and over and over . . . her whole body was jerking up and down like a boy in grammar school who had an epileptic seizure in the lunchroom. She was gasping as if somebody was hitting her, and then, after a long, dreadful howl of terrible pain, she started to whimper, and then she was quiet. I waited. There was nothing more. She was asleep.

I was ice-cold inside and out. I had my whole fist in my mouth and was biting into the back of my hand. I tried to bite it hard enough so the blood would come and I would bleed to death. Without ever leaving this bed. I wanted to die. I wanted to die. Never get out of the bed. Never live another day. Just stop breathing. Forever and ever! Amen.

In the morning it would be farther away. I wouldn't see Marianna anymore. "Marianna is an occasion of sin and an impure companion, and I won't see her anymore, and *Mea culpa, mea culpa, mea maxima culpa.*

૨૦

And I didn't see Marianna after that. We didn't telephone each other, and we both knew why. I went to Mass every morning but not to Communion . . . I knew I could never receive Communion again because it would mean going to Confession. If a priest is God's representative here on earth, he is also still a *man*. How could I tell a *man* what had happened? Maybe if there were ever a woman priest, I might be able to tell it. But never to a *man*.

One Friday night Marianna telephoned my house. It was in March, and my birthday was the week before. When I got home from the movie, my mother said that Marianna had called to wish me a happy birthday and wanted me to call her no matter what time I got in. My mother was sitting right there and could hear everything I was saying. Marianna said she was pregnant and had to see me right away. If I didn't come, she would take sleeping pills. She was afraid to tell anybody but me. I was her only friend. She was crying, and I couldn't let my mother know how frightened it was making me. I told Marianna I'd be at her apartment first thing in the morning and we would spend the whole day together because it was Saturday and no school. I hung up and told my mother Marianna had a wonderful present from her grandparents in Virginia. I told my mother that the best horses in the world come from Virginia and that was what her grandparents had sent to Marianna—a new horse! My mother wanted to know where they had sent the horse, and I told her it was shipped to the stable at Marianna's school and she had some photographs of the horse at her apartment and was dying to show them to me.

My aunt Noonie heard me talking to my mother and said, "That's all that one needs is a new horse. That little snip is headed for big trouble! Some people never know when to stop. Their kids are spoiled plain rotten. Give them everything they want, and then sit back and wait for them to get in trouble, especially a *girl*. Some kids just get everything they ask for. Just ask for it, and get it, that's what they do."

Yes, Aunt Noonie, they do. They certainly do.

The housekeeper answered the door and said Marianna had cramps and was in her room. She was in her bed with the tufted dove-gray velvet headboard. I sat on the other bed—the one I'd been in that night after Christmas vacation, when she told me everything she knew because I was a dummy, a prize dummy, and didn't know beans about boys. She was lying there in Levi's and a sweat shirt that said "Notre Dame" on it, so I couldn't see if her stomach was swollen.

She whispered it all to me and said she didn't know if it was Jerry Boyd or Tim Boyd. She had done it with both of them. With brothers. In the same family.

I had told myself, walking over to her place, that I would just act as if I were a nurse in a doctor's office. I would just listen to her story, and then I would tell her it was a matter for a doctor. I could say nothing, I was only a nurse, and she would have to talk to the doctor, and he would know some home for unwed mothers where she could go to have the baby.

But Marianna didn't give me a chance to say anything at all. She was whispering fast and shaking her fingers at me. She said she had missed two periods and a girl at school had taken her to a doctor in Evanston and he did the test and she was really pregnant. Marianna wasn't even near crying now. She was being very serious and very definite in the way she was whispering. She almost sounded as if I were being scolded. She said her mother was in New York both times it happened. They did it in Marianna's bed, and she patted the bed as if I didn't see it was there. She said it happened both times in one week. The first Saturday night with Tim and the next Saturday night with Jerry.

I asked her where her mother was now, and she said she was still asleep in her room. Marianna was telling me all this, and her mother was right there in the same apartment! That was almost as much of a shock to me as her being pregnant. Marianna said her mother didn't know. Nobody knew but me and the girl at school and the doctor who did the test and one other person. Then she shook her finger at me again and said that was why she needed my help. Because of the other person. She said I was the only one in the world she could turn to. Nobody but me could help her with this other person. I told her I would do whatever I could, but what did she want me to do?

Marianna told me to sit on the foot of her bed and just listen. All I had to do was listen. Carefully.

She said that her mother was taking the *Twentieth Century* train to New York that afternoon. She said that I had to be at her apartment no later than ten o'clock the next morning, Sunday. I would have to go to early Mass and tell my mother we were going out to Marianna's school on the elevated train to see her new horse. I would have to tell my mother it would take all day, because the el doesn't have as many trains on Sunday and we wanted to spend some time with the horse, but she shouldn't worry because I'd be home by nine o'clock for sure. Maybe earlier. *But I had to be* at Marianna's by ten o'clock sharp the next morning. She told me it was because her appointment with the other person was for eleven, and it was all the way downtown in the Loop. She was telling it like a detective story, as if we were going to blow up City Hall or something.

She said the girl at school had given her the name and telephone number of an employment agency on North State Street. She said it wasn't really an employment agency, and Marianna had to memorize the address and phone number. The girl said it was a safe place to have it done because her cousin went there and she was okay now. Marianna said she couldn't even tell me what floor it was on. It was a private secret. I would have to wait out in front of the building on State Street until it was over. She became excited telling me. Then she reached under her bed and brought out a shoe box from O'Connor and Goldberg's, and she opened it and unwrapped some tissue paper and showed me a white tennis sock. She said there were seventy-five ten-dollar bills in it. She said it had to be in ten-dollar bills.

I couldn't ask her where she got the money, but I had to ask her what it was for, and she looked at me and said the word—"abortion." "I'm going to have an abortion at eleven o'clock in the morning, and you can't do anything to stop me. If I don't have it, I am going to take poison and kill myself, so I'm going to have it, and you have to go with me." She grabbed my wrists and shook me and said that I had to.

The next morning we took the Hyde Park bus downtown and walked over from Michigan Avenue to State Street. It was hot and sticky, almost like August, and hardly any traffic because it was Sunday. It wouldn't have been so awful if there had been more people and horns and policemen's whistles, but it was very quiet for State Street.

Marianna had told me again on the bus what we had to do. I was glad she went through it again because I knew I had to be sure. It was like one night at a party when a goofy freshman from Purdue said that he could hypnotize people. He tried it on me, and I really liked the way he talked to me and told me I was getting drowsier and drowsier and would go to sleep and not hear anything but his voice and do only what he told me to do. I never did go under, but it felt like that when Marianna was telling me what I had to do. I was just listening and was going to do whatever her voice was telling me to do. I did ask her what would happen if I couldn't get a cab after she came out of the building, because there aren't many cabs on Sunday morning. We had to get her to the Congress Hotel right away so that she could lie down. She said that was what they told her. To lie down as soon as she could for two days after it was over. She couldn't go home, she said, because the housekeeper and the chauffeur were there. She had told them she was staying at school Sunday night and they could pick her up next weekend. At school she had told them she would be absent Monday and Tuesday because she had to have a mole taken off her leg. She said if she got caught in her stories, she would just be caught, that's all. She had reserved a room in a phony name at the Congress Hotel for Sunday, Monday, and Tuesday nights, and her weekend bag was enough luggage to make her look legitimate, and I could stay with her until it was time for me to go home tonight. In case she needed anything, she said. Then I could come back and visit with her after school on Monday and Tuesday, and then on Wednesday morning she would leave the Congress Hotel and take the el up to her school and tell them she felt a little weak from having had the mole taken off her leg.

I asked her what phony name she had given at the Congress Hotel, and she said it was the same one she gave to the employment agency. She pronounced it to me as if she were speaking a foreign language. It was her last name first and her father's first name last. I said it over to myself, and it did sound like a name somebody could have. A fancy first name and a plain last name. She said she thought it was a good idea because if she died on the operating table in the employment office or during the night when she was alone in the Congress Hotel, the police would be able to figure out the name and notify her mother, so she could come to claim the body.

I hadn't thought about the operating table or dying. I really hadn't thought at all. About any of it. I didn't let myself. I just thought about its being over and then I would never set eyes on Marianna again as long as I lived. If I didn't have to throw myself into the Chicago River from the top of the Wrigley Building when it was over, I would just forget I had ever even heard of Marianna. That's all I let myself think about.

When we got to the building, there was a revolving door and a regular in-and-out door on either side of it. Marianna told me to stand next to the door on the left side because she was left-handed like me and it was natural for her to turn that way, and if she was still woozy from the anesthetic when she came out of the building, she might get mixed up and faint if she didn't know exactly the spot where I was waiting. Then she gave me two dollars. She said it was for the cab fare because she might not be able to speak and I should do all the talking. Just tell the driver to take us to the Congress Hotel on South Michigan Avenue. When we got to the hotel, I should ask the doorman for a wheelchair and give her phony name. She said they were expecting her to do that because she told them when she made the reservation on the telephone that she would need a wheelchair because she had had a mole taken off her leg and couldn't walk too well. I was to let the bellboy push the wheelchair. I was to walk alongside it, carrying the weekend case. All I was to say to the bellboy was to bring the registration card to the room to be signed. Marianna gave me another dollar for the bellboy.

Marianna said the girl at her school told her they did abortions all day Sunday in the employment agency, so it might not take any longer than going to the dentist. Marianna squeezed my hand and said, "Good luck."

She pushed the revolving door and disappeared in it. It flumped around a couple of flumps, and it stopped. My blue jacket had pockets. I stuffed my hands into them and looked down to fix my feet in my spot and started to guard the left-hand door of the building. I looked up at the lovely Marshall Field clock and watched its big hand trip three times before it clicked into its eleven o'clock slot. I watched it until it said 12:10.

By then the whole middle of me up to my neck was stirring heavily like fudge when it is ready to harden, thick and slow and plopping over. But in my head there was nothing. A big bulb and the light was out and I wasn't me. I wasn't anybody. Just a burned-out lamppost of a person standing next to a weekend bag on State Street on a Sunday morning.

Marianna didn't just come out of the revolving door. She "appeared" out of it. There was no flumping noise as there had been when she went in. She was just there. In front of me. All of a sudden, like Saul, or Paul, or whoever it was on the road to Damascus. Her white coat had a gray fox collar, and she had it pulled up close and held her handkerchief over her mouth. Her scarf was around her hair, and that was all I saw. I didn't see her eyes. Just there she was, all bundled up as if it were Alaska, just standing there.

There were three taxis in a row cruising State Street in front of us, and I leaped at one and got into the back seat to claim it and slammed the weekend bag down on the floor. When I turned to beckon to Marianna, she was already getting in next to me. I lunged across her middle to close the door and gasped that I was sorry because I thought I might have jarred her down there where she had had it done to her. I told the driver to take us to the Congress Hotel. The only thing I said to Marianna was when I asked her if she wanted to lie down with her head in my lap. She didn't answer me. She sat there in the corner with her head almost hidden in the fox collar, with the handkerchief over her mouth. Her purse slid off the seat, and I picked it up and started to put it back on her lap, but then I thought the weight of it would be bad for her, so I put the purse on top of the weekend bag, and when we turned a corner, it slid off again, so I picked it up and held it. I sat there holding onto two purses. It gave me something to do with my hands.

We went past the Art Institute, and then we were there. "Congress Hotel," the driver said.

The doorman opened the door. That was where I was supposed to ask for the wheelchair and give Marianna's phony name. The doorman had the whole top half of his body in the cab, leaning in, just inches away from Marianna's stomach. One of his gold braid shoulder epaulets was wearing out, and its white cotton stuffing showed through the rusting gold threads. His face was big and red, and he was smiling and looking right at me. He asked if he could be of service and I handed him the two dollars I was holding—the two dollars that were for the cabdriver. I couldn't speak. I couldn't think of Marianna's phony last name. I knew it was her last name first and her father's first name last, but I couldn't speak it. I couldn't think it that way. I looked at the doorman and said, "I never even met her father!"

Marianna mumbled through her handkerchief behind her collar and told the doorman all the stuff I couldn't say. She even grabbed the two dollars out of his hand and gave it back to me. I knew enough to lean forward and give it to the driver, and I told him he should keep the change, whatever it was. The doorman was back in a minute, with the bellboy who was almost an old man. He was pushing a huge wheelchair. The wheels were big enough for a farm buggy. I started to get out of my side of the cab, but the driver said it was dangerous, so I had to wait while the two men helped Marianna out and backed her up and into the enormous old wheelchair. They were very nice about it. The doorman kept saying, "Easy does it," and, "Watch your step."

Peacock Alley of the old Congress Hotel was always in the newspapers. So-and-so was seen strolling in Peacock Alley of the Congress Hotel at the charity ball of Mrs. Hoop-de-doo. The whole place was full of some beautiful perfume. Such an expensive smell! The old bellboy was pushing Marianna a little ahead of me. She had said I was supposed to walk next to them, but there really wasn't enough room. Peacock Alley was narrow. The walls were square pieces of mirror and made it seem wider, but there were elegant French-looking sofas and chairs and pots with palms all along the walls, and it was too crowded for me and the weekend bag and the bellman with the gigantic wheelchair with Marianna in it.

We got into an elevator and got off at the third floor. Not one word had been said. By anybody. The wheelchair was silent on the thick carpet along the hall. And so were we. No sound at all.

Once we were in the room, Marianna told the bellman he could go. She said he could leave the wheelchair right where it was, with her in it. She said she would be in bed by the time he came back with the registration card for her to sign, and he could take the wheelchair away then. I started to give him the dollar she had told me to give him, and for the first time she took the handkerchief away from her mouth, and she waved it at me as a countess would and said, "Never mind, I'll take care of it when he comes back, Linda." I looked at him and almost explained that my name wasn't Linda. I was beginning to feel as if I had the flu.

As soon as the old bellman had closed the door behind him, Marianna yipped like a puppy and flung back her fur collar and yanked the scarf from her head and shook her hair. Then she stood up. Swiftly. Easily. The way we did when Sister Superior walked into study hall and said, "Out of your seat and up on your feet!"

I watched Marianna as she kicked her shoes off and let her white coat fall on the floor. Then she started to dance around the room like a ballet dancer. She was bending from side to side and singing like a nursery rhyme, "It's over, it's over, la la la la lala. Over, over, all fall down." She put her arms around me and pushed her nose against mine and sang, "It's over. It's over. Ha ha ha ha haha." She took off her dress and her slip and her bra, throwing them every which way. All she had on now were her stockings and her panties. She was dancing and giggling and singing nonsense words, and she curled up on the big bed and rolled around and messed it all up and kicked her legs in the air. I yelled at her to stop, that she could hurt herself and she should stop, stop, stop! I told her the bellman would be back and she should get in bed and pull the covers up. So she did, still giggling like a fool. I started to fold the spread, and she grabbed it from me and said not to be silly, this was a hotel, and she told me to get her nightgown out of her weekend bag. When she put it on, I almost died. I could see right through it, and she sat in that bed with her whole bosoms showing. I told her that the bellman would have a fit if he saw her like that, and she kicked her foot at me and said it would be good for what ailed the old geezer.

She asked me to put her toilet things in the medicine cabinet in the bathroom. I heard her call, "Come in," and I slammed the bathroom door and turned on both faucets in the sink and flushed the toilet. Let them think I was "busy." I was not going to be in that room when that old bellman looked at her in that bed with her whole front poking out at him. I sat down on the lid of the toilet and flushed it again. I grabbed a bath towel and bit into it to keep from screaming.

DEAR GOD, DEAR GOD THE FATHER, GET ME OUT, OH, GOD, GET ME OUT OF HERE. IF YOU CAN HEAR ME AT ALL, GET ME OUT OF HERE. PLEASE, GOD, PLEASE!

I stayed in the bathroom and waited for Marianna to call me. Finally I opened the door a little to let her know I was finished with whatever I was pretending to do in there. I waited, and nothing happened, so I went out into the room. The big wheelchair was gone, and Marianna was lying on her back in the bed with her eyes closed. I sniffed the air in the room. I couldn't understand why there was no smell of ether or that stuff they gave me when my tonsils were taken out. They must have given her something when they did it.

She should never have been doing all that dancing and everything. I knew she was wearing a sanitary belt and pad under her panties, and there were zillions of pads in her weekend bag. How could she be menstruating if she was pregnant? Or did she start to menstruate as soon as they did it to her in that employment agency? I walked over to the bed and wanted to ask her what they did to her up there, but instead, I asked her if she was asleep. No answer. I asked her again. Still no answer. She was lying very still. I asked her if she was dead.

Big lines of tears started moving slowly down her face. She said that something was happening. That something a few minutes ago felt as if it had popped in her stomach and she had a terrible pain and she had pulled back the covers and looked down and the bed had blood on it. She told me not to talk, that the pain was not so bad now and we should both be very quiet. I thought maybe she might be cold and I put her white coat over the bedspread. I watched her. She was sucking in on her lips so hard there was only white around her mouth and her chin was quivering, and then her whole body began to shiver. I asked if they had given her any medicine to take, and she shook her head. I asked if they had given her a number to call if anything like this happened. Again she shook her head. The tears were still coming silently. Then she said she hadn't seen anybody in the employment office but a young man sitting at a desk with sunglasses on. He had given her two pills and a paper cup of water and told her to put the money on the desk and leave it there. Then Marianna began to make a sound. It was *mmmmmmmmmmmmmmm*. She drew her knees up and wrapped her arms around them and flung herself from side to side on the bed and dug her head deep in the pillows, and it was horrible! I said I was going to call a doctor and she said we couldn't call a doctor and then she made the *mmmmmmmmmmmmmmmm* sound again and said that yes, yes, I should please call a doctor. Call a doctor! I got the phone book and looked under "EMERGENCY." I found one that said twenty-four hour service on Wabash Avenue. I said I was the sister of a very sick girl who was having a miscarriage. It was a lady's voice on the other end, and she said she would reach the doctor. Marianna said to say he shouldn't telephone us, but just to come as soon as he could. The lady asked the room number, and I had to ask her to wait while I went out and looked at the outside of the door. In the time it took me to walk to the door and back I said to myself Marianna's phony name over and over so I'd be able to speak it when the lady on the phone asked me. She said to keep the patient quiet and wait for the doctor.

Marianna said she felt as if she had to go to the bathroom. When I was helping her out of bed, I saw the blood on the sheet and said I'd cover it with a towel and Marianna said never mind that and just help her to the bathroom. I stood in front of her as she sat on the toilet. She kept her arms around my hips and held her head against me. That *mmmmmmmmmmmmmmm* sound. It was awful. Awful! When I helped her up, there was a lot of blood in the bowl; the whole bowl was dark with it. She started to stagger, and I got her back in bed and put a fresh pad on her. She wasn't shivering now. Just as if she were dead, she was lying there. She looked dead. Her mouth was hanging open, and her face looked like an old woman's face. There was spittle dripping out of her mouth, and she looked so ugly. So quiet and so ugly. I brought her a glass of water, but she didn't want it. She told me to shut up and let her ride it out. She said it like she hated me . . . "Shut up and let me ride it out!"

I sat down on the floor next to the bed, and she turned her back to me. In a few minutes she started to talk.

She told me the young man in the sunglasses at the employment agency left her alone after she took the pills he gave her. She said it was a dark waiting-room kind of place. When he came back, she said, the young man unlocked a door behind him and told her to step in there and take all her clothes off and put on the gown that was lying on the table. She said it was a regular doctor table. The young man gave her a washroom kind of towel and told her to lie down on the table with the white gown and keep the towel over her face. Then he left her alone. I told Marianna she shouldn't talk anymore, and she was quiet again. In a little while she said, "They scraped me with a big spoon, it felt like . . . I died it hurt so . . . it hurt so much I died . . . I died . . . I died!"

When she didn't say anything more, I waited and then I told her she was very brave.

The doctor gave Marianna an injection and a capsule. He said it would make her feel dopey. He wanted to know what happened. We had to tell him. Marianna did most of the talking, slurring some of the words together, and I was surprised to hear how simple it all sounded as she told it.

The doctor said she was lucky to be alive. He went over to the window and looked at Michigan Avenue; then he turned to me and said I would have to leave. He said he was going to put some packs in Marianna to ward off further hemorrhaging. I said I thought that was what had happened when she was on the toilet. He said I should go home. He would get a nurse to come and stay tonight and another one would come in the morning. I said I didn't think I should go, and he asked me to go out in the hall with him for a minute. Marianna looked as if she were sleeping.

The round-headed, pink-faced doctor took me out into the hall and asked me who was going to pay for all this "dirty work," who was going to pay him and the nurses for "saving our dirty little asses." I felt my arm swing back and then forward, and I punched him right in the chest. With all my might! And again! As hard as I could. The third time he grabbed my arm and held it. I was shaking and he was hurting me and I fell against the chest I had just hit and I sobbed and sobbed and said that I was sorry.

He took me back into the room. Marianna was sleeping. He talked to me. He said I was either insane or just plain stupid to let myself get mixed up in a thing like this. He said I was a minor and was engaged in a crime and could be sent to prison until I was an old lady. He said that Marianna could have died, that she might be hopelessly infected right now, lying in that bed; that she would be scarred emotionally for the rest of her life, and so would I, he said. He said I had *more to forget* than most people do if they live to be a hundred. "What this girl has done today is slaughter, and you have been a party to it. Butchers who kill every day out there in the stockyards would never do what you have done." He said I was a criminal-at-large at that very moment and could be locked up in sight of a half an hour. All he had to do was pick up the telephone and I would be all washed up, he said. He said that girls who do what Marianna had done were never anything but wrecks. Morally and physically. Human wrecks. The garbage of society, he said. He said that nature demanded its price and everybody had to pay it sooner or later. He told me to go home.

I went into the bathroom and combed my hair and put some lipstick on, and just as I was leaving, the doctor said that I should promise him that even if I got pregnant by a fellow with two heads, that even if I knew that all I would give birth to was a set of dishes, I would go ahead and have it and be its happy idiot mother rather than ever go through anything like this again. I told him that I would, and I left.

I didn't know what time it was, so I walked all the way to the Dearborn Street railroad station to look at a clock. It was twenty-five minutes after four.

I couldn't go home. I had said I wouldn't be home until nine o'clock. I went inside the station and bought a copy of *Photoplay* magazine and sat down and listened to the noises of the people, and I read. Page after page after page. I read words. Word by word. Just words with no connection to them. I skipped all the pictures and just read words.

I had to go home. I had to. I felt as if I were getting the flu again. It would be almost seven o'clock by the time I got there on the bus and I could stop at Walgreen's for a Coke, and when I got in my house, I'd say that we didn't stay as long at the stable at Marianna's school as we thought we would. I'd say that it was boring to look at horses all afternoon and there wasn't anything else to do out there on Sunday. I'd say it was dumb for me to go in the first place. I'd say I sure found out I wouldn't want to pay all that money to worry about an old horse for the rest of my life. I'd say I thought rich kids like Marianna didn't know what to do with themselves. I'd say I didn't think I wanted to see Marianna anymore. I'd say that she must have a few screws loose somewhere.

I needn't have bothered thinking up answers because nobody asked me any questions. I knew I should tell it in Confession. I'd stand in line for Confession with old people and little kids, and as the line moved up and it was getting closer to my turn, I knew that when I got into the box I would lie! Again! I never told the really bad things in Confession. Never! When I got in there and peered through the grating at the profile of the priest, I knew that if I really started to tell the whole truth, I would cry my heart out. I couldn't do that. People have to whisper their sins in Confession so that the others outside in the line don't hear them. How could I whisper the whole thing about Marianna? It would take a long time to tell, and I knew, I really knew, that the priest would never understand. How could I kneel in there and embarrass a holy man with the story of the dirty thing I did? He might understand the old ladies in line. They didn't do what I did, and neither did the little kids.

Sometimes I'd get to the place in the line where I was going to be the next one in the confessional box and I'd pretend I had a wristwatch on and I'd look down at it and act as if it were later than I thought and I'd leave the church as fast as I could! I'd sometimes pretend I suddenly felt faint so I wouldn't have to take my turn.

In bed at night I would close the covers around me like a big round loaf of bread with me in the middle of it, and I'd try to whisper my sins to God. It made me very, very unhappy.

7

GUESS IT WOULD BE APPRO-priate to say that, genealogically speaking, my people have never been prone to illumination before the fact until it is absolutely necessary. Better to keep all things secret from everybody until the last possible moment. Little catchphrases (burned into my soul at my grand-mother's knee), such as "Nobody needs to know everything about you," and "It is safer to trust a stranger, but don't trust him farther than you can throw him," and "What people don't know won't hurt them." That's the one I hate! *What people didn't want me to know has hurt me more than anything in my lifetime, for all of my lifetime!*

My generally hysterical aunt Noonie was part of my first experience of being made a fool of because people didn't want me to know something, people who believed that my not knowing wouldn't hurt me. Didn't those people realize that people like me usually find out what has been kept from our knowing and that when we do, we are mortified and enraged because we believed the lies they told us? My aunt Noonie was right there when it happened to me the first time, and I never believed anything she told me after that, and I never learned to like her very much. I've always wanted to play some kind of dirty trick on Aunt Noonie just to get even. I've been nurturing this resentment since the Christmas before my sixth birthday.

Aunt Noonie and her sweet-smiling, long-suffering shadow-hus-band, Alf, had taken me to Marshall Field's store to see the Christmas windows and to meet Santa Claus. The windows were fairyland, magic and marvelous, but when we got upstairs to Santa Land, I wanted to go home. There was a long line of little people standing on a narrow red carpet between long ropes of peppermint-candy-like barriers. Ahead of them, and several steps above them, on a platform covered with bales of cotton and broken-up sparkly things, sat a big something in a huge red velvet chair. One by one these little people were led by an oversized dwarf in a cutesy little purple and gold costume . . . right out of any normal child's nightmare . . . up the steps and closer to the big "thing" in the red chair.

I had been able to cope with the story of Santa Claus. I even enjoyed things about him like his "little round belly that shook when he laughed like a bowl full of jelly." But I was not ready for what Marshall Field's had to offer me in the way of Jolly Saint Nick. He was a grouch! I could tell by the way he lifted me up onto his lap, where I did not want to be. I was a skinny kid and not very big, but he didn't have to do that. He certainly didn't have to dig his knuckles into my flesh as he hoisted me up onto the lap he didn't have! I arched my back to keep as much distance as possible between us. He was saying something to me (and beyond me to the next two little people in line behind me . . . an economical move on his part . . . saved needless repetition).

This salivating State Street Santa, who was wetting his cotton beard as he talked, told me and the others that he was going to come down our chimneys on Christmas Eve. I looked around to see if my ensuing friends were going to protest. They weren't, so I didn't. I wanted to tell this overpowering gentleman that we didn't have a chimney; he'd have to cut a hole in the roof, or, as I wanted to suggest, he could just ring the doorbell the way other people who had things to deliver did. But since I didn't want to fight that battle alone and since it didn't seem to bother my companions, I could only conclude that they came from richer families who all had chimneys, so I pretended that I had one, too, and I thanked Santa for planning to come down it on Christmas Eve.

Then he did an awful thing. He asked me to lean into him and whisper into his ear so that the others couldn't hear. He wanted to know all the things I wanted for Christmas. I had a little trouble finding his ear, there was so much of that pulled-apart cotton all over him, but there it was, finally, emerging from the fuzz. I put my mouth close to it, as though I were making a long-distance telephone call. I thought I was merely whispering loudly, but apparently my aspirate strength punctured something inside because he pushed me away and told me to try again . . . more gently this time. In being cautious, I made a great mistake. I actually looked at the ear I had just blasted.

There were hairs growing out of it . . . black and gray hairs! I stared in horror at the hirsute shell of Santa's ear. I told him whatever he wanted to bring me was okay . . . just anything he had left over he could drop down our chimney if he could find it. He wanted me to be more specific. I was beginning to cry, and I looked out past the group of little people and saw my aunt Noonie and uncle Alf standing with all the other grown-ups who were enjoying this cruel spoof at the expense of their frightened and embarrassed children. They could see that I was crying. They were laughing. I could see all of uncle Alf's phony teeth, and aunt Noonie was doing what she always did when she thought something was funny . . . she was poking him with her elbow. It was Christians and Lions time at Marshall Field's. That was the first time I ever felt like a horse's ass!

Of all the horses' asses I have felt like since, the Santa Claus horse's ass, perhaps because it was the first, is still the worst. Watch any group of little kids in line to see Santa Claus . . . read their faces. If I ever DO commit murder, and it is not unlikely, it will be because somebody has played me for a fool and is laughing at me! I am nobody's horse's ass. And don't you forget it!

🙚

It isn't so bad if it is really an ass of a horse who is doing the laughing. I've had that happen and could see a certain clever irony in it. In one of those dead, except late-at-night, TV series, I was playing a pore desert rat of a woman whose last possession was an ol' varmint of a moth-eaten donkey. We wuz dyin' of thirst out there in the desert of the old Republic Pictures back lot. Thar waren't no water, the coyotes wuz a-comin', and them ol' vultures wuz a-flyin' low. You put that up there on your nineteen-inch TV set, add a few snatches of musical score stolen from vintage Dmitri Tiomkin, and you've got your basic somewhere-in-the-top-twenty rating.

It was a blisteringly hot San Fernando day. It was a hundred degrees hotter down in the gully of the old Republic riverbed. No breeze, just still, heavy hot . . . under very hot color lights. The "donkey-actor" with whom I had to work had such scorn for me that it was ridiculous. It is very hard to call your agent and say you refuse to work with a stuck-up donkey! It would be equally hard to bring him up before the union on sex charges. He was obviously in love with his trainer. At sight of him, the nervous neighing started, all falsetto and frilly, and then, slowly, and with all the rigidity of stale celery, his masculinity or what was left of it would appear from under his aft section to dangle dreadfully before our eyes, and in full view of the camera! It is risky to incorporate such sights into your average family-type show, so our director insisted that the trainer hide behind the sound truck, out of sight of the donkey. During the scene I was supposed to send the donkey away forever. I was supposed to put my arm around him and, through my blacked-out front teeth, explain that he would have to go it alone. I was sending him away because I was goin' to die, parched to death. Without me weighin' down his pore ol' back, he might stand a chance of gettin' to water somewheres! The "little gem" of a scene read more easily than it played.

The entire morning in the blazing, breezeless gully was spent trying to get the stupid donkey to hold still long enough for us to do anything. I was supposed to tell him the whole sad story, then kiss him on the nose. He was supposed to kiss me back and nudge my shoulder. Then I was going to slap his rump, and—the script said— "the heartbroken, dying animal, realizing there is no other way, shakes his mane in a last-minute rebellion against fate, and then with as much spirit as he can muster, he trots poignantly into the vast wasteland."

It kind of grabbed me when I read it, but the donkey wanted to play it his way, which was to cut me out of the scene completely. He managed to maneuver his massive head into a position where he could flutter his long, uncurly eyelashes right in front of the lens, blocking me out altogether. We couldn't call his trainer because he'd start that foolish neighing again and go all to pieces on his underside. A couple of the wranglers on the set taught me to secrete a sugar cube soaked in whiskey into the donkey's ugly mouth, out of sight of the camera, thereby allowing me enough time to kiss his hide-worn nose, on which there were usually three or four big flies! It didn't work on the first several takes because the stupid donkey, after he'd eaten the whiskey-sugar cube, thought there must be more somewhere in the region of my crotch. That had to be discouraged. We had to shoot the scene in very brief shots. We finally worked the sugar-whiskey trick. I got to kiss him good-bye. Maybe the donkey was a bit boozy by then, but he did seem to feel something toward me. Then honey was smeared on the side of my face that was hidden from camera, and more honey was spread on my jacket's shoulder area. My friend, the four-footed pervert, drew close to my face and shoulder, sniffed, and backed away. He was supposed to kiss me and nudge me nicely, but he merely backed away. The jokes among the crew were now fairly raunchy. Motion picture crews, as a breed, will latch onto any sort of mediocre joke and wring it out until it cracks. It was obvious that the donkey was revolted . . . whether by me or by the honey *on* me was debatable. Everyone on the set was roaring with laughter, prompting the donkey's trainer to come out from behind the sound truck to see what was going on. The donkey spotted his love and lewdly projected himself and began to neigh wildly. It sounded as though he were laughing at me! More loudly than everybody put together! Long after it had ceased to be funny, a die-hard property man called out for the whole company to hear, "Well, Miss McCambridge, if anybody asks you what you did all day, you can always say, 'I spent the whole morning trying to kiss my ass!'"

The donkey never did kiss me back; we just let him trot uncertainly off into the vast wasteland and back into his trainer's arms where he probably died in some kooky love-suicide pact!

Still, I find something to admire in a *horse* that makes an ass of me. BUT if a "hume bean" does it to me, I am prepared to kill him dead.

A couple of people have come close! The jury is still out. They know who they are and they know they are on probation. The ax could fall at any time. "You never know when God (or Mercy) will strike." *Boing! Boing! Boing!* Just like *Inner Sanctum!* Just like on the radio!

8

LAST YEAR ON A STEAMY AF-ternoon I was gasping my way along Peachtree Street in Atlanta wondering why. A polluted city in humid weather discourages me. I think there should be a better payoff for inhaling that stuff than just exhaling it. I was dripping and soggy. Perspiration rolled into my ears, and it felt good. It was cool in there.

I snapped viciously at a man who recognized me. He wanted to visit with me in that city-sized sauna. He was a man of indiscriminate age, somewhere in the middle, I guess, and he had that same look that so many others like him have when they talk to me about "remembering radio." I don't mind it when middle-aged people do it, but when the senile ones tell me they remember listening to me when they were six years old, it bothers me. I used to try explaining it by saying that I started very young, but these people don't really want to listen to me; they want me to listen to them remember radio. I find them everywhere I go. The man on Peachtree Street was typical. He waved his arms in full-sweeping gestures and made nasal-screeching sounds. He was describing "the giant killer bats in that cave in South America" on the *I Love a Mystery* program. That show was broadcast in 1943! Maybe earlier!

His eyes were flashing; he was sweating, flapping his arms, very agitated now, determined to relive for me the grizzly adventure I'd had in the dark cave somewhere in the Andes!

How could I tell him that the killer bats were nothing more than a sound man flipping strips of canvas in front of a microphone, and the screeching sounds were made by twisting a cork on a thin layer of gravel in a cookie tin? And that those of us in the dark vault of the canyon-cave were really four actors standing around a mike in the old CBS studios on Sunset Boulevard in Hollywood?

It always amazes me that people all over the country have retained for so long and so vividly the visions they themselves created merely from sounds! Radio is truly the theater of the mind. The listener constructs the sets, colors them from his own palette, and sculpts and costumes the characters who perform in them. They don't remember what they saw on TV night before last, but they remember forever what they heard on radio! Radio was the best. The best for actors, too. You didn't have to stay geometry-thin; you didn't have to be injected with silicone; if your eyelids drooped, they drooped. Tall leading ladies didn't have to stand in trenches to accommodate small leading men. Hairpieces were considered faggy. It was better, more human, less puppet.

Even now I go to a lot of trouble to work the CBS *Mystery Theatre* into my jigsaw schedule whenever I possibly can. For me it is an exercise in courage, in fidelity. It is a one-hour show, and it calls for a degree of concentration and creativity that is distinctive. Very few superstars in Movieland could cut that kind of mustard.

We of the cast, along with the producer-director and the sound man, gather 'round a work table in Studio 6B at Fifty-second Street and Madison Avenue in New York City at 9:00 A.M. We waste no more than fifteen minutes in general bitching and in congratulating each other that we don't look a day older than we did forty years ago, when we all sat 'round just such a table in this same studio, hired by this same producer-director, Himan Brown. This man, for whom I would kill, has always been radio's number one life support. He is determined that radio drama be kept alive if it kills *him*, and one day it probably will, right in the middle of throwing a cue at one of us doddering old actors.

At 9:15 (never later) we go to work, and the marvelous gamble begins. Himan Brown deals out the scripts, like a poker game, calling out the character names each of us is to play. Then he starts his beaten-up old stopwatch, and we begin . . . "cold." All bets are down. None of us knows, while we are acting out page 10, what may be expected of us when we get to page 11, or 23, or 42! It's more fun than anything. And we all love to watch each other as we discover our "character" from moment to moment. Sometimes abrupt altera-tions in style, accent, or interpretation occur in mid-sentence. We are full of surprises, and we are all very good at it. Not merely because we are "old pros" (I hate that term. Why do people always say it with such lofty condescension?). No, we were always good at it . . . good at impulse, adaptability, flexibility, and pure *chutzpah!* Run that by most of your languorous ladies and limp Lotharios who appear in the top ten TV shows . . . disaster!

Once the first script reading is finished, Himan Brown gives us, in Gatling-gun style, the cuts to be penciled, the direct cues to be quoted. He makes a couple of broad suggestions, and he goes into the control room as we go up to the mike and we DO it . . . trusting each other, vulnerable, risking, involved, and electrically concentrated. It is pure surgery, precisely performed; and, at 11:30 (never later), slightly over two hours from the time we first saw the script, the show is finished . . . and we are all richer for the experience. Not for the pocketbook because we all do the show for union scale. We leave the studio convinced that we are wonderful because, indeed, we are! Wonderful practitioners of our craft. We do it becaue we love it and because we are among the very few who know how.

In radio you had to be a tiger or you didn't last. If you didn't keep your toes curled under, you would fall off the edge of that marvelous world. For me, nothing in films, or theater, or certainly TV has ever touched the magical kaleidoscope of radio.

You could be anything in front of that microphone, and that is what was expected of you. In the old pre-union days you might have to play three or four people on the same show. Now you can only be two! Another actor gets a job. Hooray!

I remember settling an argument once between the two people I was playing. We could all do that! I was never as good on dialects as most actors on radio were. Every dialect I did sounded a little Irish. But that was what was so great; we were willing to try . . . try anything! And sometimes it was gorgeous.

A great actor, by anybody's standards, was Everett Sloane. Everett was restricted to offbeat, even weird parts in films and the theater because God made only one Tyrone Power and Everett would never turn in the street if someone called, "Hey there, handsome." He'd know it wasn't meant for him. But in radio nobody was more enchantingly romantic than Everett. I have looked into his eyes, behind their thick glasses, and swooned for the beauty there, and that, combined with his voice and his characterization, would put Gable to shame.

I have wept years of appreciative tears for Everett's work, and I have wept equally as much for his unnatural death—a broken-hearted man with failing eyes peering out from a not-commercially-beautiful face!

It wasn't only the actors in radio who were remarkable. There were the sound men—always set up in a corner of the studio, surrounded by turntables on which they cued up, in split-second timing, bombings, thunderstorms, tidal waves, and gentle crickets for nocturnal love scenes, usually followed by earsplitting car crashes augmented by hammering and shattering glass panes in a screened coop! These fellows needed a dozen hands, and they worked all of them at once. And inventive. . . !

One night on *Lights Out*, probably in 1938 or '39 at NBC in Chicago, the producer-director Arch Oboler was fortunate enough to have engaged Boris Karloff to play . . . what else? . . . a vampire! I was the victim! Every radio actress in Chicago was green with envy . . . and all radio was in Chicago in those years.

Lights Out was broadcast LIVE (everything was *live*) at midnight. It was gory . . . gloriously gory . . . week after week. We did it in Studio D in the Merchandise Mart, and Oboler turned off all the big lights. The giant warehouse of a studio was black except for a gooseneck lamp over the microphone for the actors, and a hooded light over in the corner where the sound man worked. Even the control room was dark. Oboler had a small spotlight on him so we could see his cues through the glass, and it was really spooky in there. I had just spent sixteen years with nuns, and there were nights when I felt queasy on that show. It got sort of Old Testament in gruesomeness.

Boris Karloff was the most docile, gentle man who ever lived. Boris Karloff wouldn't hurt a fly. But the script called for him to break my neck and drink my blood. During rehearsal he made all the right slurping and gulping noises, laughing satanically, and I, helpless maiden, groaned and pleaded and slowly passed out, but the *sound* was wrong. It was rotten. Less than effective to the horror of the scene was the sound made by hacking with a cleaver at raw spareribs on a butcher's block. It was even stranger to watch. Tommy Horan was the sound man. He later became an executive at NBC. There he was in his nearly blacked-out corner, hacking away like Lizzie Borden at the red meat, bits of it flying crazily all over the studio. It didn't work. He tried cracking his knuckles, which didn't sound too bad, but he said we had better not risk it on the air because he couldn't guarantee they would crack every time he jerked them.

Then it happened! Tommy Horan discovered some old peppermint Life Savers in his utility chest. He put them, one at a time, on their ends, into his mouth between his back teeth, and nearly biting into the mike, he chomped. He chewed. He ground! It was a terrifying sound. You heard little tiny neckbones breaking into bits. Boris salivated and slurped, and I postponed my end as long as I could . . . and it was glorious! People I meet currently remember that show! I have never mentioned the Life Savers. They wouldn't believe me. And no matter what heights Tommy Horan attained in the front office, his finest hour will always be that crunching horror his molars made—the eerie sounds of my peppermint Life Saver neck breaking while Boris Karloff slurped up my blood.

❧

The wonder of sound! I believe the most distinctive, the most telling facet of any actor's ability is the way he sounds. What is this person's sound that it separates him from all others? What sound is there in him that strikes the fire in us? Hitler's sound, the sound of Churchill, of Roosevelt, of Jack Kennedy, of Adlai Stevenson, of Everett Dirkson, the sound of Ethel Merman. Sound paints the picture, tells us the whole story of the person who is making the sound.

The empty auditorium at Mundelein College was acoustically quite *unsound.* But only when it was empty. It fascinated me. I was a sophomore, in college on a scholarship, and had been cast as Viola in *Twelfth Night.* Sister Mary Leola directed me to lean against the arched doorway on stage right (forward of the proscenium and almost to the edge of the apron), to deliver the soliloquy about the mixup among Olivia and Sebastian and Viola and Orsino . . . lovely Shakespeare mishmash . . . lovely speech.

At unscheduled times when I had a free class period and when nobody else was using the auditorium, I had the whole vacant vault to myself. When it was full of people, the acoustics were great. But in the emptiness there was booming and echo . . . a perfect place for me to work on my voice, using the meter of Shakespeare, acceding to its demands . . . assuring that enough breath be stored to carry through to the completion of the thought, without strain . . . making sure that the parenthetical or descriptive phrase that interrupted the narrative was reunited to it in exactly the pitch and tone at which it had been left!

Shakespeare is a gambler's game. I was hooked at seventeen and it has never changed. In these latter years it is less risky because I can rely on my "system," but not invariably, not at all a sure thing every time. Most recently, in a smaller auditorium at a great medical facility, the Mercy Hospital in Pittsburgh, I was addressing the staff at their Founder's Day observance. The Mercy Hospital of Pittsburgh was founded in 1847 by seven little nuns from Ireland. Today it is a vast complex of superb standing. What better opening could I have chosen than Portia's speech "The quality of mercy . . ."? The hospital's Mercy, my Mercy, God's Mercy . . . I used it all. The audience can't have known the fast cover-up I had to do to make applicable the line "Therefore, *Jew*, [author's italics]/though justice be thy plea, consider this. . . ." Unless the speech is delivered to Shylock, the word "Jew" can be puzzling, but Shakespeare needs the "beat" of the word to fit his rhythm—the simple silence of a one-beat pause is hollow—so between the "therefore" and the "though" I hung a *hum* . . . a short *mmm* sound to bridge the gap which "Jew" had left. There aren't many places in Shakespeare which allow for such chicanery! I didn't break the meter. I skipped like a stone on a pond through the next line—"That in the course of justice, none of us/ Should see salvation"—and then I could lay way back on the lines that would hit home with this audience . . . the staff of Mercy— being recited at by Mercy—about Mercy! "WE DO PRAY FOR MERCY;/ AND THAT SAME PRAYER DOTH TEACH US ALL TO RENDER/THE

DEEDS OF MERCY." I began the line with a full voice, impassioned in the plea, and then, lollygagging along with all the time and oxygen in the world, I deliberately contemplated, with leisurely emphasis, the miracle that the "same prayer" doth teach us all. I hesitated almost too long to be certain that I had saved enough breath to complete the line with proper effect and still have breath left over. Sister Mary Leola poured that into me. "Never use it all. Always let them think they have only seen the tip of the iceberg." She quoted James Agate, the British critic-genius . . . "Because the character is at the end of her tether is no reason for the actress to be at hers."

I had to learn how to do it by myself in my empty college auditorium. I literally learned to play my instrument by ear. The reverberations that hit back at me from the walls and the deep hole of the balcony let me know that nasal tones are scarcely ever effective, that each word deserves its completeness or it is received as garbled garbage, and that there must be clarity and power in a vowel well turned out!

A couple of years ago I returned to that auditorium to deliver the commencement address. Forty years after I had spent the lonely hours there discovering what a human voice is, how to use it, how much I needed it to express who and what I am, I was back there, doing it again.

While delivering the address to the graduating class, I enjoyed a particular and private gratification . . . "Age cannot wither her, nor custom stale/Her infinite variety. . . ." I could still do it; even *better* could I do it! "Let it out, Mercy, let it far out, but hang onto it like a fish on a long line, then tone it down, let it roll around just under the surface, clear and rippling, suddenly let it leap out of the water and catch the light of the sun before it plunges down into its 'tomb' in the 'sounding sea' . . ." all without effort, all without strain! Even better, after forty years, than the long, long ago in the same auditorium over in a corner of the apron stage practicing Viola's speeches in sophomoric isolation!

ॐ

Shakespeare demands *risk* from his enactors. Any performer who does not risk is not an actor. He merely performs. For a merit scholarship student in theater "risk" was rudimentary. It never occurred to me that I should be embarrassed if I made a fool of myself. It was the only way I knew how to do anything. *Do* it, and in the doing of it, it may turn out to be triumphant, in which case everything is peachy. If it turns out to be disastrous, go hide in a corner and beat yourself for a while. Nobody gives much of a damn for very long, one way or the other.

It was in the middle of my life that I seemed to have lost that technique. I became fearful and tentative and cautious and dull, dull, dull.

But back in college I was very well off in the risk department; I was nowhere near running out of risk. Risk was running out of me from every pore, and a beautiful black-eyed nun knew how to deal with it. Sister Mary Leola Oliver was as slight as Mia Farrow, as fiery as Tallulah Bankhead, as stately as Lynn Fontanne, as witty as Beatrice Lillie, and as talented as all of them put together! I know she must have awakened at dawn to praise Almighty God, but I know she must have thought in terms of theater for the rest of the day, except when her humble adoration called her to her prayers. Sister Mary Leola invented the Verse-Speaking Choir. I think she invented me, in large part.

She loved to act, to design sets and costumes, to coach a dance group, to light a stage, she loved to live in her theater! With her God! Sometimes she would gather the outer skirts of her black habit into a flounce secured to the rosary that hung from her waist. She would pin back her veil to clear her face, and she would set our Mundelein stage aflame. Only her students saw how great she was! She danced, she orated, she whispered, she shouted, she dared, she pleaded, she flirted, she scorned. The theater was denied a wonder when God chose her for His own. I'm so glad He shared her with me.

And heaven help the student who played the part Sister would like to have played. That student was usually me. Sister would always find enough wrong with the way I was doing the "big scene" so that she would finally have to get up there and play it for me, at least for one rehearsal! There was a little "ham" in Sister. There had to be.

A VIP from NBC was a captive audience to a performance at Mundelein College of Sister Mary Leola's Verse-Speaking Choir. It was extraordinary, the choir. Sixteen voices, eight lighter ones, eight deeper ones, all female, all reading poetry in unison, deftly directed by the petite nun, occasionally augmented by a solo voice, which was mine. The VIP from NBC was impressed, as well he might have been. He invited the choir and me to the Merchandise Mart studios the next day. None of us had ever seen a microphone other than the ones the singers with the big bands used at Chicago's night spots, and few of us had ever seen a Chicago night spot. We spoke our verses into these contraptions, and within an hour the Verse-Speaking Choir was signed to a full year of appearances with the NBC

Symphony Hour, and I had signed away the next five years of my gloriously gifted self to the National Broadcasting Company!

I was (but barely) eighteen with a large silver cross around my neck, in my dark blue uniform, with its white collar and cuffs and full-pleated square skirt decently calling attention to my non-patent-leather shoes.

The program director of NBC sent for me to meet with him in his office. His secretary sat me down and said he would be right back. The secretary had suggested that I sit on the couch, but I sank down so far that when she left, I got up and sat in a straight leather chair. That was a smart move. The chair was right for the moment; the couch wasn't right until a few years later. The door opened and the man walked into his office and my heart fell flat on its face.

He was the handsomest thing alive. A bit shorter perhaps than Clark Gable, but meatier, more substantive, less pinched around the eyebrows. This man's smile had already begun to appreciate a joke, long before the punch line. He moved across the room to the chair behind his desk with a smooth and surly sort of swagger that any convent-bred girl could see had "sin" written all over it. His hair was black and gray and glistening and plentiful. There was a sharp little mustache to complete the set. He must have been born bronzed. And nobody needs teeth that white and even . . . and the graceful hands, the gray-hazel eyes warm with the comfortable awareness that he was God's gift to women, maybe God's only worthwhile gift to the world in general, and I had just reached eighteen and he said that he was to be my mentor and would teach me all I needed to know!

9

I HAVE NEVER BEEN LESS THAN unqualifiedly certain that the man who taught me all that I needed to know about radio was the best man for the job. What he didn't know wasn't worth knowing anyway. He taught me the ABC's and the XYZ's of radio technique, and I ate it up. He was generous, this attractive man. He had been a college teacher and had not lost the knack. He was protective of my courses at school, in which I had to maintain a high average in order to hold the scholarship. He arranged my day in ideal fashion.

Typical of my schedule was a morning bus ride from my home on the Far South Side at South Shore Drive to the beginning of the el train, which carried me downtown and around to the north side of the Loop and up to Loyola Avenue, which was nearly the end of the line. From that station it was only three long blocks to Mundelein and sociology class. I would perform as a student for two course periods, then hightail it back to the el station and head south to the Merchandise Mart and NBC, where I would perform as the preacher's daughter on *The Guiding Light*, hoary old soap opera that is still jerking tears from desultory folk at home! Then back on the el train up north to readin', writin', and play practice, and back down to NBC for a part on whatever evening show he had lined up for me, then back to the South Side on the last el train of my day to the end of the line, and onto the bus, and finally home! I travelled 144 miles a day on public transportation. I did all my homework on el trains. I had no idea I was being unusual. It seemed like a very exciting way to live, and besides, I was putting money in the bank . . . my own money . . . a practice at which I never cease to wonder!

On a TV film I did recently there was a young and eager wardrobe woman. There is hardly ever a young or eager wardrobe woman. This one was bright and bouncy and happy as a clam. She said she was "being paid to dress grown-up live dollies!" Beautiful! Exciting way to live!

In college most of my way was free because of my merit scholarship, and downtown, in those cavernous NBC Radio studios in the Merchandise Mart, the cleverest, most beautiful man in the world was watching over me, and I was being paid for playacting. I probably would have walked the 144 miles a day!

My radio mentor was my devoted friend, before all else. The "all else" came much later on, after each of us had tried our best to avoid it. If he had asked me to spend my life with him, I'd have jumped at the chance, but he didn't ask me, and I knew that he wouldn't ask me, and it ended as it had to, bittersweet and fateful in New York City long years later, when he was a VP in Rockefeller Center. His office looked down on the golden Prometheus statue in the plaza. It was a winter evening; skaters were whirling around on the rink. We stood looking down at them. He said, "This is a great spot for an assignation, isn't it?" I agreed.

It had all the recognizable aspects of an assignation. Network executive, young actress, after-hours office with casting couch, Manhattan rendezvous, and all that . . . all the elements of assignation. We had known each other for a decade. He had been my mentor in Chicago, he was promoted and transferred to New York, I had gone to California, and now we were together once more.

We stood in the twilight holding hands, and it happened as naturally and as certainly as we knew it would. It was not an assignation. I hold him in my heart, and I am grateful. I think he must have died by now.

&

He was the first of the older men who moved into my life, caused quite a commotion and moved on or were removed from the scene, usually before I thought it was time. They are alike in that they have all been dapper gentlemen of considerable success in their chosen fields, all witty, all masters of the spoken word, almost all shorter of stature than is considered chic, all determined to make more of me than I made of myself; all of them, to prove Freud's theory, variations on the theme that was my father. All belonging to the same school of devastating charm, all impatient with the multitude of meaningless demands with which we shackle ourselves and each other into servitude, all inevitably irreverent, all something of the scoundrel, all partakers of the feast that was and is my love.

Younger men I've known, two of whom I've married, were not-yet-ripened versions of the same mold. Attractive bravura with just a touch of pomposity gave both of them a reasonably accurate facsimile of the effortless urbanity the older ones had earned the hard way; both splendidly handsome, both the brightest young men of their pack. We shared a few good years, but I don't think I should have been married . . . to anybody. Whilst the man of the cloth was reciting the troth I was pledging, I thought about that, both times. It must have crossed my grooms' minds as well, because while I've married for only a total of two, they share (at last count) a total of six mates. I can't have been the only "lemon in the garden of love where they say only peaches grow."

All the dapper gentlemen, all like my father. . . . Young and old.

My Grandfather McCambridge left considerable land behind him, which made it possible for my father to wear Borsolino hats. In Joliet, Illinois! Weeks before he enlisted in the infantry in WWI, he went into Chicago and had a photographic sitting dressed in full cavalry regalia which he had rented at a costumer's on Lake Street. My father and my mother had their riding habits made by Marshall Field's, herringbone with velvet trim of forest green and handmade black boots and monogrammed riding crops. There was only one horse. The truck would bring the horse into town, and Mother would mount it out in front of the house and proceed to canter down the street on her way to the park. My father would wave good-bye to her with his fancy riding crop and then would repair on foot to Paddy Flynn's saloon on the corner, where he could sip his whiskey and watch through the window for my mother's return from her ride, at which time he would rejoin her for the trip back into the house, where he could change into something more comfortable.

Not long ago Joliet honored me as a native daughter at a banquet. Old gentlemen, two of them, came to me separately at the party, to tell me they had known my father. They said, "John Patrick McCambridge was a young prince," and, "There was never another like him."

One of the really old fellows remembered the night my father, at age twenty-three, made a grand gesture to care for the indigent men of his fair city. My father and a bunch of the boys were whooping it up in harmless, if somewhat rowdy, fashion at Paddy Flynn's when my father announced he would like to host a train trip to Canada for a few of his best-loved friends, all of whom were bellied up to the bar at the time. The less stalwart backed off, pleading that they'd have to talk to their wives about a thing like that. My father was indignant. It had to do with separating the men from the boys of this world. Only three men piled into my father's touring car for the trip to the railroad station. One of them had to be dropped off along the way. He was heaving his cornflakes, as the saying went.

My father told the sleepy ticket taker that anywhere in Canada would do; he just wanted three tickets on the next train north that night. There were no trains for the rest of that night. No trains anywhere.

My father and his two "men" friends sat down on one of the grand old oaken benches to plan their next move. And then my father saw, in the gloomy shadowy light of the Gothic room, scraps of humanity who were sleeping on the benches. Men huddled against the night, thinly cushioned bones against the hard wooden pallets. My father hadn't an idea in hell that people lived like that. He cried. My father cried, at injustice, at cruelty; my father cried for many reasons, especially after a little whiskey.

Across the street from the Joliet, Illinois, railroad station was a hotel called St. Nick's. Never a palace, it was nonetheless a building of some size with scores of rooms containing proper beds for weary bodies to lie in. My besotted father and his raggedy crew made their way across the street, and my father purchased, my father bought the St. Nick Hotel and declared it "home" in perpetuity for all unfortunates who had no place to sleep. "Just send the bills to Happy McCambridge." The newspaper carried the story the next day, my mother carried the matter to the lawyer, and my father regretfully withdrew his claim to ownership of the St. Nick Hotel. But it was a grand gesture by a young prince who is remembered to this day in his hometown as having been unique. "There never was another like him."

In Adlai Stevenson's second campaign my father met the governor's plane in Chicago. I was aboard with the governor, and we were running a little late, so everybody was hustled into the open convertible cars for the motorcade downtown to the Palmer House. All of the top-down cars had banners with the governor's name across them.

Robert Ryan, my father, and I were hurried into one of the cars. We had to sit on the canvas top which was folded down behind the rear seat. It is a rocky ride because your feet are resting on the seat and there is not much leverage and a motorcade moves swiftly with a motorcycle escort.

I sat in the middle, and Robert Ryan and my father flanked me. Governor Stevenson was in a car three or four behind us. He was the *pièce de résistance;* he came last! But his name was on all the cars! And as we moved through Chicago's dirty outer rim and on into the glory of that zestful glob of a city, hundreds of Chicagoans lining the streets saw the banner on our car, saw the little fellow with the balding head sitting up there on top of the back seat, and they gathered that my father was Adlai E. Stevenson, and they cheered wildly, and my father waved, accepting the huzzahs, loving it, loving every impostering minute of it! You bet, Happy McCambridge! Hurray for you, sir! You've got my vote, sir!

I have saved my father's eulogy, written by the Reverend Charles F. Hamel, CSC, of Notre Dame. It reads:

. . . If there be one characteristic mark that stands out above other noteworthy memories of John McCambridge, it is his visible pleasure in the simple things of life—common joys and common, everyday people.

He was extremely patriotic and never tired of recalling the battles and vicissitudes of World War I—for which he volunteered and in which he served valiantly.

John McCambridge liked people, not all equally well, but most of all those who were vital, and human and articulate, no matter what their status or position in life. He didn't particularly care for dull people, nor did he strive to cultivate them. He enjoyed thoroughly people who were interesting or interested; he could go on and on recalling vibrant people and stimulating events that remained indelible in his fertile memory.

He had an insatiable thirst for knowledge, especially history, and haunted the libraries of every city where he might be spending a week or two. Serious reading was at once a pleasure and a necessity for him: food and heady drink.

John hated sickness and consequently hospitals; it seemed to him such an utter waste of time to just stay in bed all day. It was indeed a most kind act of Providence that he was taken from us while he was so enjoying the Notre Dame-Michigan State game.

John McCambridge certainly wanted death to come that way! God seems to have wanted it to come that way, too! So, it is most right and fitting that we, all of us, should want it no other way!

Let us be mindful of him in our prayers. I'm sure that his prayer for us will be that we share the grace of his timely and happy departing: boots on like the soldier that he was; ready and waiting for God's call. It wasn't really Taps—it was Reveille that he heard the bugle sounding.

May his soul and all the souls of the faithful departed, Through the mercy of God, Rest in peace. Amen.

My father and the other men I have treasured knew how to take advantage of a situation. They always rose to the occasion, never with malice or ridicule; they simply added a flair to a foolishness in which they had no design but were nonetheless participants. Audacity is the quality most needed at such times, and all the older men I knew had it in abundance.

Governor Stevenson on a few rarer occasions would pick me up at the theater or on even rarer occasions would take me to Sardi's. At stage doors and in front of Sardi's there is always a clump of ragtaggle slavishly devoted autograph experts who keep asking for your signature over and over again. It must be that for twenty-five of me they can get one Jane Fonda. These collectors know every bit player who has ever appeared in any film in the twentieth century. They recognize them all . . . immediately. How could they be expected to recognize the U.S. ambassador to the United Nations, the man who was very nearly President, not once but twice? Eddie Albert or Telly Savalas, sure! But Adlai who? Sometimes the pushier ones among the hounds would shove their grubby books in front of the governor and ask him to sign anyway. You can never tell, today's nobody might be tomorrow's Clint Eastwood!

I watched Adlai E. Stevenson sign, on three different occasions, in three different books, the words "George Raft." He did it with flourish, thanked the dim-witted solicitor, and took my arm and helped me into his waiting limousine. As the chaffeur pulled away, good old George Raft looked back at the abandoned commoners and gave them that lofty circular salute that the queen uses on her way to the opening of Parliament!

It is the irreverence that I find irresistible. From the time my son was a small child he has always had it. Like an older man, he has always made wry comment on what fools we mortals be. He was no more than four years old when he and I found ourselves at the absolute rear of a big old Bloomingdale's elevator. There were elevator operators way back then, dressed in ill-fitting, fraying uniforms and constantly harping, "Step to the rear of the car, please." We were at the *very rear*! Ten thousand New York shoppers piled in with us, and we began our crammed ascent to Furniture, Bedding, and Rest Rooms. I have always felt sorry for small children in elevators. Their eye level is usually somewhere in the region of all those adult behinds. My son decided to fight the system from his powerless level. In a full and commanding tone he called out from the lower depths, "Excuse me, but did you know there is a child in here? Well, there is, and it's me, and I can't breathe, and I can't see, and I want to get out. I want to get out right now. So stop. Just stop!"

The elevator operator did what she was told. At the next floor the heavy doors opened, the crowd leaned back on either side, and the small boy, head held high, departed from the cage, followed by his proud mother. The boy turned and looked back at the "huddled masses yearning to breathe free" and said, "Thank you."

Nothing delights me so much as a person, unsupported by a group, unprotected by statute or regulation, merely a person declaring himself out of step with the mob and not giving a damn who knows it. My son has always had it, thank God.

When the unhappy city fathers made their desperate attempt to revitalize the poor dying Hollywood Boulevard of Broken Dreams and seedy storefronts and dreary done-in people, somebody had the catastrophic idea of implanting bronze stars in the sidewalk! Great bronze stars immortalizing Jack La Rue and Laura La Plante and Fifi D'Orsay.

My star is very near my dentist's office, which used to be (where else?) on the corner of Hollywood and Vine! Where everything was supposed to happen and nothing ever did! There was a nice Protestant bank on one corner, a ghoulishly garish coffee shop on another, and gracing the third corner was, and still is, bless its tacky heart, a most unattractive department store called the Broadway-Hollywood. The fourth corner, completing the square, which could just as well have been in Cleveland, was a cut-rate drugstore, above which, on the eighth floor, was my dentist's office.

My son was about fifteen. We were to share a dentist appointment. I knew that MY star lay in our path between the parking lot next to the old Brown Derby restaurant and the Taft Building, where the dentist was. I knew, but I was sure my son had no idea, nor could he have cared less.

I'd thought up my scheme the day before. I would, when we approached *my* star, stop. I would make no break in our conversation; without any kind of interruption, I would take a piece of Kleenex from my purse, kneel down on the sidewalk and polish my star, and go right on talking! Imagine my son's chagrin! Imagine!

Not at all! Not for a minute.

My son stood there on the most famous sidewalk in the glamour capital of the world and casually watched his mother make a fool of herself. He held up his end of whatever our conversation was with complete nonchalance, oblivious of the people who were beginning to gather. He was merely a young man waiting for his mother to finish her chore as star polisher. There was nothing for me to do but get to my feet, smooth out my skirt, and proceed to the dentist's office in the company of this monster I had spawned in a fit of wild abandon. Neither of us has ever mentioned the incident. We wouldn't dare!

❧

My son's father had his own kind of flair; his own audacity. After my graduation with honors from Mundelein and my move away from home came my fateful meeting in the NBC drugstore in Chicago with a very fancy young fella who was an announcer at CBS. My marriage to this same fella came two weeks after I had met him. My mother's reaction when she heard he was the son of a Congregationalist minister was predictable . . . she announced she had just held my funeral!

For a year and a half I played on every soap opera that came out of Chicago, and in those days all of them did . . . and I did all of them! But my best acting took place in our elegant honeymoon apartment overlooking Lincoln Park, where I played cook and housewife. I was not well cast in either role. One night I followed the cookbook exactly. Lamb chops and peas became mallets and marbles. There was comment from my mate as he was served. I threw both our plates full of marbles and mallets out the window eight floors above the sidewalk of Lincoln Park West. Another time when I followed the cookbook, it was a roasted chicken. It shriveled up and died in the oven. I peeled it. The whole bird was served peeled. One could hardly eat such a sight. We hired a cook-cum-housekeeper. There was a swimming pool in the basement of our building. I spent the cooking times down there.

The dark and handsome husband was twenty-three, as was I. We spent long hours formulating our plan of attack on the American theater. He would write the great plays, I would star in all of them, and history would be made. We quit everything to think about it; we bought a new convertible and drove off to Mexico to think about it. We thought about it in Monterrey and San Angel and Cuernavaca and Taxco and Acapulco and Chilpancingo and Pátzcuaro and Guadalajara and Morelia and Fortín de Las Flores. Beautiful places to think. My idealistic husband wrote prizewinning short stories and began a novel that would not end until our marriage was a thing of the past. The novel persisted; the marriage died, as did the dream of conquering the theater.

From Mexico we went to California, where our son was born. I was given a great job on Carlton E. Morse's I Love a Mystery. Norman Corwin hired me, and I worked with Bing Crosby and Bob Hope and Jack and Mary Benny and on all the drama and adventure shows. One night just before Red Ryder hit the air, the boy who played Little Beaver had to go to the bathroom . . . he HAD to. So I played Little Beaver. "Get 'em up, Red Ryder! Hi, ho, get 'em up!"

My husband worked on the novel and grew a beard. He had never told me that he had a beard in mind. I have always had a hard enough time working through a mustache, but a fuzzy-wuzzy face is not what I promised to love, honor, and oh, boy! The beard was very becoming, but I wasn't sure I liked what he was becoming. He was Tolstoy!

Tolstoy was back and I got him! He began to sift the nonessentials from our life. Growth of character could come only through adherence to frugality; we must strip away the gloss of relaxed comfort. What, after all, was more important? A rigorous devotion to principles of the highest order or the useless waste of precious energy on ephemera?

He stayed home and thought such things and worked on a novel, and I divided my time between radio and my fine baby son.

New York beckoned, in the form of an offer for me to play *Abie's Irish Rose* on the full NBC network in front of an audience with an orchestra in Studio 3B in Radio City!

My husband went on ahead to find a place for us to live. I followed cross-country by train with a seven-month-old child, a huge black motion-sick maid, and a constipated cocker spaniel in the baggage car ahead. There were very few pit stops for dogs between LA and NYC. Our dog was trained on grass—refused to oblige otherwise. There is no grass along the tracks in Albuquerque, none in Kansas City. In Chicago we found a patch of green as we drove from one station to another. I asked the cabdriver to pull over and keep the motor running. The dog did it on the grass, and we were swept away onto another train, the *Twentieth Century Limited*, which hesitated in Altoona but not long enough for our dog, and I didn't see a smidgen of green anywhere. It was a terrible trip. The baby's formula, which was supposed to have been kept fresh in the refrigerator in the dining car, had turned rancid. I had to boil milk in the galley, lurching around in front of the stove as the train bumped over the rocky roadbed. The maid threw up for 2,000 miles, and we were all three cozied down in a stale-smelling dust-plushy compartment.

I fell into my husband's arms at Grand Central Station. Soon we would be settled into our sophisticated new place with probably a gorgeous view of the Manhattan skyline. All would soon be magnificent.

On the TV show *All in the Family* the Archie Bunker family occupied our New York home. I'm sure of it! It looked exactly the same. Row upon row upon block after block of joined monstrosities on Narragansett Avenue 'way up, 'way 'way up in the Bronx. In the middle of one of the blocks of the monotonous rows of houses was the nest chosen for us by my husband. The only view was across the street . . . at another row of ditto houses!

In that house my Tolstoy worked on his novel and thought large thoughts. I was Abie's Irish Rose. World War II was in its second semester, and young fathers were being drafted. The young father in our house was a conscientious objector. A real one. If ever there lived a soul more opposed to violence than my Tolstoy, it has to have been Jesus Christ!

The American Friends Service Committee helped him with his application, and Tolstoy went off to nonfight the war. I was mountainously admiring. It was a far cry from our dream of conquering the American theater as a brilliant pair, but I knew he was moving toward his own reality, which in many areas was not reality at all, not most people's reality, but it was and always has been his. It seems to me that he had paid a terrible price for it, but he has had to do it his way. He could be Tolstoy, but I could never be Mrs. Tolstoy. I love, to this day, the flashing light he shared with me, the uncomplicated lovemaking which resulted in our perfect son. Beyond the affection I feel for the long-gone young man is the undeniable respect I have for his dogged determination! Against all odds, and forsaking all else, he lives for his work. I suppose he will die for it. I must admire that kind of stubbornness. I don't want to live with it, but I wish it well, God help it!

I went to visit him a few years ago when he was living on the island of Ibiza with his third wife and his fourth or fifth child. I was making a stupid movie in Spain, and when it was finished, I took the boat from Barcelona, beyond Majorca to Ibiza. I spent a restless night in a humble hotel in Santa Eulalia on the coast. Next morning I attended a funeral in the village church for a small girl who had died the night before (still no embalming on Ibiza), and at two o'clock there appeared in the doorway of the hotel bar, Tolstoy! My God, how beautiful he was! Gray now, a lion's mane of beard, the curly hair above the burnished brow, sun-bleached pink shirt, no buttons (by deliberate design, no buttons), rough-woven cotton pants, and leather things with tassels at the toes . . . a touch of Morocco, I guess. There was a golden chain 'round his neck from which suspended a flexible golden fish . . . Tolstoy was all very well, but a man has to look *right*, doesn't he? Again the irreverence, which for me is fatal. We had a wonderful afternoon of bitter coffee and Jordan almonds. We talked of our mutual admiration, we complimented each other on our son, we cried a little for all we had been and all we never were, and we said good-bye and I sailed back to Barcelona. And today Tolstoy lives in Cádiz de La Frontera, and we remain fond . . . on our own terms.

On his recent trip to New York to see his publisher, I invited him by letter to use my apartment. I was out of town with *Madwoman of Chaillot.* Being Bill, he was happy to save the money a Manhattan hotel would have cost. He returned to Spain long before I got back to New York.

When I opened the door to the apartment I knew that he had been there. The place felt like Bill. Nothing was visibly different except for a pretty new bottle of Miss Dior perfume on my dresser, with a note written on the backs of several small laundry-list blanks from the Melía Apartotel in Alicante on the Costa Del Oro. He wrote that he had read something of mine from my bookshelves. He thought I didn't write as well as he did, but he felt there was a spark in me, that there had always been. He wrote that we had pursued fireflies together somewhere in a dark wood long ago. He noted our aloneness, he congratulated us both on our son, and lamented our having been born in an age which had so little space for our particular excellence. He hoped it was my feeling too, for if it were not, it meant that I didn't hold myself in the same high regard he felt for me. He wrote that he loved my courage.

There is only one bed in the apartment. It felt, that night, too large for one person . . . for this person. What I needed was a smaller bed, or . . . no, that was it . . . what I needed was a smaller bed. To this day, I just haven't gotten around to it.

When I was Abie's Irish Rose, during the Bronx time, I was still making a feeble stab at the frugality and hair-shirt routine which Bill believed was vital to character expansion. I wasn't a howling success at it.

On Saturday nights at midnight I finished the second show of *Abie's Irish Rose.* In those days we did *live* repeats for the West Coast, usually three hours after the first show, which only beamed as far as the Midwest. Such as it was, and it was highly successful, *Abie's Irish Rose* was what we now call prime time! And it was Saturday night *"live,"* for real, and such as I was, I was the Star . . . the title-role celebrity! Except in radio it was different.

Three blocks away from our studio were Broadway actors taking curtain calls, removing their makeup, waltzing into Sardi's or the Plaza, being recognized and admired by the populace. Meantime, back at the NBC ranch, I was gathering up my coat and umbrella and saying good-night to the cellist and saxophone players who were putting their instruments to bed in their blue-lined boxes. Then it was out into the bleak emptiness of the third-floor elevator area and down into the entrails of Radio City to catch the subway to the

Bronx. Subways in those days were not hotbeds of crime, but they were hot, and they were woefully depressing. Only the lonely ride the subway at midnight on a Saturday night in Manhattan, and I was Abie's Irish Rose! But a cab to the Bronx wouldn't be Tolstoyan. I DID take a cab from the Fordham Road station past the zoo and the university, piercing the shell of fog rolling in from City Island, and then home at last to a doorway indistinguishable from all the others!

"*Shhhh*. Very late, almost one-fifteen. Tiptoe time. Cold! Oh, God, it's cold. He's got the heat turned down to Arctic again. I'll bet the baby has kicked off all his covers. Big old black Daisy is snoring loud and clear all the way down here through her closed door and from under all her blankets which she pulls over her head. Dear young husband is deep in his nocturnal trance; sleeping dog is deaf; and I am Abie's Irish Rose. Tiptoe, tiptoe up the stairs. Undress, quiet as a mouse, in hallway outside bedroom door. Oh, my God, it's cold! *Shhh*. Creep in nakedness into boy's room, replace discarded covers, kiss sweet little face, sneak back down the hallway, into the bathroom. Water tap is still clanking like crazy. *Shhh!* Use just enough water to moisten toothbrush and one good swallow afterward. Oh, God, it's cold. *Shhh!* Pick up heap of clothing from floor in hallway, fold it over railing and slowly, *shhh*, slowly open bedroom door and grope way to the bed. Back into the space that has been saved for you. The sheets! Oh, God, it's cold! And I am a title-role celebrity! I am Abie's . . . Irish . . ."

As soon as young Tolstoy went off to nonfight his war, I moved my son and maid and dog downtown to a fancy sublet on East Fifty-seventh Street, where I could see the East River and feel more like Abie's Irish Rose. Of course, by that time the show was off the air, but there were other shows, tons and tons of other shows. Good radio actors had "conflicts" with themselves, overlaps of rehearsals from one show to another. I was Big Sister, and Nora Drake, and the bad girl on some shows and the good girl on others, and once on *Inner Sanctum* I played a loony elevator man. There were no women in the script that week, but I had to use the fee from that show to pay my rent, so Hi Brown let me play the loony fella. I was great.

10

❧

*R*ADIO IS REALLY WHY I AC-
cepted the role of the Demon in
the film *The Exorcist* in 1973.
Because it is a 100 percent radio performance in a movie! Of course,
the special effects department of Warner Brothers deserved its Oscar
for the brilliance of its magic visual tricks, by my job was to supply the
sounds that matched its pictures. That's why I wanted to do it, for the
magic that I could bring to it in sound—my radio sound!

Except for playing *Who's Afraid of Virginia Woolf?* on Broadway, I
think *The Exorcist* stint was the hardest work I've ever done. I mean
sheer physical work! There were nights when, after recording all day,
I was afraid to drive over the pass from the valley to my home in
Westwood. I was wiped out . . . I couldn't be sure of handling the
car. So I would sleep in a motel near the studio.

One of the hardest sequences was the invention of the sound for
the biliously green vomit that spewed in projectile surges from the
possessed child's swollen mouth. The visual effect was revoltingly
done by the special effects men. They used a basin of pea soup with
cornflakes scattered in it! The cornflakes covered with pea soup
looked like bumps of food from the child's stomach. The icky mess in
the basin was sucked up by syringes into two plastic tubes coming
around either side of the headboard of the child's bed and then
behind her head, from which point they were glued onto her cheeks
and covered with makeup to look like whorls of bruised or welted
skin, and thence they were put into her mouth, with tiny end spouts
facing out toward the camera.

At the proper fraction of a second the special effects man behind
the bed squeezed the syringes; the bumpy pea soup flowed forcefully
up through the tubes and gushed like a green geyser out of the child's
mouth onto the holy cross embroidered on the vestment of the
exorcist-priest! Dreadful *sight!* But I had to make the *sounds* to
accompany all that!

After much useless experimentation, I knew I would have to do it the hard way. I asked them to bring me from the studio commissary sections of overripe, almost mushy apples, and a dozen raw eggs, and a stack of paper cups. A scrim was used to protect the nest of microphones in front of me, each recording a separate sound track. A tarpaulin was spread beneath me to protect Warner Brothers' rug. I lined up six paper cups on the table next to me and broke two eggs into each cup. Not stirred, just deposited. I felt the apples with my fingers; they seemed squishy enough. Then I had the operator in the projection room run the footage of the vomit sequence on the great screen in front of me. He ran it over and over until I felt I had exactly memorized the frame where I had to match the spew! When I felt I was ready to go for a "take," I would load my mouth with apple sections, munching them to a not-quite-mealy consistency; and then, from a paper cup, I would add, in my distended mouth, two eggs—yolk and gluey stuff. At the instant before the pea soup and cornflakes erupted on the screen, I would swallow the glob I'd been holding, down to mid-gullet, flex my diaphragm muscles, and gag it up onto the nest of microphones! On the sound track you can hear the bumps that the apples and the yolk make! I had to do it many times before it was absolutely right. It made me so dizzy and weak that I would have to lie down for an hour between throw-ups, and then I'd go back and have another go at it.

Part of it was really funny. Warner Brothers and Billy Friedkin, the director, were determined that the whole endeavor be kept secret. Nobody on the lot was to know I was there! Nobody! Billy Friedkin said it would spoil the mystery surrounding the movie if people knew how we were doing it. I believed him, like a fool. Thanks to Billy Friedkin, there was so much mystery surrounding my work in the movie that he gave me no screen credit at all! The furrier got credit, the jeweler got credit . . . I got nothing! In the production office they had shown me the artwork for the line of screen credits at the end of the film. My name was on a whole separate card . . . big . . . bold . . . very satisfying. But that's as far as it got . . . that lovely card!

After more prepublicity than Coca-Cola gets in a year, The Exorcist premiered on December 26 at the Bruin Theater in Westwood Village near the UCLA campus. They were editing the film until two days before it opened. They had to open it by the twenty-sixth in the Los Angeles area in order to qualify for the Academy Awards of the year. (As it happened, at awards time The Exorcist was nominated in eleven categories, everybody but the janitor was "up" for an Oscar. But on the great night, "May I have the envelope, please?" produced only two winners—screenplay *and* special effects . . . in which I played a large part. There was no category for what I did, but if it were labeled anything, it would have to be special effects.) But back to opening night in Westwood. I lived in Westwood, so I walked in old slacks and a sweater and sneaked into the theater. I got there very early and sat in the back on the side with my popcorn. I saw all the bigwigs from Warner Brothers come in and sprinkle themselves among the college kids who bulged the walls of the theater. Everybody wanted to be first to see *The Exorcist* . . . including me. It was, of course, a grotesque, sensational smash! Time for credits came. I waited for the burst of applause that would accompany my card:

AND MERCEDES MC CAMBRIDGE

as

THE DEMON

It never came! There was the furrier's name, the jeweler's, everybody's but the janitor's . . . and the house lights came up, and it was all over! I was stunned; I was livid; my heart was thumping so loudly that I could hear it. I ran out into the lobby, which was swarming with the Warner's crowd all congratulating each other. Ecstasy time! One of the publicity men grabbed my arm and shouted, "Great, isn't it? Isn't it great?" I slapped his face, hard, and ran for the street. I could hear him calling, "Hey, Billy, Mercy's here. She's crying."

I was just outside the big theater doors when Billy Friedkin stopped me. He was saying, "Let me explain, please." I pulled away from him, running toward the parking lot. He pushed through the crowd, yelling, "There wasn't time to work it out . . . I told you we wouldn't have a film without your work. You made it *go*, for Christ's sake." I was looking for my car. I'd forgotten I hadn't brought it. I walked to the parking area, and I got into a car that I thought was mine (you had to leave your keys in the car in that lot) . . . and I started it up. Billy was still after me as I drove the stolen car out onto the street. I couldn't see. I couldn't breathe. At the stoplight I realized the car wasn't mine. I had to drive it around the block and put it back in the parking lot. I just left it there and ran all the way home. It was the night after Christmas, and all through the house, not a creature was stirring, not even that louse Billy Friedkin!

The blacks in Mississippi have a great saying: "What's going around is coming around." It works every time . . . *if* you can wait! God bless the Screen Actors Guild. It went to bat for me, and beyond the first twenty-six original prints of the film *my credit was there!* Not the way it was designed to be, not the way it was shown to me in the production office, but it was *there*. Orson Welles said the dirty trick was the best thing that could have happened. He says if the original credit had been where it was supposed to be, nobody would have raised a fuss, but the way it turned out, everybody's attention was called to my part in the film. Orson once said he wished he were a Stoic . . . I think his wish came true. It fits his character, but not mine. In the dispute before the Screen Actors Guild, Warner Brothers were truly pussycats. They took ads (full-page ones) in the Hollywood trade magazines noting the value of my contribution to the film. Executives of the company phoned me to apologize, but nasty Billy Friedkin, the boy wonder, insisted that the question of my billing "was not set down in the letter of my contract." He was right! Since then I have never signed a piece of any kind of paper without seeing Billy Friedkin's face in the middle of it.

But "what's going around IS coming around," and eighteen months after *The Exorcist* had been released, and was grossing eighty zillion dollars a week, in worldwide distribution, Warner Brothers decided to make an album of the sound track! Great idea! Make a mint! Scare millions of people out of their minds right in the comfort of their own living rooms! All the actors in the film signed release forms, permitting the studio to use their voices without further compensation. But what did their voices mean on an LP album? A lot of talk, that's all. What would *sell* the album was the vocal contribution of guess-who? They sent me the release forms. I sent them right back! They raised hell. I shrugged. They tried to shame me by saying all the other actors had signed the release. I told them all the other actors weren't the Demon and I WAS, and it wasn't "in the letter of my contract" that I had to allow them to make a fortune on *my* work! They took it to arbitration before the board at the Screen Actors Guild. They were willing to offer me, in an unprecedented gesture of corporate munificence, a teensy-weensy percentage of the album sales. I said no. I said I wanted a new Mercedes-Benz, 30 percent of Fort Knox, and, as a bonus, the entire month of October! Otherwise, I said, there could be no album utilizing one peep from my throat! AND there never has been! A lot of money washed right down Warner Brothers' drain and withered Billy Friedkin's black old heart!

I cannot sustain hate for longer than a couple of years. I don't hate Billy anymore. He's taken his lumps in the last little while. I decided to remove my heel from his windpipe and go on to better things!

But back to the studio where I was "fashioning" the Demon! They were hiding me, as I said, and I thought it was a wonderful idea. It would make such a surprise when everybody found out! I believe the damnedest things!

They had parked an unmarked, dilapidated, lopsided old dressing-room trailer just outside the recording studio. I think it was probably used by Ben Turpin. It was only slightly larger than an outhouse. It was my hiding place!

The security man would open the recording studio door, peer up and down the studio street, and, when the coast was clear, I would dash past him and into the broken-down dressing room to rest between vomits and other rigorous exercises in demonology.

Inside the weary old dressing room it was like being in an iron lung! The rump-spring studio couch was out of early Tennessee Williams. The floor was bare and splintery. There was a folding chair facing a blackened mirror. The drawn curtains were institution green. There was an archaic plug-in heater, and in the wardrobe was a single hanger for a man's trousers. I was sent regularly into this place to rest. And hide! I found myself saying to the dangling, uncovered light bulb over my head, "I always knew I'd grow up to be a movie star!"

To punish myself, I would part the ugly green curtains to peek at the dressing room parked across the street. It was the Taj Mahal! A mile long and just as wide, geraniums in window boxes, dainty little fringed awnings, gleaming white and blue paint, a great limousine nestled against it, and a hand-painted nameplate on the door . . . "Barbra Streisand," it said. She was making something called *For Pete's Sake* in a mammoth set which neighbored my recording studio. I have yet to set eyes on Barbra Streisand (well, that's not altogether true. Billy Rose and I walked out after the first act of *Funny Girl* at the Winter Garden in New York . . . I wanted to stay, but Billy said it was garbage, and I figured Billy, of all people, should know what Fanny Brice was really like. I almost married Billy myself there, for a minute). But I would peek out of my hovel to see if I might catch a glimpse of the end of Barbra's nose as she was carried in a Persian sedan chair from her palace to the camera, but it never happened. We were sisters, in a sense, because she was as successfully hidden as I was. When you are Streisand, nobody is allowed to see you because you might catch ordinary-people disease, but when you are the Demon, nobody is allowed to see you because Billy Friedkin is going to give you the shaft!

I guess I was so involved with the creation of the Demon that I never suspected anything was fishy. I was really *into* it. In the text of the novel the Demon's breathing is described as unearthly and eerie, audible (through the closed door of the possessed child's bedroom) to the exorcist-priests who were sitting on the staircase outside. How was I to make such sounds? How would a devil breathe? I spent nights with my tape recorder, trying to get something that would freeze blood. It all sounded hokey . . . some of it laughable. Then I remembered Stanislavsky, who said we could *use* anything we had ever experienced. One of my leftover fathers-in-law said it, too: "Anything that happens to you that doesn't kill you will be good for you." They were both right.

I've always had bronchitis. As an infant it nearly returned me to my Maker. I've been administered the Sacrament of Death three times for it (not counting a couple of other times for a couple of other reasons). Bronchitis is a way of life with me, and when I get excited, I wheeze! I've always hated that sound. In college, whenever a guy kissed me, I wheezed at him. It was less than lovely for both of us. I've learned to control it, but not altogether successfully. What I do when I feel the wheeze coming is try to transform it into what I hope sounds like a lustful moan. It doesn't always work. Sometimes I just have to lie there and wheeze through it. Sex is sensational, but I have to survive, too. Death by copulation is not for me.

Pure Stanislavsky worked for the Demon's breathing in *The Exorcist*. I wheezed! I used it! That which had almost killed me turned out to be good for me. On eight different sound tracks, set at varying decibels and intensities, I wheezed. In tonal chords. On one track I wheezed in middle C, on another in E, on another in G sharp maybe, and then into C again. I wanted it discordant and harsh and continuous. The continuity could only be done by careful splicing from one track to another. You can't sustain a wheeze for very long— maybe a half minute at most—because before the wheeze is audible, the chest bellows need to be nearly empty. It means you have to *strain*. I did, to the point of wetting myself and soiling Warner Brothers' carpet. The inelegance didn't bother me because the sound was spectacular. The discolorations were unfortunate, but you can always buy a new rug. Where are you going to find another bronchial condition that produces hair-raising sounds to send audiences screaming in terror or fainting dead away? At three dollars a ticket, you can carpet every sound studio in America!

Truman Capote told me I was the only good thing in *The Exorcist.* Perceptive person, Capote! But it made me happy because it was pure *radio*— and radio is still the best!

I've tried over and over to think of theater as the best—I jumped into it headfirst. I had been in New York from Chicago only three weeks when I got the leading feminine role in the Lindsay and Crouse production of *The Hasty Heart.* All the tales I'd heard about how difficult it was to get into the theater seemed foolish to me. I had done it in less than a month!

During rehearsals I never doubted for a minute that I was good in the part. I worked very hard. And on the ninth day I was fired. The Messrs. Lindsay and Crouse were distressed because I was green and inexperienced. It was my first part since college, and I knew they were right. It was what the director said to me that had me bewildered. He said he had to let me go because I was "pregnant with warmth," and until I gave birth to that quality I was "as ugly to watch onstage as a woman large with child." His nickname was Windy. That's what I thought, too. The play went on without me to become a smash hit.

Not long after that I got my second chance. One night Sidney Sheldon, who went on to become "the thinking man's Harold Robbins" and has sold more books than the Bible, took me to the Stork Club. We sat in the Cub Room, which was the rarefied section reserved for the "in" crowd. Doris Duke, richest and surely thinnest woman in the world, was directly across the room. When she turned sideways, you couldn't see her at all.

Sidney and I were impressing each other with all sorts of harmless lies about our plans for next season. The owner of the Stork Club, Sherman Billingsley, came to our table and said that the gentleman three tables to our right wanted to know if I was an actress. "Only the best there is," I said. I looked at the gentleman who had presumed to ask the question. He was a pudgy-faced man in the company of a prissy-faced lady. He had very little hair, and hers was severely pulled back from her face. They looked like two shorn sheep. They were smiling at me. They sent word asking us to join their table. They were Marc Connolly and Jean Dalrymple, coproducers of a play, in rehearsal, with Franchot Tone and a beautiful young thing who couldn't cut the mustard. She was Dina Merrill, another of the richest and thinnest women in the world, and dazzlingly lovely! Even today!

There, in the Stork Club, two Broadway producers laid eyes upon me and invited me to their hotel next day to meet Franchot. I read with him, got the part, and went into rehearsal immediately. It was *Hope for the Best* by William McCleery. The part was perfect. A keen, bright, honest young journalist girl with alpine ideals and a temper to match. There was a monologue about the way her father hit a baseball. Oh, God, what a speech! I pretended to stand on the mound, wind up the pitch, check the guy over on second base, then sock it to them. It was a whole wonderful speech, a tribute to an "ordinary little guy who does something extraordinarily well." The speech stopped the show every single night. Franchot had to stand there and wait for the applause to die down. Uncomfortable feeling, I imagine.

We opened in New Haven, and my notices were sensational. I didn't understand why the character-woman actress had a better dressing room than I had, and I thought I might have been offered a solo curtain call, but I was so high on the show that it didn't matter.

On New Year's Eve we opened at the National Theater in Washington. On New Year's Day I got fired! The notices were, again, sensational, but Miss Dalrymple and Mr. Connolly had decided that "it was inconceivable that Franchot Tone would fall in love with someone who looks like you," and besides, the show was not all that solid and they needed another "name" to go into New York. Jane Wyatt had already arrived in Washington when we opened. She saw the show! She studied the moves, pegged the laughs, and began rehearsal on New Year's Day. All that miserable week I played the show each night and at the matinees, and Jane worked during the day with the cast, which was a little weary by the time it got to me.

The D.C. critics John Maynard and Jay Carmody wrote special pieces about my work and the rotten business I was in, and on closing night the producers deigned to give me a solo curtain call. I declined it. The curtain rose, the audience applauded, and the curtain was held, waiting for me. The audience began to call for me, but I was locked in my dressing room, crying my heart out. I was fired, not because I was a bad actress, but because I didn't look beautiful enough for Franchot Tone! The fact that I didn't have a name didn't bother me, but I didn't know that I was uglier than Jane Wyatt or any other actress. I thought I was gorgeous. Until then.

ếa

Next, Elliott Nugent gave me a part in a play he had written for his father. It was called *A Place of Our Own*. The morning after the opening, our *New York Times* review was headed "Eviction Notice." We closed after four or five performances. Next was Arthur Koestler's play *Twilight Bar* for George Abbott, who said he thought that "there were about seventy-five laughs in the piece that we weren't getting out of it." I never thought it was meant to be a funny play. We closed in Philadelphia without ever seeing New York. Then there was the Sam and Bella Spewack play for Kermit Bloomgarden with Frank Lovejoy and Kirk Douglas, who asked to borrow my eyelash curler one night. The play flopped.

I might have had a part in another play which ran for months, but the author—and only he and I will ever know who he is—chased me around his office until I finally bolted. He had on a seersucker suit, and at one point when he had me cornered on the couch, I tried to push him away. I said I didn't see how men could stand to wear those suits. They looked like pajamas, I said. He got very passionate and gaspy and said, "Oh, my God, I wish they were." I got out of there fast.

But I'd never been in a play long enough for the flowers to die in the dressing room. I always took them home, and they lasted for days after the whole thing was over.

Radio paid the bills during the interims of my stabs at theater. Radio saved the lives of many actors who were "between shows." Radio made it possible for me to afford to go abroad. It was time.

11

જ

AT THE BEGINNING OF THE war I had married the boy I had known for two weeks. When he came home after it was over, we were strangers. The marriage sputtered and died.

I was in my late twenties with a five-year-old boy and a desperate need to find myself and get things back in order. There was a man to be made from a small boy. That was up to me. There was the rest of my life. That was up to me, too.

After the seedy little sequence of New York flops in the theater, I felt sure that if I could get to England, success awaited me. The cards had to be stacked in my favor this time. I'd been through my baptism of fire, and now there would be a perceptive British producer and a gifted British director and I would lose my middle-western accent and rise to great heights and all my friends back home in New York would be seething with envy and would be going around saying, "What do you know? She made it." "In London, my dear!" "At Covent Garden, no less, they threw roses! She's the new Siddons, for God's sake!"

❧

We took two rooms near London's theater district, so that I might share Olivier's air, but the little hotel in Upper St. Martin's Lane was no place for a child. It was a nice hotel, but there was no space to play and no place to eat. Many of the guests slept all day, and John couldn't keep quiet that long, so we moved. To the Pembridge Carlton in Pembridge Square. It pleased me to write home and give that address, but actually it was an old four-story boardinghouse in Bayswater. Its outstanding feature was the square, quite large and treeful, where John could be in the sun and air. There were many children, and he made fast friends fast. They played a small boy's version of cricket, and it was no time before John was happily bruised from head to foot. He even talked differently. He never said "r" anymore.

Our room was a "combination"—two beds, two lumpy overstuffed chairs, a phony fireplace, two bureaus, and a sink. The chairs looked like bears dressed in cretonne, lying on their sides. They were treacherous to occupy. Arms sprang up and almost devoured us in the folds. The beds were like that, too. The fireplace needed a shilling to make it glow artificially, and the taps in the sink made a dying sound.

The house was occupied by old people—quite old. One lady, whom everybody called Mrs. L., was over ninety. She lived on the top floor, as we did, and she adopted John. An Oriental bell clanged at mealtime, and when John heard the gong, he would leap across the hall to Mrs. L.'s door, practically knocking it down, and then they would walk down the four flights of stairs, hand in hand. When they reached the bottom floor and walked into the dining room, she wasn't even breathing hard.

She had stayed up in that room of hers all through the Second World War, and when the air raids came, she submitted to the trip to the basement shelter the first few times and then gave it up. It was too much trouble. She sat out the blackouts in her room and waited for them to be over so that she could light her fireplace and make tea. Windows were shattered, a bomb was dropped in the square, and she sat up there in the dark, waiting, alone.

She became my built-in baby-sitter. She read to John in a voice full of expression and fantasy. She smuggled Algerian oranges to him. When I went to a movie, he slept on a couch in her room until I got home. They were devoted to each other, but they had fights.

One night John had left his shoe in the middle of her floor. I was in our room, and both our doors were open. She and John were playing Chinese checkers. John thought he was letting her win, and she told me she was deliberately playing badly because she thought it made him feel like a big man. She got up to get something and tripped over John's shoe. She gave him the devil: "Blast you, John, what is your shoe doing in the middle of the floor? How can you be so careless?" He grumbled. A few minutes later he went to the sink to get a glass of water. Her upper plate was lying on the edge, and he knocked it off with his hand. "Blast you, Mrs. L., what are your teeth doing in the middle of the sink? How can *you* be so careless?" It was funny. They spoke the same language and understood each other perfectly. She was ninety, and he was five.

Another time Mrs. L. had brought a small glass of vinegar from the kitchen. She was going to use it as a rinse for her hair. John drank it—not all of it—but enough to set up a howl. Mrs. L. was certain he was going to die, but I took him to the WC and made him stick his finger down his throat and forced him to be ill. Then I got some warm ginger ale from the kitchen, and he sipped it slowly and he was okay. We went back upstairs to our room, where Mrs. L. was all undone with worry. John lay propped up in bed, finishing the ginger ale, and I told her everything was all right. I told her about the time he had drunk more than two ounces of witch hazel.

He was less than three and I was talking to Arch Oboler on the telephone and John came up to me with the empty bottle and said, "Good juice, Mom." I cut Oboler off and called the doctor and said that this time it was witch hazel and what did I do about it? He told me to give John a full glass of milk, to help absorb it, and I was to follow that up with black coffee with aspirin because he said it was likely that John would be drunk from the alcohol content. I did all the things the doctor said, but John got swacked just the same. He had a little toilet-seat arrangement that had a yellow duck painted on the front of it. He had never mentioned the duck before, but that afternoon he fell in love with the silly thing. He wanted me to kiss it and he wanted to take it to bed with him and that little old duck was the greatest pal a fella ever had. He got fuzzier and fuzzier and finally went to sleep—for three hours.

It was summertime in England, and it got dark quite late. About ten o'clock. Old Mrs. L. was usually asleep before ten. One morning after breakfast she and John got into a heated dispute about the moon. He was helping her tidy her room, and she asked him if it was the time of the full moon. There was a silence. I could hear John take a deep, patient breath, and then he said, "No, Mrs. L., this is the daytime. The moon shines at night." A sigh from Mrs. L. and then: "Yes, John, but is this the time when the moon is full?" From John: "I just told you this is the morning. There is no moon in the morning. Just in the night." She was getting testy: "I want to know if the cycle of the moon is complete at this time?" John almost screamed, "How can the moon be out in the middle of the daytime?" I let them go ahead. They never did settle it. Each was sure the other was a little dotty.

જ્જ

I had three letters of introduction to people who might help me get a job in the English theater. One was a Mr. Davis in the J. Arthur Rank organization. He was a handsome man, and he couldn't have been kinder, but he only had to do with films. I wouldn't have been averse to signing a contract right there, but I was obviously somebody he had to see rather than offend the person who had given me the letter, and we had a stiff social chat and I left his palatial office no better off than when I went in.

The second letter was to a man who *was* the theater in England. He produced or managed or handled just about every show that was running that season, or any other. He was, of course, very busy, but he gave me a few moments of his time. That's all he gave me. He said, with indifference, that the summer was a very bad time to look for work in the theater and that if I came back in the autumn, something might turn up. He was affable and precise. Like Elyot in

Private Lives. Smart, clipped, rich. He was Binky Beaumont . . . he *was* English theater.

The third letter was to an agent, a Mr. Warren in Piccadilly Circus. Like American agents, he turned out to be very difficult to see at all. When I did get an appointment, his phone kept ringing, and he told me, in between calls, that it was next to impossible for an actor from America to work in London because of a labor-permit law. No American could fill a part if there was a possibility of a British actor's doing it, he said.

He thought it would be wise for me to go back to New York and wait until I was sent for. By whom? I wondered. I thanked him; he was in the middle of another phone conversation, and I walked out and into Picadilly Circus and looked at all the marquees on all the lovely theaters.

John kept saying he was hungry. All the time. He had reason. There wasn't enough milk, no butter, no real eggs—we had duck eggs once a week—and the meat was next to nothing. Desserts were watery puddings or an ersatz ice cup or a cake made, I think, of real sponge. I was hungry, too, but it was worse for John. He ran in the square all day and played midget cricket and reacted to everything with a giant's energy. He didn't complain. He just mentioned it. Often. "Hungry!"

I hadn't realized how far things had gone until one Saturday night. Our ration books allowed us, as tourist-guests of the British Empire, a quarter pound of sweets per week. The English had even less, I believe. John and I would walk to the sweets shop up on Bayswater Road every Monday morning, with our books. The man would take our coupons for the next seven days, and we would look at the chocolates and the caramels and the peanut brittle, but we always settled for the sourball mixture. It seemed like more because it was bulky and the tart taste never let you forget you were consuming it and if you got tired of sucking, you didn't have to throw the rest away—you could put it back in its wrapper and save it for the next time.

We governed ourselves all week. Folly to gorge and be left wanting. "Willful waste makes woeful want, and I may live to say that how I wish I had the bread that I once threw away!" Grandfather McCambridge.

John was better at this form of discipline than I was. He always had a couple of spares at the end of the week, and I was usually a full day without any. It was hard to get through a whole Sunday without a sourball.

On this Saturday night it was late, and John was asleep. I wanted to be, but it wasn't something I could do. I was reading a book of James Agate's, and my stomach was growling. What I craved was a can of Franco-American spaghetti and a slice of French bread.

John kept his white sack of sweets in his drawer in his bureau, and I kept mine in the other. Mine, as usual, was finished. I knew that John had saved some. He had told me that I would be sorry.

I looked over at him. He was rolled up in his big lumpy bed and was breathing heavily and steadily. I knew he wouldn't hear me. I wouldn't have to turn on his light—there was enough of a beacon from my bed lamp. I knew what I was doing every moment of the time. I didn't know how I would face him in the morning, but I didn't care. If we'd had enough sugar in our diet, my system wouldn't be forcing me to do it.

I stole out of my bed and sneaked across to the bureau and opened the drawer silently and picked at the sack gently to keep it from crackling. I looked back at John. He was fast asleep. I was safe. I made it back to my bed without waking him, and I lay there and chomped on two sourballs I had stolen from my own son.

Mea culpa. How low had I fallen? My mother fixed my lunch, and I carried it in a paper sack. On my way to school I always stopped at the church and fed one of the statues. A banana for Saint Anthony. A sandwich for Mary. Potato chips for Saint Joseph and a cookie for Saint Theresa . . . And now I stole from my son!

When John and I awoke next morning, I made preparations to go to Ireland—where we could eat. For a whole week. The theater could wait.

John never mentioned the sourballs. John has always been great at letting matters lie where they lay!

We took the night train to a misty village in Wales called Fishguard. It was well named. The odor of the fisheries was awful. It was pouring rain. There was a great to-do about papers and tickets. It was a very wet procedure.

At long last we were crossing St. George's Channel. It was a vicious body of water. We tried to sleep in leather chairs in the lounge, but it was crowded and blazingly lighted, and several passengers felt unsteady. It was so unprivate. If they had cut the electricity, we could have suffered freely. But in the glare from the chandeliers we all felt obliged to be civil and properly un-nauseated.

People are interesting when they are all in the same fix. I wish we could put all the representatives of the argumentative nations in the world on one rough voyage, in one large room. Peace!

One lady on the boat was a nagging-backache-aged flirt. She was trussed up into a tailored suit of blah blue. It had been too tight to wear, but I was sure she thought she would lose those extra pounds overnight, and then she would be svelte again. Her blue hat had a teaser veil which crossed her face at the widest part. Her lipstick had been applied hours ago, and the difference between what she thought her mouth looked like and the way it really looked was tremendous. And she didn't feel well. But the smile! And the crossed knees! And the willingness to have a party if anyone so much as dared suggest it! The circumstances were not ideal, but as they say, woman's work is never done, and one can't tell where opportunity, like God, may strike.

John said he couldn't sleep because he was too tired. He asked me to tell him the story of the night he was born. He loved to hear about it, and each time it was "just once more!"

ঽ৯

It was Christmas Eve in Hollywood. I was working on the Rudy Vallee Sealtest Hour. I wore a red and green maternity dress in honor of the season. The men in the orchestra were making book as to whether I'd have the baby on NBC's red or blue network. I played Tiny Tim. Only the studio audience could see how incongruous it was. I was so pregnant! John Barrymore was on the show, and he reached around the microphone and balanced his script on my middle.

When the show was over, Mr. Vallee gave everybody presents, and everybody wished everybody a Merry Christmas. I went home to decorate the tree with Tolstoy. Suddenly labor began in earnest and four and a half hours after I'd been on the air, I gave birth to John, the first baby born in Los Angeles on Christmas—it was seventeen minutes past midnight.

Before I got to the stage in labor where the go-to-sleep pills took over, I could hear the carolers on the lower floors of the hospital. They would fade away, and then, when they turned a corner or climbed a flight of stairs, the sound would be rich and full and very beautiful. The labor room was dark, but the window shade was up far enough for me to see a long row of palm trees silhouetted against the sky. I thought about Bethlehem. The weather must have been about the same. I thought about that holy night.

Then the pain made my cry, and I sobbed over and over again, "Mary, please help me. Mary, please help me."

Dr. Krahulik was sitting in the corner of the dark room. He was counting the regularity of the labor, and I must have been getting pretty noisy because he came over to my bed and put his hand on my brow and said, "They say that Mary was only fifteen the night Christ was born. She was without a bed. There were no nurses or doctors or pills. She must have been frightened. She must have been very brave." I didn't make another sound after that.

And when I woke up, it was Christmas morning and I had a seven-pound son and I felt hallowed and rich and immensely grateful.

It was too good a thing to pass up, so I called everybody who had been on the show with me the night before, and I shocked them all by saying, "My son and I would like to wish you a Merry Christmas." They were all flabbergasted.

John Barrymore wasn't at home or was asleep or something because I had to leave the message with his Japanese houseboy, but that afternoon a wire came to the hospital, and it read: "Congratulations to you and the other Wise Man. Imagine his surprise when he found that the star he came to see was you. John Barrymore." Everybody always tells about the bad things Barrymore did. I found him a kind and considerate man. When my son was three months old, I had a photographer take thirty poses of him. People would look at the first two or three and say what a dandy baby he was, but not Barrymore. He looked at all of them and had something to say about each of them.

When I'd finished his birth-time story "just once more," John was happy and went off to sleep.

☙

Toward dawn we arrived on the coast of Ireland at Rosslare. It was like its English neighbor town, Fishguard—wet and smelly. The authorities didn't care as much as the British had about our passports, and the routine was swift and uncomplicated.

The Irish have a way of looking at a woman, even on a drizzling and dreary morning. I was offered hot coffee and biscuits, and we were escorted to one of the "finer" compartments on the train that would take us to Dublin. I told the charming customs fellow about how my mother's people had come from County Mayo. He'd been as attentive as if they had come from Timbuktu. He told me I had sad eyes. He stored our bags in the rack and couldn't do enough for us. He called John "laddie-o" and said he hoped we'd find fulfillment and happiness for the rest of our lives. He said it in a way that sounded as if it were a sure thing. I had the feeling that if I could have spared the time, and if the rain had stopped, my entire life might have changed, but the train was huffing and puffing, and suddenly we were away.

The Irish called the train the "slow and easy." It wasn't exactly easy, but it certainly was slow. It took us until four o'clock that afternoon to travel 200 miles. But it was a darlin' trip! A darlin' trip! We stopped everyplace. The people at the mossy little stations in the towns up through the counties of Wexford and Wicklow talked with us, often boarding the train to rest their feet for a bit. They must have done it every day, and like all Irishmen, they were professionals at the art of meeting people. It was a form of interview. Where were you from and what did you work at and how did you find Ireland and were there many wealthy Irishmen in the principal cities of America and did you ever meet Pat O'Brien?

There's a thing about the Irish. They are full of the fear of the Lord and the joy of living, and they don't know how to combine the two, but they'll sure have a good time trying. I thought if I should suddenly disappear from the face of the earth, I could leave John with these people and rest assured that they would keep him wholesome and hearty and well loved.

Our track-side companions would stay aboard the train long after it had left their station. They knew it wasn't going very fast. They would finish what they had to say and then step off lightly. They waved at us until we were out of sight, and then it was time for the next station and a new group of staunch citizens who had a great deal to talk about, and wasn't it too bad there was so little time?

The rain was over and a half-trying sun was warming us and we bought cheese sandwiches and milk and I was happy to be in the land of my fathers.

I had a right to be chauvinistic. I was born on St. Patrick's Day, and I always felt that the parade on Fifth Avenue was just for me. My father, John Patrick McCambridge, was so proud that I was born on the great day that he and a chum went off for three weeks to celebrate!

My father was a noble young Irishman. My grandparents had sent him to St. Bede's School, and before he left home for college, my grandmother got him to a priest and made him sign a pledge that he would not touch alcoholic beverages for an entire year. My father went along with the idea, but he insisted that a rider be put into the contract—excepting wakes, weddings, and funerals. Grandmother and the priest agreed. So my father went to his place of higher learning and promptly subscribed to every newspaper within 100 miles of the school. Each morning he would read the obituary notices and the society page. Then away he would go in his sporty touring car with a barrel of beer in the back seat. He didn't have to know the people. The important thing was not breaking his pledge. The important thing was to have a good time.

My father went through his inheritance in less time than it takes to tell it, but everybody called him Happy, and he had more friends than anyone in Joliet. He invited them all to a big meeting hall where he was to read poetry to them. He had been "on" for only a few minutes when the hall caught fire. That was his only attempt at show business. My father was a real blade, and all the women were crazy about him. The thing he liked best about himself was being Irish. He felt sorry for people who weren't.

He told people he'd been in Ireland many times. And the devil in him got away with it. He had read enough about it to know the entire geography and much of the history, and he spent many an evening of travelogue conversation about the old country.

He had a fine story about our ancestors, and I never met the man who didn't believe it. It went back to the Cambrian Mountains in Scotland. "Of course, you know where that is," my father would say. What kind of ignoramus would say he had never heard of the place?

"Robert Bruce had a brother, Edward, a younger and far more daring lad and the handsomest man of his time." This set his audience up to accept the fact that all the McCambridges came by their good looks naturally.

"At any rate," my father would elaborate, "when Robert became the big muckety-muck, he handed over portions of Ireland to his little brother, Edward." This was meant to be an endearing part of the story. Loyalty among brothers and all.

"And young Edward," my father said proudly, "chose for himself the county of Antrim, where he settled down with his finest soldiers. They were called Cambrians by the Irish."

Here he would always sigh, showing tolerance of the hearty lads.

"They married the fair colleens, and their families became known as the sons of Cambria or McCambridges."

I believed the story until I grew up. I don't know yet if it was a complete lie, and there was no point in asking because I'm sure my father believed it was all true. Once in a while he would run into trouble with someone who said the story proves that we are Scottish—not Irish at all. But he had an answer for such as themselves.

"The Bruce incident was hundreds of years ago, and all the Scots in the Cambrians has long since been absorbed by the stronger Irish strain. My God"—he always shut them up with—"it would be like saying we are not all Americans when our families have been here for a hundred years or more!"

I asked my son if he didn't think his grandpa would have liked this country. He said, "If there's enough cigars and coffee and people to listen." And there were. I saw men on every platform who could have been my father. They snapped along with a bit of a chip on their shoulders, and they always had a ready and ruddy smile. I wished my father could have been with us. I have since learned and verified that the earliest record of our family is on a tombstone in Antrim. In Gaelic it reads "Malcolm McAmbroise—1511!"

Fierce is my feeling of Irishness. It always has been. I have for long years spent as much time as I could manage on university campuses as artist-in-residence or lecturer or visiting actor with a student cast. It is good for me. I like being met at an airport by three or four young people in wild garments who whisk me off to their campus in the official station wagon. Sometimes I am quartered in fancy digs reserved for VIP's like William Buckley. More often I am tucked into the end of a dorm someplace, preferably not too near the cafeteria or the bowling alley . . . both noisy, both smelly. Sometimes I stay for a couple of weeks, sometimes only overnight. At Catholic University of America in Washington I stayed for a whole year. What better place for an Irish Mick like me? I worked as artist-in-residence for the great and good and godly Father Gilbert V. Hartke, O.P. I did Medea there but the high point of the year for me was altogether Irish.

Father Hartke said that the Irish Cultural Society had invited me to appear in the great Constitution Hall on St. Patrick's Day along with the Air Force Band!

Glory Be To God, will you look at me now! I wrote and recited two poems about Irish women. The first poem is a prayer of a Belfast woman before she goes to sleep. It is late. The streets outside are ominously still. Her family is bedded down and she kneels next to her bed, hands clasped on her lumpy mattress, and alone with her God, I think her thoughts might be these:

And now at the close of another day
I've made it to the end!
I don't know what the night will bring
But I'll take whatever you send!
I hope I drop off right away for
I can't afford to think—
If I open up that tin of worms,
I'll never sleep a wink!

Oh, Fiddle-dy-dee, Dear God, it's me.
Most Holy One on high!
How did you ever let yourself
Get stuck with such as I?
Are you weary of all us malcontents
Who do little more than grieve?
Time after time I find that I'm
Here tugging at your sleeve!
If there were somewhere else for me to turn,
I would spare you all this woe
But you're the one who put me here,
So where else would I go?

Oh, Fiddle-dy-dee, Dear God, look at me.
All artifice and sham!
For all the show that others know
You see me as I am!
And I've spent this day in running away
From the one thought in my head—
Except for maybe an hour or two
I've wished that I were dead!
And that's a sin, a horrible sin
I know that very well.
And if I die before I wake,
I'll surely go to hell!

And I quiver with fear in this terrible year
And I flee from pillar to post.
The people are going mad in the streets
And the children suffer the most!

Oh, Dear God, did you see that which happened to me
Today when I started to run?
I'd rounded the bend of our street at the end
And there was the lad with the gun!
It was Frankie McPhee, now he's always known me,
He's no more than seven or eight.
But his people fight on the other side
And his eyes were filled with hate!
And he shouted my name, I was covered with shame
When he cursed me, he's only a boy!
But it made me see red, though I knew in my head
That his gun was merely a toy!

Dear God, how can we sleep when the wounds are so deep
When we're tearing each other apart?
Is there Mercy enough in your Almighty hand
For every Irish heart?
Will we ever be free, Dear God, help us to see
That we're wrong as much as we're right!
For whatever we're worth on this troubled earth
Bless all of us through this night.
I take leave of you now and I give you my vow
I'll do better, I will, on the morn!
Dear Father above, with all of my love,
I thank you for having been born!

Oh, Fiddle-dy-dee, do you hear the "mewee?"
Well what do you know about that?
I'll have to get up and open the door,
        I forgot to let in the cat!
Amen!

The second poem states my own case, my own prayer as an Irish
woman.

Thank you, God, for all of the strains
Of Irish blood within my veins.
For all the McCambridges, all of the Weirs,
All of the Connors and all of the Clares,
All the Mahaffeys and all the O'Tooles,
Some of them brilliant
Some saints and some fools.

For the full-breasted women, the earth-scented men
From Galway and Cork and from Antrim's bleak glen.

The north and the south both are blended in me,
All the rage and the passion; the need to be free
From the well of emotion, the grief and the gall,
The guilt and the glory, I live with it all.

God, a person born Irish bears somewhat of a curse,
But not to be Irish is a fate even worse,
For from out of the pain in an Irish soul,
Insistent as the ocean's roll that pounds the shore until it's raw,
Came Sean O'Casey, Bernard Shaw, Eugene O'Neill, Behan, and
          Yeats,
All of them Irish, all of them greats.

Watch an Irish girl dance, hear an Irish lad sing,
Watch their father observe them as proud as a king.
Watch him nurture his young,
Watch him care for the old,
Watch him share all his warmth
Through a night that is cold.

Watch his wife growing thin, hear her laugh, hear her cry.
See her suckle her babe as she croons "Toora Lie."
Watch her work with her hands, watch her tend a lame horse,
Watch her bear life's misfortunes as a matter of course.

Through the centuries of struggle, the plight of the poor,
What country but Ireland could so long endure
The history troubled? It's currently grave,
Not the land of the free, but the home of the brave!

God, if there's reincarnation (and well there might be)
Whatever you have in your books about me,
If you *do* send me back to this planet of men—
Please be merciful, God, make me Irish again.

                        Amen—Amen

For young John and me in Dublin our favorite thing was an elephant named Sarah in the zoo at Phoenix Park. She had just turned fifteen when we met her. She was appealingly clumsy like all fifteen year old girls. We went to visit her several times, and often she wasn't at home—in her enclosure. The big gate would be ajar, and Sarah was gone. We would wander around the great zoo until we tracked her down. She paid social calls on the other animals. She had ground privileges. Strolling among the people on the paths, she would stop at the cage of one of her confined friends and rub her forehead on the bars for a while and then waddle off home.

Sarah had a house in her enclosure and a play yard. People would give her coins, and she would drop them in a tin pail and go over to her table and pick up a pie plate full of cut-up potato sections. She carried them back to the person who had given her the coin and delivered the plate with her trunk. Then she would allow herself to be fed the potatoes. When she finished, she would reach for the empty pie plate and carry it back and put it on the table. Her keeper talked to her as he would to any lady. No commands or shouts, just pleasant chatter. And she listened. You could see her listening. John and I were devoted to her. Sarah was our dearest Irish friend.

And how we ate! Our first dinner in the posh Gresham Hotel was all the things we hadn't had for so long. I had a steak and a baby lobster. John had chicken and ham, and we shared a mountainous baked Alaska. We were giddy with gluttony. Later we danced. The top of John's head came up to my stomach, and when we got to a corner of the dance floor, he would push his head and turn me the way he wanted to go. It was a kind of walk-dance done in relentless one-two rhythm. When we got back to our table, I held his chair for him. He thanked me politely. It was a glittering evening.

The room rates at the Gresham were a little rich for our pocketbook, and the man at the desk told us about a clean and comfortable rooming house. It was far from the center of town, but the buses ran often, and he was sure we would be happy there. He called the landlady on the phone, and she said yes.

The accommodation that she said was just the thing was on the under-the-ground floor. The windows were up against the ceiling. The lower half of the room was buried in the old sod. It was damp and cold, but the beds were friendly, and there was a heater we could fill with shillings. The hot water was available from six-thirty to seven-thirty—morning and night. Our manageress brought us coffee with hot milk and rolls and jam each morning at six. We would eat, have our hot baths, and go back to bed until the day warmed up a little.

Our principal occupation in Dublin was the consumption of food. I figured in a week's time we would regain the zest we had lost in the rigors of London's rationing. John wished that all the old ladies from the Pembridge Carlton were with us.

It rained and misted constantly and was stingingly cold. I thought that must be why the Irish had such red faces. And the grass was so green it looked phony. I bought John a big burly sweater made by the ladies on the Aran Islands. It was butter yellow, and it cost only nine dollars. He didn't want to take it off. He looked like a miniature wrestler in it. He wore it everywhere, even out to dinner.

We ate Chinese food and French food and Italian food, but mostly we ate steaks. They were not too expensive, and we needed the energy.

We were staring down into the Liffey one day and commenting on what a dirty river it was when a lady in a chic black suit, carrying a gray silk umbrella, started talking to us. That happens when you travel with a small boy. I guess people think if the child is clean and combed and cheerful, you can't be too bad. This lady asked us if we had seen anything of the Irish countryside. We told her about our train trip on the "slow and easy." She said if we were going back that way, we should stop for a few days at a place called Glenealy, where there was a typical Irish mansion which had been turned into a hotel. She said we could pick up the train from there and continue to Rosslare to catch the boat.

So we were leaving Dublin. We went out to the park to say good-bye to Sarah. I told John she would miss us because an elephant never forgets. He said elephants only remember elephants . . . they forget people.

The hotel in Glenealy was beautiful. It must have been a grand estate at one time. The rooms were high and majestic, and the staircase was dark and massive. The grounds were full of stalwart old trees, and the food was even better than we had had in Dublin. I told John if we ever got rich, this is what we should have—this lovely house in the gloriously green county of Wicklow.

There was sun every day, and John rode a young horse from the stables, and I began to think about God. That was a sure sign that I was in a happy state. Whenever I seem most content with my lot in life, that's when I think about God. Not my Guardian Angel, or Christ crucified, but awesome, mystical, Almighty God. It was easy in that place with those pensive and peaceable people. There weren't many guests, and we drank Irish coffee after supper, and there was always a fire and an involved tale to be told. I told John that was the way I thought we were all meant to live. In an easy going, good-natured, untortured way. It was more money than we should have spent, but I felt we owed it to ourselves. John said it first. A bit of the Irish spirit of philosophizing had rubbed off on him, too, and he said it was all right to be spending the money because to love thy neighbor as thyself meant you should appreciate and care for the person you were; otherwise, you wouldn't be doing much in loving your neighbor. He felt that was pretty profound. That was it! The Irish are profound, even if they're wrong. There is no halfway attitude about anything, and I told John it was a good way to be.

The only thing of any consequence that happened on our return trip across the Irish Sea back to London was that two nuns were arrested for smuggling. They weren't really nuns, and they were loaded with loot.

I have often wondered what kind of customs officer suspects such ladies in the first place. They can't have been Irish ladies. Irish ladies would have had "*guilt*" written all over them.

After John and I got back to London, I faced the awful truth. It wasn't going to work—my finding a place in the British theater. I didn't know anybody, and nobody knew me.

Orson Welles was at the Dorchester, and I phoned him because I had worked with him on his *Mercury Theater* radio program back home, but Orson was in town only to find somebody with a bag of money who would finance a film he wanted to make.

Mr. Warren, the agent, gave me no further encouragement, and I knew it was next to impossible to get a part without an agent. I could have gone the rounds of the producers' offices, but I was too old and too tired for all that hopeless hopefulness. That was fine if you were eighteen.

And then I thought—what if I did get a job? Would it pay enough so that I could rent a flat and hire someone to care for John? Salaries in London weren't as high as they were in New York.

There would be parties—if I happened to be invited to them—and that would mean clothes and hairdos and a coat that was special. And endless talk about "our" kind of people and name-dropping and long lines of adorned ladies who would make me feel dowdy.

If it meant trying out for a part—standing on a stage with some knowledge of what I was doing there—I would be all right. If it meant reading for a man in an office for a role that I had spent an hour's study with, I would be fine. But to walk into a big cocktail session and stand around posing and impressing—I couldn't do it, even if there were somebody to take me. A wise man in New York told me that most of the business in our business was conducted at cocktail parties. I knew it would be the same in London, and I knew I wasn't very good at it. There wasn't anything to say that meant anything to anybody. I had watched girls do it and had read about the jobs they got as a result, but it wasn't anything I would ever be any good at. I only wanted to act!

I should have realized all this before I left home. But I truthfully thought England was different from New York. It might have been, but I was either too dumb or frightened to find out. I envied our Pilgrim fathers who really found a New World. I was afraid that my bold venture was only a repetition of what I had left.

I thought we had better go home. I'd have to be a radio actress again, and that seemed a shame—to end up suffering soapily five days a week. I might not find it easy even there. Before I left, I had been rash and brash in telling everybody what I thought of them. I had really insulted only a few, but they were producers and agency men, of course, and they were the boys with the jobs I'd be looking for. I could just see them welcoming me back. Even to my friends I had sounded off about how they were wasting their talents and energies acting in junky stories which would degrade them until they became very rich dullards. I would have to eat hunks of humble pie, but what the dickens, everybody makes mistakes.

At least I'd tried. Not very hard, but I didn't know what I could do. A lone married lady doesn't go pub-crawling in Soho. I wasn't invited anywhere because I only knew strangers who told me what a sweet little boy I had.

I was very restless. It made John jumpy. We would go home to America.

❧

It was the last night aboard the cheap-rate Liberty ship on which we had sailed from Southampton. There was no slot for our docking until morning, so we floated in the harbor of New York. It was a chilly night, and John and I took our blankets up on deck and watched the lights of home. I was full of all kinds of thoughts, like "I'll lick you yet, New York," and through the night I made new resolutions and discarded old ones. We had come a long way, and now it was all over.

A garbage barge floated by, and John said he would like to be captain of one of those someday because they had such nice little houses at one end of them. The one going by had geraniums on the window ledges. John asked if he had to go to school, or could he go right out and get a job? He said that somebody had to support us, and he thought I was getting pretty old. He said he would hurry through school, and then he'd be ready to take over. I told him I might get married again sometime, and he said, "Maybe," but I knew he was thinking nobody would want a decrepit old lady like me. He fell asleep leaning against me, and I wept. I didn't know why. I reminded myself that my father had always said, "If you wake up in the morning and don't hurt anywhere, you are the richest person in the world!" He was right. We were healthy and back in the land of opportunity, and it would be no time before we got back in the thick of things—please, God!

I picked John up—he was getting heavy—and carried him down to the cabin and undressed him and put him in my bunk. He didn't wake up. I got ready for bed and climbed up into John's berth and lay awake, thinking about New York.

The first thing we did was rush to the Algonquin. For years all I ever did as soon as I got to New York was rush to the Algonquin Hotel. The times when John was with me were special treats for him. He had an easy talent for room service (from his maternal grandfather, no doubt). He liked bath towels to be used no more than once, and all the little bars of soap you could unwrap.

We ate a huge breakfast and took a taxi to Macy's where we charged new suits and shoes and underwear and the works. The bill wouldn't come in for at least a month.

We got back to the hotel and showered and changed and arranged ourselves. The Algonquin is just the place to be when you have been away for a long time. Everybody is glad you are back. Mike, the bellboy, and Paul, and the nice cleaning man on the second floor. We sashayed into the dining room for lunch, and handsome Raoul, the maître d', was concerned because we looked so thin, and he ordered for us, and Harold Clurman came up and kissed my hand! Nothing had changed.

And that was just fine. That night I called a few friends, but I didn't want to see anybody. I realized I was tired, terribly tired. Tired from a long time.

I got John to bed and told him a story about a pony and a bird and then I sat in the dark room and wondered what would happen. There were so many things to do, to organize, to get settled. I thought John was asleep, but suddenly he said, without turning in bed, "Mom?"

I asked him what he wanted. He yawned and said, "You won't feel sad if I tell you something, will you?" I told him I wouldn't. He said, "I won't be able to see you so often now." I asked him what he meant. He said, "Now and all the rest of the time. Because now there will be school and all the children to play with and you will be alone." I told him that was pretty silly. Of course, I wouldn't be alone. Then he said that I could go to a party sometimes or to a dance and have some fun that way. I told him not to worry.

Then he said, "We sure did a lot of things, didn't we?" I asked him what he liked best, and he said, "Mrs. L." Then he sighed and said, "All the places are the best. All the places in the whole world are the best. And so are all the people. All the people in all the places." I told him he was right and that he should stop talking and get to sleep, and he agreed and rolled over and sighed again.

We were home.

12

&

I WENT BACK TO RADIO . . . this time, smack into the ample and open arms of Orson Welles and the last seasons of his radio *Mercury Theater*. Orson was exactly the therapy I needed. Massive force that Orson is; he can rouse the dead—and I needed rousing. He made me think I had something "special" to contribute, to share. Orson has a genius for that, too. He can spark you into stretching yourself, into being better than you think you are.

One day in Hollywood, when I was minding whatever was my own business, of the moment, the phone rang, and it was Orson Welles. He was filming *Touch of Evil* in the late fifties, I guess, and he wanted to know if I could come out to the set in time for lunch. Sure I could. Did I have a pair of black slacks and a black sweater? Sure I had. Did I have a black leather jacket? I said I wouldn't be caught dead in a black leather jacket. He said never mind, come anyhow. I went.

At four o'clock that afternoon I was back in my house minding again whatever was my own business. I had been in a movie in the time between Orson's phone call and the stroke of four.

That's what it is like to work for Orson Welles. A phone call or a cryptic telegram giving no information whatsoever serves as the summons, and if you are like me, you drop everything and go to wherever Orson is . . . no script, no talk of money, billing, nothing . . . go!

The *Touch of Evil* experience was typical. I arrived on the set in my black pants and sweater. Orson waved at me and forgot about me. I sat on a stool and watched the action. There wasn't any. Janet Leigh and a bunch of greasy-looking hoodlums were cluttering up a very small set that looked like a broken-down motel room. Nothing was being filmed. Orson was thinking. People were just hanging around, waiting for some kind of direction. Finally one of the assistant directors came over to me. He was in shock. He said, "He's going to cut your hair. I mean, *he's* going to do it . . . himself!"

Very quietly I said, "Yes, I know." I expected him to faint. He nearly did. I decided to play the whole misadventure in that attitude . . . unflappable! So far nobody else had said anything to me. No representative of the studio had asked me if I wanted to be in the picture; no script person had given me a page of dialogue; no costumer or hairdresser or makeup expert had been anywhere near me. I was a black-clad object over in the corner on a stool, that's all! And if Orson Welles was harboring the faintest notion in his gloriowsky genius-brain that I was going to ask him why I was there in the first place, he was, oh, so sadly mistaken. I would sit there, unnoticed and unpaid, forever. And not one eyebrow would I twitch in frustration.

At one point he looked up from his script as he was lighting a cigar, and he waved at me again. I waved back. The son of a bitch is just going to let me sit here. I never stopped smiling. When he did approach me, arms outstretched, he greeted me as though I were Stanley and he were Livingstone; he was so pleasantly surprised to find me in his line of vision. Imagine meeting me here! Such a small world! I was placid.

He asked for a light to be brought over to my corner so that he could see what he was doing. So far he hadn't done anything. I beat him to the draw. I said, "I understand you are going to cut my hair, Orson."

Orson said, 'No, no, no, no, no, no, my sweet dear girl, not *cut* your hair; I am going to *trim* it ever so slightly to give the perfect effect to the character you are going to play for me." I had to ask if he knew anything about cutting hair. He said that wasn't important since so little actual hair was involved. I explained that little as it might be, it was all I actually had and I actually hated to lose it.

A small cluster of people had gathered to watch the shearing of the sheep in black. The instrument of torture was brought. Orson clutched the scissors as a surgeon does a knife, and he executed a few very brief snips of perhaps a grand total of twenty hairs. I like to think it was less than what he would have liked to do. He stood back to see if he had achieved the desired effect. It was evident that he was delighted. Then he called for the black shoe polish. Like a five-year-old with finger paints, the man rubbed the foul-smelling goo into my hair until he had made thousands of shiny, tiny ebony curls and ringlets of what had been a mousy brown head! He asked for a pencil and dipped the eraser end into the shoe polish and applied it to a mole on the side of my left cheek. He put some of the icky polish into my eyebrows, and I will always think he was on his way to adding a mustache, but I stayed his hand and froze him with a look that must have terrorized him!

They brought a black leather jacket from somewhere, and I was "ready." Orson said he wanted a heavy, coarse Mexican accent. I said, "You've got it!" He asked me to walk across the studio like a tough, masculine, hood-type broad. I said, "You've got it," and I did it. He said, in a statement terse and unadorned, that he wanted me to burst into Janet Leigh's motel room with all the other hoodlums. As their ringleader I was to give them the go-ahead to have their "group pleasure" with her, and I was to say in gruff accent that I would hang around and watch. Simple little drawing-room comedy scene. Charming! I said, "You've got it!" I did it. And at four o'clock that afternoon I was back in my own house on the top of Bel-Air, minding whatever was my own business of the moment. And it turned out to be what Orson wanted it to be: a short shot-in-the-arm lift to the picture. Orson knows what he wants, even when he has no idea of why he wants it!

I'm one of a host of people in a film of Orson's that has never been finished. I don't see how it can ever be finished. Those of us who began the film when it began are either dead or unrecognizably older. People change over a span of a decade or more.

The filming turned up from time to time in strange places and stranger situations. One scene was shot in the San Fernando Valley on Mother's Day, in a battered rented yellow school bus filled with life-sized cloth dummies dressed in GI raincoats and frizzy blond fright wigs . . . sixteen of these things strapped into the seats of the beaten-up old bus! The actors were Edmund O'Brien, Cameron Mitchell, Paul Stewart, and I.

It was a hot valley-Sunday morning, and weaving up and down peaceful little streets called Ethel and Dorothy and Eunice was a bus full of strange things to come across on a Mother's Day. People on their way to Sunday service watched us pass. Sitting next to the bus driver on a makeshift stool and facing the rear of the bus was a monster, naked, bearded, and smoking a large cigar! Orson was naked only to his waist, but the churchgoers had no way of knowing that. Gathered around him and over the head of the squeezed-in driver were several half-nude young hippie-type fellows holding camera equipment. We would travel up Dorothy Street and back down Ethel, then across Eunice to Agnes and then back down to Harriet Place. Orson was shooting every blade of grass on every street. It was hot, and we were hungry and thirsty. We said so.

Orson ordered the poor rented bus driver to stop at a pizza palace. There were some customers seated at the outside tables under the garish sun parasols. It must have been unsettling for those people to see our group pile out of our conveyance, leaving behind, and strapped into their seats, the sixteen dummies in the raincoats and blond wigs. Orson refused to alight from the bus. That was just as well.

After we'd been nourished, if that's what it was, we clambered aboard our prairie ship once more to continue the exciting trek up Dorothy and down Ethel. Orson had called out to the strangers at the tables, "Don't anybody leave . . . we will be back." We drove 'round that way fully two hours later. Some of them were still there.

After that episode in the never-ending filming, Orson disappeared again. Somebody said he was in Yugoslavia; somebody else said he was not, he was hiding in a rented house off Benedict Canyon. Nobody knew. Nobody ever knows. That's how Orson wants it.

Then, two years later, came the call. "Mr. Welles wants you to join him to continue the picture in Cave Creek, Arizona. Your ticket to Phoenix will be prepaid at Los Angeles Airport, and you will be met in Phoenix for the drive to Cave Creek. Bring your suit (same old costume)."

Cave Creek, Arizona! Halfway up a cliff, and fitted into the rocks like a finely made gold inlay between two teeth, were an enchanted house and swimming pool so beautifully designed that there was not the slightest disturbance of nature's intention in the vast desert. If a great boulder was in the way, the swimming pool went around it; nor did the house itself intrude on its surroundings. The place was heaven, and Orson was in command of it.

John Huston and his then-current spouse arrived from Turkey. Hoary John and voluminous Orson embraced each other in front of the huge picture window against the backdrop of the russet, wasted monumental rocks. It was historic and geologic, and I was thrilled to be there.

John Huston kissed me and said, "My God, Mercy, you are the only one of my friends who doesn't shake."

He and Orson sat facing each other in the late-afternoon light. They asked me to stay. They discussed John's role in the film. He would play the part Orson must have written for himself, but decided not to enact. I sat close to the two brilliant moviemakers and listened to them draw each other out about the character. They both wore elaborate King Lear-sized beards. John asked Orson if he thought his beard would be right for the part. They agreed and disagreed and finally decided that it might not be the correct impression to portray a great film director with a full beard. It wouldn't seem right somehow! And there sat the two great film directors with full beards giving two wrong impressions of what a real-life great filmmaker should look like.

Orson was on a diet of canned stewed tomatoes that season. The rest of us weren't. When you say things to Orson Welles such as "Listen, Orson, we all think it is just grand about you and all the canned tomatoes, but the rest of us are less than captivated by the cuisine around this place . . . none of us wants to die in the desert of malnutrition," when you say things like that to Orson, his great face registers such incredulity . . . the lips part, the jowls drop, and the eyes go all-over mistylike! You have injured him now, perhaps irreparably. He will attempt to pull himself together, but the wound was so sudden, and from YOU, of all people. The mighty jaw juts forward, the head tilts slightly, and the grand exit from the room takes place! The King of the Jungle has been struck with a slingshot! He will retire to his lair, where he can clean the ugly gash in his magnificent hide!

All you have said is: "We need better food than we are getting at the hands of the local Cave Creek cooking experts."

Orson was not visible until noon of the following day. He shuffled majestically into the great sitting room in his purple circus-tent robe. His smile was beatific. Before us was a man who hadn't been ruffled by anything since the fall of the Maginot Line in World War the Twoth! He was particularly pleased to see me. It was obvious that I was his favorite. He exhaled mightily, letting all the breath rasp out of his barrel chest, and then so softly, so caressingly he cooed at us, "I trust

"Sister Mary Leola's Verse Speaking Choir, 1937." (Photo courtesy of Mundelein College.)

"En route to Oscar." *All the King's Men.* (Courtesy of Columbia Pictures. Copyright © Columbia Pictures Corp., 1949.)

"Son John and Mom playing 'Hallelujah!'—a hollering game."
(Photo by George Karger, *Life* magazine. Copyright © Time Inc., 1947.)

"The great man."
Celebrating Adlai E.
Stevenson III's fifty-second
birthday, 1952. (Photo by Bus
Jackson.)

"A horse had just been hurt. Nobody much cared!"
Bullfight, Mexico, 1955.

*"Two very close friends on the
ranch in Texas."*
Jimmy Dean on the set of
Giant, 1955. (Photo by Sid
Avery.)

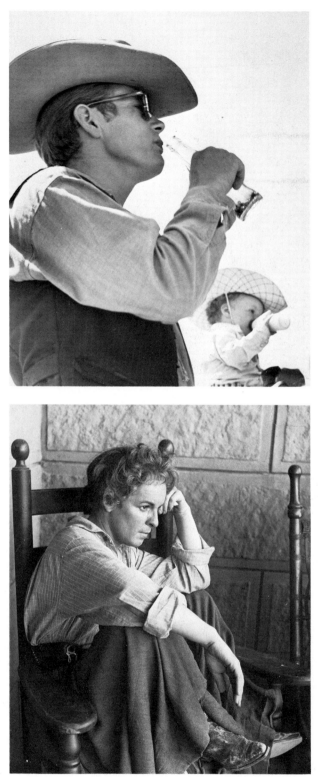

"Life is a bitch, it really is."
From *Giant*. (Photo by Floyd
McCarter. Copyright ©
Warner Bros., Inc. 1955.)

"Better watch out, Joan Crawford. I'm a little upset!"
From *Johnny Guitar*. (Photo by Charles Albright. Copyright © Republic Pictures Corp., 1959.)

"Elizabeth is wonderful in this film."
From *Suddenly Last Summer*. (Photo by Charles Albright. Courtesy of Columbia Pictures. Copyright © Columbia Pictures Corp., 1960.)

"A veranda full of talent . . . and me."
From *Suddenly Last Summer.* (Photo by Charles Albright. Courtesy of Columbia Pictures.
Copyright © Columbia Pictures Corp., 1960.)

"Performing the foul deed with the reluctant George."
From *Angel Baby.* (Photo by Charles Albright. Copyright © Allied Artists Pictures Corp.,
1961.)

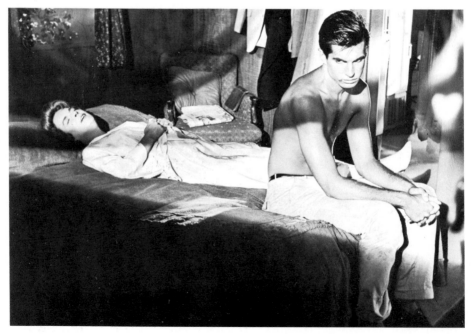

"A great day for the Irish!"
With Mayor and Mrs. Daley, St. Patrick's Day, 1967.
(Photo by Dan Lydon.)

"Sir Malcolm Percy—King of Beasts, 1967."
(Photo by David Mobley.)

"Can't you see I want you to love me? I'm so nice!!"
(1978.)

that you will be pleased to know that I, at great effort and considerable expense, have been able to secure for your delectation not one, but two, highly regarded chefs of the Cordon Bleu." And then he added, "The Cordon Bleu of Fresno, California." I didn't dare look at anybody in the room. I couldn't afford it! One snicker in that room at that sacred moment would have cost me my head.

Hours later the dusty road leading to our desert castle was a thick cloud of billowing sand out of which emerged a pickup truck containing pots and pans and two long-haired, tattooed, barefoot, bead-adorned refugees from the Haight-Ashbury in San Francisco via Fresno, courtesy Cordon Bleu.

Chicken Divan on paper plates in 100-plus-degree-heat placed in front of you by an arm which says, "Up yours," is an enrichment of sorts. One night we had some kind of rare sauce over beef, and Orson and John Huston washed down the beef, the sauce, and at least the top shreds of the paper plates with very good wine as they outdid each other recalling meals they had enjoyed in Hong Kong, in Kashmir, and on the island of Minos in that dear cave near the sea!

There is a special bond between Orson and John. Each has acted under the other's direction. They go back a long way together. Each has maintained his uniqueness, his mark of excellence, each has been large enough to fail, and neither has been successfully imitated.

One very late night John and I were doing a scene for Orson, or trying to. The crew was exhausted. All of us had been on continuous "call" for sixteen or seventeen hours. Dinner had been ages ago. The barefoot chefs had long since emptied their paper plates into the bulging garbage bags and had taken off for another night of wild revelry in Cave Creek, where the only sound after 10:00 P.M. was the rattle of a nervous snake.

Orson was medium-cranky, I was all-cranky, and John Huston was drinking 140-proof Polish vodka.

The scene, which we had shot ten zillion times, was still not what Orson wanted. He had three cameras working at oblique angles, in less than half-light, and the action was contained in a rise by John from a three-legged wicker bathroom stool to his full height. I was framed in the doorway, and as John rose, I was to turn back to him and say, "What other girl?" End of scene. Not your average De Mille extravaganza . . . man rises, woman turns, says three words, and good night, folks! Not with Orson. It might have been the parting of the Red Sea with a cast of thousands!

John Huston is tall tall tall. Orson wanted him to rise slowly, which is hard when you are that tall, especially if you are rising from a short stool. Lean, lanky John balanced himself beautifully over and over again. I timed my turn in the doorway to coincide with his movement so that we were both caught in frame precisely. We were right! Time after time after time! Orson said there was something wrong. "What, Orson?" He said he didn't know, but if we kept doing it, he'd find the problem. We were ready to die! We kept doing it, and he found the problem. I was it!

Orson blamed it on the dancing lessons I had as a child. I thought he had lost his mind . . . he was right! While John Huston was straining his tendons to rise slowly into full figure, I was turning to him in the doorway, but I was *pivoting!* It was mechanical . . . like a clay figure on a turntable. There was no body movement, no shifting from one foot to the other, and it flawed the picture. It was a phony turn! I did it right just before daybreak. Orson was buoyant! The last thing he did before calling it a day, and a night, and almost another day, was to address the spare form of his fatigued friend Mr. Huston, who was folded like a fallen puppet on the ridiculous little bathroom stool. Orson boomed, "Very good, John," and from his crumpled position John boomed back, "Thank you, Orson." Two lifetimes of learning the art of filmmaking were summed up in six words spoken in significant mutual respect:

"Very good, John."

"Thank you, Orson."

❧

Much of our time in dear old Cave Creek, Arizona, was given over to staying awake while Orson developed his next move. We drank gallons of prefabricated iced tea and lolled on the rocks that jutted dramatically around the swimming pool. Some of us were beginning to look as scaly and leathery as the rest of the iguanas and gila monsters of the area. Each of us had long since exhausted the actor's store of tall tales of past triumphs. Like in the song from *Oklahoma!*, we lay on our blistered backs and watched the hawks doing their lazy loops in the sky, except I think our birds were vultures. And some of them were flying low. Orson stayed in the house.

Conversation was out of the question. It was too hot to talk. All of our jokes had died! Once in a while one of us would attempt to jostle the rest of us with a simple declaration such as: "Did you know that there is a famous plastic surgeon in Rio de Janeiro who only lifts behinds?" Everybody either knew or didn't give a damn because there was no reaction whatsoever. Then some persistent but foolhardy gold mine of useless information would add to his own ignominy by saying: "I heard that Jackie O. went down there and had it done and had to lie flat on her face for eight weeks!" Somebody else came to life long enough to say: "If you have to lie in one position for eight weeks, Rio is a hell of a place to have to do it."

Somebody else closed the subject forever by saying that Rio was the only place where you could go and have the Sugar Loaf lifted from your own mountain. Everybody in the pool!

On such a desultory day did Orson choose to order Rich Little and me to stand by to position ourselves on the roof of the house at sunset. The great man explained that he wanted to capture the magic moment immediately before the desert sun slides like a giant egg yolk down the other side of the world. There IS a light in that instant that is the color of a new lemon. The light is blinding just as it disappears. That's what Orson was after. It meant an entire afternoon of elaborate planning. He wanted to shoot it with his three-camera technique which meant that the clumsy equipment had to be carried or hoisted onto precarious perches. One huge light fell onto the stone patio . . . great hunks of broken glass in the pool, in the iced tea, in the folds of the lounge chairs and, worse luck, we had one less piece of expensive equipment—way out in the middle of nowhere.

If I have to climb into heaven on a ladder, I shall have to decline the invitation. I cannot go anywhere on a ladder. Never could. Going up is sheer agony, and going down is impossible. I cannot do it. I did it, of course, for Orson. Orson couldn't do it for me, or for heaven or for anything. His girth is not ladder material. So he stayed down there on level ground in his billowing balloon of a bathrobe, shouting at me to keep going . . . I was almost there.

The view was terrific. I could see all the way to Milwaukee. Rich Little fairly leaped up the ladder. He's a Canadian, and Canadians are inclined to leap a lot, particularly if anyone is watching. I was married to one of them. When you've seen one leaping Canadian, you've seen them all. Rich Little wasn't about to get any "bravos" from me. I was anything but happy up on that roof because I knew the descent on the ladder would be my last mortal endeavor.

Orson directed us, inch by inch, to a spot where we would be etched against the magic lemon-green brilliance of the sky when the exact moment came. He threatened to kill us if we ruined the shot because it meant that a retake would have to wait until tomorrow at sunset, when the sky might well be overcast and the light would be all wrong.

It gave me a funny feeling. I was playing a scene with the incomprehensible universe, for heaven's sake. I had no chance to rehearse with the sun; I had no idea what its timing might be; how could I retain any spontaneity, any fresh discovery in a scene where I was at the whim of a big yellow blob of fire that would surely be upstaging me anyhow?

The three cameras and their crews were at the ready. Rich Little had smoothed his hair for the ninety-sixth time. All we needed now was the sun which, we hoped, had read the script and knew its cue to do its thing!

Orson had made it painfully clear that Rich Little and I were to stand with our backs to the sun, our shoulders barely touching. Orson growled that the shot was absolutely critical in its focus for all three cameras, and therefore, even the slightest movement from us might knock us out of frame. I gathered that what he wanted was two statues on a roof. But that wasn't what he wanted. Every time you figure you know what Orson wants, it turns out to be anything but what Orson wants. This time he wanted us not to move, BUT, he yelled as the magic moment came nearer, "I want you both up there to be still as stone. I want you to give me the feeling that you are being jostled; I need that feeling from both of you."

Rich Little mumbled, "Oh, my God."

I mumbled back, "It's simple. Think jostle, but don't move."

Rich Little hadn't worked for Orson before and was therefore not to be blamed for asking a question like "How do we do that, Orson?" When Orson feels that a question is so stupid that it doesn't deserve an answer, he stares at the inquirer with what can only be called gentle horror! He wants so much to believe that the questioner is above the sort of thing that has just escaped his lips.

"Sweetheart," he called to Rich Little, "listen to me, my friend. I want you to keep your bodies rigid from the waist up, but I want your lower extremities to be jostled. Is that clear to you up there, my children?"

In a million years I will never know why Rich Little felt he had to pursue this meaningless quest. He asked Orson *why* our lower extremities were being jostled.

That did it! Orson threw his great bearded head back and confronted the heavens. I think he was addressing God, directly. He shouted, "Why must I be challenged in such things? Why? Why? Why?"

Rich Little stammered something civil about merely wanting to do it right.

Orson sighed to the ocean depths within him and said, "I need your shoulders to be still, your hips to sway ever so slightly, a rocking on your heels that is barely noticeable . . . all of this will give me the effect I need with the midgets that will be milling around your feet and between your legs."

Why did Rich Little have to ask, "What midgets, Orson?" Orson was beginning to look the way Christ must have looked when he found the money changers in the temple.

He refused to communicate further. He beckoned his assistant cameraman and relayed the message through him. It wafted up to us: "Mr. Welles says never mind what midgets. Mr. Welles says he's going to be filming them in Spain next month."

Only a certain breed of actor should ever even try to work for Orson Welles. I'm glad I'm one of that breed.

PART *Two*

13

*

ORSON IS ONE OF THE HIGH-est peaks in my life. I seem to stumble onto my peaks as often as I tumble into my valleys. I might never have stumbled onto an Oscar if it hadn't been for a pushy friend of mine, Elspeth Eric. She hangs onto a notion until she has whirled all the life from it. My grandfather used to do that with chickens, by wringing their necks. It was a violent pinwheel of feathers and then a flinging to the ground, and that night we ate supper from the remains.

My friend hasn't the violence, but she can't let go of an idea. Good or bad she pursues it to the end.

We had lunch at Sardi's. It was late 1948. I'd only been home from my London un-triumph for a few months, and already I'd landed a part in a play on Broadway. I may not have belonged in London having luncheon at the Savoy with Sir Ralph Richardson, but I damned well belonged in New York having luncheon at Sardi's with my friend Miss Eric. I have always entered Sardi's restaurant in one of two attitudes. If I am merely meeting someone for lunch or being escorted to dinner as a non-performing-on-Broadway person, I assume a bemused air, as though I feel, in some fashion, out of place, intimating that I enjoy the ambience of theater and its folk, and hope that my eyes reveal that somewhere in another life I might have been a part of it all, but regrettably I am only passing through.

If, however, I am appearing in a play and can manage to get to Sardi's before the play closes (which has been, on occasion, too soon to reserve a table), I enter Sardi's with my other attitude. I guess it could best be called "Prize Bitch!" I learned it from the experts whom I watched making *their* entrances. The ones with real class avail themselves of the "bitch" bit only when they are in a play. The seedy, "never will make it in a hundred years" ones enter like that all the time. They almost never, if ever, have been on Broadway, but they keep surviving on the Yul Brynner or Anne Bancroft pills they take, and they keep sweeping into Sardi's and usually sweeping right out again after making a quick round of the tiny bar and the rest rooms upstairs. Who knows? One day Mr. Big will grab them up and make great stars of them overnight! Right? Wrong!

My friend Elspeth mentioned over the canneloni (no restaurant but Sardi's should be allowed to serve canneloni) that a cattle call had gone out for that very afternoon at the office of Columbia Pictures. A cattle call is one of the most disgusting things in show business. Little people with big heads send out the word that they are ready to take a look at all the "flesh," review all the "bodies," all the "puppets" in New York. "Just run them all into the corral, and we'll sift through them in no time."

I disdained Elspeth's stupid suggestion that we join the livestock display. I was, after all, in a play . . . a running play . . . not playing to capacity, but alive and well. It was *The Young and Fair*. Julie Harris was in it, as was Frances Starr, a theater *grande dame* from the Belasco era. It was a good play; my personal notices were peachy, and the salary wasn't bad. Why would I demean all the wonder of me by showing up at a Columbia Pictures cattle call? My friend prevailed.

On the floor of the Columbia Pictures offices, the elevator doors opened to what might have been the dayroom at any state institution. When a herd of actors gets together in one place, particularly when they are all looking for the few jobs that might be available, there is a special kind of jubilation . . . overdone . . . overplayed. The laughter is pitched too high; it jangles loudly, and rings false. There is much posturing and sucking in of stomachs and lifting up of chins. Topcoats are never fully on, nor are they left on chairs or hooks. Everybody wears his or her coat on the shoulders. Old actors, new actors, fat actors, skinny actors, holy actors, tipsy actors, actors of every hue— all of whom left their names "with the girl at the desk," as did my friend Elspeth and I. There was no place to sit, almost no place to stand. Our "lowing herd" could not "wind slowly o'er the lea." There was no room to wind slowly o'er our lea where everyone was lowing and blowing a lot of smoke at everyone else.

"The girl at the desk" would call out a name: "Darrylynn Obecheck." The two-footed animal answering to that name scurried into the chute, and the door to the Colosseum was opened and shut behind her. No need to fret . . . not for very long. In less time than it takes to call off the married names of Zsa Zsa Gabor, Darrylynn was back among the herd. Given the good old boot, she was. Thumbs down for Darrylynn. Back to pasture, old girl!

I watched this happen over and over and over again. Men and women, and children of all ages and sizes, fed into the jaws behind the great door and vomited up almost immediately. "An actor's ego is his stock in trade." Every actor's ego in that awful room died a little that day. Having been dismissed from the presence of the mighty ones the actor had to walk the distance to the elevator. It was a long trip. He might wave to a friend or stop to peck a kiss onto the forehead of a girl he knew, but his feet kept moving. With luck the elevator would be right there, at the floor; otherwise, it was best to take the fire stairway down a flight. The main thing was to get out of there with some crumbs of his dignity.

I was livid when "the girl at the desk" intoned loudly, "Mercedeees McComber . . . Mercedeees McComber . . . next!" As I passed her, I caught a snootful of a scent I recognized as the "West Village Whiff." It has been the same since I can recall. Muskey-oxey-stale-camel-caravan-old-Turkish-blanket smell. West Villagers all smell like that, and she more than most.

She opened the great door and looked at me. I looked at her. I was waiting for someone to say, "Come in, Miss McComber." Nobody did. I stepped in sideways, and the door closed behind me.

The room was paneled in the typical dreariness of a boardroom in any prestigious organization. The long gleaming table was hemmed in by twenty vacant leather chairs. At either end of the table, a continent apart, was an occupant in a king-sized upholstered chair. One occupant was a little guy with a broad face. The other occupant was a big guy with a narrow face. Both faces medium attractive, California brown.

I wasn't asked to sit down. They didn't say anything. They didn't tell me their names. They had the wrong name for me. It was a good beginning. The little guy with the broad face said, "Miss McComber, you are—"

I took an aggressive step toward him and said, "No, sir, I am not."

He looked down the long table at his colleague, and then he lifted his gold pencil to his mouth and set it between his teeth, like Carmen and her long-stemmed rose. Sun-browned as he was, the gleaming cylinder made him look like one of those African tribal chiefs in *National Geographic* magazine who wear jeweled spikes through their noses. This little guy looked as if he had missed the mark and caught it right in the kisser. He talked at me through the barrier. "I beg your pardon," he said.

I said, "Thank you."

I was standing where the net would be if the room were a tennis court. I looked back and forth at the players, waiting for somebody to serve. It was their ball game, not mine. Nothing! I looked back and forth, two times each. Finally old gold-pencil-in-the-face said, "You say you are not . . ."

I retorted, mincingly, "No, sir, I am *not* Miss McComber [which can be said mincingly to some effect. So I said it again]. I am *not* Miss McComber, and I don't care if you ever find out who I am. I don't care if I ever find out who you are. I think it will be just dandy if we maintain our anonymity all the way around." I held them for two back-and-forth looks, and then I said: "I don't know what you are here for, but I want to tell you that if you were planning to film the Last Supper with the original cast and if you offered me a million dollars to play a part in it, I wouldn't be interested, thank you very much." The little guy had taken to wiping off the saliva on his gold pencil with his fancy-Dan handkerchief. The big guy at the other end looked at his watch. I pointed to the waiting room beyond the door. "I have been sitting out there in that stagnant room, jam-packed with people who live by their wits, and I have watched you shoot them down, some in two minutes time. In, out! In, out!" My mouth was getting dry. "Who in hell do you think you are, gentlemen? Why did you make this foolish trip? If you want pretty faces, go back to Schwab's drugstore on Sunset Boulevard. If you want cowboys, go back and talk to John Wayne, but don't come riding your palomino ponies into New York City and mow down a whole room full of live actors in the space of one afternoon!" I lowered my voice to a basso and divided my parting shot equally between them. I looked at one end of the tennis court and said to the big guy, "Thanks for the use of the hall, gentlemen." Then I looked down to the little guy and said, "I bid you a joyous farewell." I had timed it so that the last word, said lingeringly enough, would carry me all the way to the door. It did. I reached for the doorknob. I missed. I had to fan at it. My hand shook.

The big guy with the narrow face applauded. Slow, deliberate, harsh clapping of his hands. I turned to him. Instinct, I guess. The little guy with the broad face was smiling—broadly, without the pencil. He said, "That was great. Really. Absolutely great!"

He asked me to sit down. I declined. The big guy said, "Oh, for Christ's sake, sit down!" I sat, in a huge board member's leather chair in the middle of the table where the net would be if it were a tennis court. They introduced themselves. Little guy . . . Robert Rossen, one of the best film directors there has ever been. Big guy . . . Max Arnow, head of talent for Columbia Pictures. Two VIPs, two moguls of the movies, and I had just told them to go take a flying leap for themselves!

They finally got my name right. They thought it was a little "cumbersome." I said it might be cumbersome, but it was a far cry from McCombersome. I shouldn't have bothered with that.

Mr. Rossen asked me if I had read *All the King's Men*. The book was firmly entrenched on the best-seller lists, it had won the Pulitzer Prize; Robert Penn Warren was one of my favorite poets. Of course, I had read it. And loved it, thank you. They wanted to know what I thought of the character of Sadie Burke. I didn't say anything. Mr. Rossen got up from his regal throne and came around to me. He moved the chair next to me and leaned against the table. He cupped my chin in his hand and said, "You could play the pants off Sadie Burke. You just did it."

And that's how I won an Oscar. In a seventeen-minute role in a three-hour film, my first film. A pushy friend took me to a cattle call . . . I behaved in an Irish manner . . . and Ray Milland said, "May I have the envelope please?" and then he said, "And the winner is Mercedes McCambridge for *All the King's Men*." And when I accepted the gleaming golden boy from Ray's hands, I said, after thanking the deserving ones, "Mostly I want to say to every waiting actor . . . hang

When the jangling jalopy pulled up in front of the Algonquin, I felt the jubilation that can come only with affluence. This time when I registered at my old stamping grounds, I would ask for a room with a window! A complete bathroom with a larger-than-mite-sized tub that had not yet lost its stopper from the end of the long chain that hung down from the faucet. I might possibly ask for a suite! On the front of the house, not on the dismal side of the building. Columbia Pictures was picking up the tab. My sky was their limit!

Mike, the Irish-Mick bellman, was on duty. He delivered me to the desk, commenting, in familiar manner, on my "ritzy" new suitcases, my "Mrs. Astor" coat, and he gasped obligingly when I showed him the miniature Oscar on the golden chain around my neck! Mike said he always knew I'd make it. He said the night he watched me pick up my statue on TV, he turned to his wife and said, "I always knew she'd make it."

Doddering and dear old Mr. Mitchell, the night clerk, was drooping through the last minutes of his long, lonely vigil. In another hour he would be home in his own little bed and not a moment too soon . . . a lifetime spent as a night clerk in a mid-Manhattan hostelry . . . and one that catered to show folk and authors and poets and musicians. He must have seen everything three times over and over and over.

How sweet, then, for him to brighten so warmly when he saw me! Always! He'd always greeted me that way! Always I would have returned broke or with my tail between my legs from another show that had closed somewhere out of town, no longer on its way to Broadway. Mr. Mitchell never embarrassed me by asking what kind of accommodation I desired. We both knew it was never a question of desire. It was a place to lie down out of the cold . . . the cheapest room in the house . . . and there were spells when I had to owe them money due at the end of the week or, in a couple of instances, month.

The cheapest room in the Algonquin was room 200. I say "was" because the hotel has gone quite grand now, and they probably wouldn't dare put a "hume bean" in there! Room 200 is immediately to the right at the top of the old cracked marble stairway from the lobby. In my various tenancies of room 200 I always felt I had no right to use the elevator the way the regular guests did. I always took the dark stairs. Room 200 is as "rear" as you can get within the structure. The old tailor's shop is next door, and there are three doors that surely were sealed . . . never once did I see them open! Room 200 was sort of 4½ feet by 7, give or take a quarter of an inch. The original architecture provided a spaghetti-thin slit of a window, but subsequent improvements made it useless. A huge tunnel of an incinerator tower, or furnace exhaust pipe, blacked out all but a few wisps of light. In order to know how to dress for the day, I had to call Bertha on the switchboard downstairs to ask if it was raining or snowing or shining bright blue!

The closet had room for four coat hangers, not coats, just hangers. The bed had been miraculously riven in half from what must have been its original twin size. There were no chairs . . . no room for more than a backless, armless stool that fitted under the toy-department desk in the corner; well, almost in the corner. The brutally sharp point of the desk protruded into the passage to the bathroom, and during the night great bruises were initiated as I answered nature's call.

Having arrived, even unbruised, within the bathroom was hardly worth the hazards of the journey. A man-made room if ever I saw one. A man must have marked the X where the commode would rest. He must have pantomimed the activity of urination and then decided on the spot. I have no reason to think that he was wrong. But for a woman who would only expect to be pausing briefly as she availed herself of this particular facility for that particular function, it became more difficult. Man OR woman would have to slide into position on the throne by jackknifing around the sink and easing into place, but a man would know that he was likely to stay for a while so that the maneuvering was not all that demanding. But a woman had to go through all that twisting and tucking no matter *what* she had to do, biologically speaking. I've often wondered how many people bother to consider their good fortune in being able to back up to a toilet in full height and then just sit down on it!

Room 200 boasts, as well, the only "step-up" tub I've known. There is a six-inch platform on which it lies, what there is of it. It may have begun life intending to grow into a bathtub, but something must have happened. In mid-length it bumps into the wall, and that's the end of it. Getting in and out is a feat because the platform has no room for a person's foot. You have to lope into it, not leap, a long slow-motion loping up, over, and hopefully in, and if you are lucky, just as successfully out!

Room 200, for all that it was and wasn't, qualified as a legitimate part of the Hotel Algonquin. There is even a small and select cult of those of us who have called it "home"—Tennessee Williams,

Dorothy Parker, Myron McCormick, Wolcott Gibbs, me . . . all members of the 200! But now I was a fabulous Academy Award-Winning Actress! Room 200 was in another life.

Mr. Mitchell turned away from me as I was signing the register. He faced the slotted shelves where the room keys were kept. I saw his arm descend and reach into the low-down box marked "200"!

He graciously handed me the key. Same old familiar key! How could I say, "My dear old friend, Mr. Mitchell, sir, I am not broke anymore. I have not just flopped in from Philly. I am a gigantic celebrity as you see me here before you. I need a room like other famous people have!"

I went "home" to room 200!

There is no sadness to equal a rented mink coat hanging in a wedge-shaped closet so confining that both arms of the coat brush against the plaster that is flaking off the walls!

I had to escape. I needed a plan. One which would liberate me from this dark little dungeon but which would not offend the management that had so faithfully sheltered me in the past! The last thing I wanted them to say about me was that I was too good for old 200 now. That's what I thought, but I didn't want them to think that's what I thought.

Once again God must have figured I'd suffered long enough. The phone rang (yes, there was a phone, one of Mr. Edison's earlier models). It was Earl Wilson's office. He, the much-sought-after and widely-read gossip columnist of the New York *Post*. He wanted to interview me that day at noon. He never liked to meet in public places because people were always after him to write about them in his column. Could we have the interview in my suite, where we wouldn't be bothered by pests? Oh, yes, Mr. Wilson. Oh, sure, in my suite. Right, Mr. Wilson. Oh, my God, Mr. Wilson.

But wait! My salvation was at hand!

I ran down the dark stairway to the desk. Earl Wilson was coming! I would have to be moved to the fanciest front suite right away! Right now! Old Mr. Mitchell had been replaced by the daylight crew. They calmed me down, which was not what I wanted! They arranged to have me "use" the best suite long enough for the interview, and then I could go back to room 200, and the whole charade would be "on the house" . . . wouldn't cost me a cent! Not at all what I wanted!

I waited in the lovely suite for Mr. Wilson. Imagine staying in grandeur like this! Victorian and mahogany and draperies and curtains and a chandelier. And a bed big enough for two people, at least. I couldn't look at the bathroom. I might fill the tub and hold my head under the water until it was all over for me, thank God!

Mr. Wilson arrived. He was not impressed. Obviously hotel rooms as opulent as these were in his everyday experience. Then I looked at the ashtrays on the various tables. Each glass receptacle held a full untouched book of Algonquin matches! Obviously nobody lived here!

I confessed to Earl Wilson as though he were the bishop of Rome. I led him to room 200. I asked him to make himself comfortable on the tacky little stool under the poor excuse for a desk. I sat on the sawed-in-half bed, and he asked me the questions he was obligated to ask me about how my life had changed since I'd won an Oscar!

14

It WAS ANOTHER PRIZE I WON that year that changed my life far more than the Oscar ever did. I was married for the second time. A handsome man of many talents who schooled me in the sybaritic philosophy of life—a man who brought style and specialness to everything he touched. Performance was all!

I took great delight in the fact that Fletcher Markle had an extraordinary aptitude as an orchestra leader. He was more than a leader; he was a true conductor of orchestra . . . virtuoso! And it was never just anybody's orchestra, it was likely to be vintage Stan Kenton or early Michel Legrand, or Percy Faith, and now and then old Dorsey or Nelson Riddle. My own favorite was his interpretation of Legrand's complete movie score of *The Umbrellas of Cherbourg.*

Our evenings of musical appreciation took place in our own living room. There was always only the one appreciator . . . me! Son John was away at school. The musicians were not gathered in the usual pit; they were clustered unseen deep inside the great speakers of the giant gramophone contraption that had set us back such a pretty penny.

Outside was the tourmaline-lighted swimming pool gently disturbed by the evening breezes, and beyond it, extending into forever, were the eighty-five trillion dancing lights of the City of the Angels, and far off to the right, the drop-off of the world into the dead night of the sea.

"Martini time" had long been over; Ella Butler, world's greatest housekeeper, had once more fed us well and had gone off to her bed. For himself and me, my lord and master had poured the finest scotch and water that money could buy. All was in readiness. Another memorable night at the podium was about to begin.

In my own little corner of the couch I made myself felinely comfortable. Cool libation on table, plenty of cigarettes, shoes off, small cushion at small of back. Perfect!

There was a special anticipatory excitement watching him in the moments prior to performance. He kept his baton on one of the bookshelves at the far end of the room. As he returned with it, he whipped it in the air a few times to make certain it had retained its snap. There would be the stop en route at the counter of the bar to fortify himself with one final swallow of satiny scotch, then the deep *ahhhh* and the last few steps to the record player, wherein lay the magic!

He always dropped the needle onto the disc at its very outer rim, which would allow him the few seconds he needed to assume his position in front of the fireplace and to risk the instant he always saved for me, his slavishly devoted audience . . . the sweet indulgent smile he flashed my way just before he lifted his arms and confronted the downbeat!

He usually conducted in his shirt sleeves; on warmer nights he sometimes conducted in his shorts, but his shirts were so elegant and his shorts so chic that none of the arch formality was lost.

For me, the most theatrical part of any bullfight is the opening procession into the ring: the tempo of the blaring, tinny paso doble and the sensuously arrogant slow stride of the *matadores* and their *cuadrillas*. Only perfectly-put-together people march in such parades. Such a person was my maestro. He was a well-fashioned "hume bean," and he knew it. If it was a gift from God, he wasn't about to use it less than well . . . never boastfully, never in any way that could possibly offend anyone's sense of propriety or decorum, merely quietly acceptant of the unfortunate reality that all men are created far from equal!

Maybe all great conductors have to be that way. A mousy milquetoast has no place on a podium, nor has a burly truck driver.

John Wayne never could have made it as a symphony conductor; no more could Alan Ladd. Mastroianni, maybe; Cary Grant, certainly; and beyond any shadow of a doubt, the man to whom I was wed. Stokowski may have had more pizzazz, Bernstein more fireworks, but no maestro, except perhaps Toscanini himself, could have been such a spellbinder; nor could anyone have blended more hypnotically with the musicians who responded to his baton; nor was such response ever more deeply appreciated by a conductor, who was visibly elevated to such seductive heights. In the softer passages of the score, the muted strings pulsed through our living room sustained by the tender, aching support they received from their loving leader in front of the hearth. Then the forceful brass section, insisting on the right of its might, booming, its reverberating power fed from the force of his twisting torso, his thrusting pelvis. Best of all was the left hand held close to his lips to communicate that the music must now whisper in transcendental tone; rhythmically undulating hand; closed eyes; barely breathing.

I loved it! It was a whole show! I enjoy looking at beautiful things, and it is particularly nice to hear pretty music whilst looking. A handsome man, who couldn't read a note of music, was having a glorious time conducting forty or fifty gifted horn players and fiddlers, and I, his lucky woman, was happy to be lapping it up, lasciviously.

I wonder if life can ever be like that for long. I wonder if there could have been a way to live on and on like that. To work at your work while you are working at it and come home to private concerts in a beautiful house atop a beautiful hill, full of beautiful food and drink, watching a beautiful man playing orchestra leader. I know there was innocence in such decadence, if that's what it was. I know I would have appreciated it more if I had had the slightest notion that it was ever going to end. I think if I had gotten the message that the princess-fairy-tale chapter would inevitably close some following Saturday night, I might have marveled more at the make-believe!

I'm glad I am a woman who once danced naked in the Mediterranean Sea at midnight, wrapped in the slippery strong arms of the captivating young pirate whom she adored, or thought she did. We tried to make love, but we kept losing our balance and tumbling under the water. We laughed ourselves into exhaustion and shivered into our robes and found our way along the deserted path to the hotel's beach elevator. It was the old Hôtel Provençal, in Juan-les-Pins, in the not-all-that-exclusive part of the French Riviera, but we had a lovely suite, yellow and blue, and we were the "road company"

Scott and Zelda Fitzgerald for that season, walking their walk, talking their talk, and convinced, as they must have been, that this time two people so perfectly matched had finally broken the code; had surely found the secret!

There was a waiter at the Provençal, a Basque from the French Pyrénées. A stunningly caramel-colored, broad-grinned, black-eyed beauty. Not very tall, but such a swagger, such style. The first time we saw him he served our dinner in the grand old dining room. There was no ignoring him. His presence at our table commanded our attention. He was so easy about everything, so smooth.

Late that night we called for some brandy and some soda in our room. He brought it to us on a small tray balanced on his left hand. We were in bed. He scarcely noticed. He opened the bottle of soda, asked if there was anything more, smiled as he wished us good-night, and left. Next day he served us lunch. My husband asked him when he slept. He had a charming laugh, and he said, "Sleep? Oh, no, monsieur, I sleep never in the summertime. I sleep only in the winter."

We adopted him, and one day we gave him the thrill of his life! The Riviera grapevine bristled with the news that down the road apiece from us was hidden the undisputed sex goddess of that era. Rita Hayworth was incognito at La Réserve in Beaulieu!

I had not known Rita Hayworth, but my mate had known her, not biblically, of course; he had met her when she was Mrs. Orson Welles and when he himself was Mr. to the Mrs. who preceded me. They had all been in Mexico together while Orson was making *The Lady From Shanghai*. Now, in the post-dissolution period of both marriages, one ex-wife and one ex-husband were in temporary residence in neighboring towns of the Côte d'Azur. Oh, happy happenstance! Oh, the globe-girdling glamour of it all!

Miss Hayworth was out, but our telephone number would be left with her secretary. Within the hour Rita called. She was overjoyed to know that her friend Fletcher was in the region. How soon could he come to lunch? Oh, he had someone with him. Mercedes who? Weeellll, if he knew of a spare man, would he bring him along? Tomorrow at one, okay? Okay!

Spare man? What spare man? But of course, who else?

At dinner that night we asked our adopted brother, the dashing waiter, if he would be good enough to join us in our room at midnight for a conference of sorts.

At first he refused. Flat positive "thanks, but no thanks" refusal. At

Rita's name his caramel suntan turned to flame. He pounced around our room, slapping his hand to his forehead, beating himself, and saying over and over, "Rita Aywort! My God, Rita Aywort! Rita Aywort and ME? My God, Rita Aywort!"

We calmed him with some brandy, and Fletcher talked to him in a manner that a pediatrician uses to prepare a five-year-old boy for a tonsillectomy. He said that nothing but good could come from this experience, that, far from being an ordeal, great pleasure would be derived to everyone's benefit. Our nervous friend, whose name was Jeán Nery, protested that he had no argument with the pleasure element, but it was difficult for him to deal with the exquisite agony even the contemplation of such an adventure engendered. Jeán, our Gallic and gallant *agent-d'amour*, was briefed in stern fashion. There were to be no false statements, no blatant misrepresentations of any kind . . . we were all above that sort of thing. He would be introduced as our good and dear friend; which he was. Our friend from the Basque country near Spain, where high in the Pyrénées Mountains he spent his winters; which he did. Where there roamed the finest herds of sheep in Europe; which there did. Where his family had been ranchers for generations; which they had. They hadn't owned the vast ranches or more than a few of the sheep, but we were not claiming that they did. We were only not stating that they didn't!

It was during this time that the late Aly Khan was chasing Rita all over France. We pointed out to Jeán Nery that we wanted to adorn him with a glow of intrigue to offset the brilliant effect of the ruler of all the Moslems. That idea made the difference with Jeán. That he would challenge the famed and fabulous Aly Khan for the favors of Rita Hayworth put fire into his blood. He accepted! We asked him to arrange for a car that we could hire for the next afternoon. He was insulted! But of course, we would travel in his car! It was in splendid condition! That would give us time to stop en route to Rita at a favorite café to take an apéritif in celebration of the day! Beautiful! Until tomorrow, then, good night and rest well, my dear, dear friends!

It is difficult specifically to name the exact color of Jeán's car. The genre was Renault; the style, very small convertible coupe *sans* top; the upholstery was casual patchwork; and the radio antenna flew a lady's black satin garter at the top of its mast; but the paint job might best be called rusty pink, with variegated shades of vein-contained blood!

Jeán was fitted into the driver's seat smiling beatifically as he artfully brought the little horror on wheels up to the grand porte cochere of the Provençal. He looked gorgeous. Wisteria silk shirt, open down to there, brown peek-a-boo body, hairy-ape-type chest framed in wisteria blue. White duck pants, generous genitalia all but exposed beneath the cloth, which, at long last, had finally reached the perfect state of warp nearly parting from woof! One good rip and away we go! Jeán was wearing a scent that made him arrestable; a little too much of it perhaps, but the open Mediterranean breezes would waft enough of it out to sea to make it breathable by the time he reached Rita. Breathable but fatal!

There really wasn't room for three of us, but if I balanced myself on my left buttock and if Fletcher could then slide the left side of his pelvis under the right side of my behind, we could close the tiny door on the right side of the tiny car. I had to ride sideways, which is a good trick along the lower Corniche when the driver is a typical Frenchman whose aggressions and repressions are all released once he gets his hands on a steering wheel. I didn't see much of the seacoast, which was to our right, but I got to learn a lot about the contour of Jeán's earlobe, and I made a mental note to talk to him later about what looked like a pesky pimple in a fold of his neck.

The planned stop at Jeán's favorite café was foolhardy because it meant we had to pry ourselves out of our coach and, ultimately, would have to stuff ourselves back into it. Jeán wasn't bothered by the cramped situation, and he obviously thought his car was beautiful, but he just as obviously seemed most discomfited over something. Jeán had cold feet. So we had two apéritifs to remove the chill. He offered a sad little suggestion that we go on without him and explain to "Miss Aywort" that the wealthy Basque sheep rancher had died during the night. He said he would wait there at the café and get drunk with his friends until four o'clock. Then, he said, he would start to drink strong coffee, which would sober him up sufficiently to make the drive back to the Provençal in time for him to serve dinner at seven. He said we should take the car and enjoy ourselves and forget about him until we came back to pick him up no later than six o'clock. It *was* a sad little suggestion, so we all had another drink and Jeán became more malleable, and we piled back into the bruised little Renault with all the age spots and ruptured blood vessels. It was easier the second time.

Rita Hayworth on the French Riviera in the almost-ended 1940's was very likely the eighth wonder of the world. Rita Hayworth's smile when Rita Hayworth is happy could illumine the Black Hole of

Calcutta into blinding sunlight. Her red-gone-blond-gone-sun-streaked hair was loosely gathered up from the nape of her neck like a Gainsborough lady. She was waiting for us on the terrace. She leaned against the railing, which was all that separated her from the Rock of Gibraltar a million miles away. She was wearing a white piqué sundress with an enormous full skirt and no visible means of support in the mammillary section, which in her case was, of course, legendary and in this case was, of course, quite real.

At sight of her, Jeán groaned. I recognized the sound. When a man has had his way with me, when the mission has been accomplished, when the ardor is finally spent, there is that same sound that Jeán was making. I knew it as a sound of termination, of completion, but poor beautiful Jeán hadn't even begun yet!

Rita squealed with happiness to see Fletcher. She was so sweetly effusive, all child! I thought she was wonderful.

There was something of a sticky wicket as we entered the dining terrace for luncheon. The maître d'hôtel recognized Jeán as a fellow waiter. He raised his arm as though he were going to slap Jeán on the back, but thinking better of it, he drew his hand back and straightened his tie. Rita said to Jeán, "Oh, Monsieur Nery, you must come here often. I'm sorry I have not met you before."

Fletcher was about to jump in with a cover-up story, but Jeán beat him to the punch. Sometime during the few minutes between his first groaning glimpse of Rita and the moment with the maître d', Jeán must have made a private pact with his own demon. In reply to Rita's naïve remark he said, hunching his shoulders and leaning toward her, "No, no, Miss Aywort, it is hardly likely that you would have seen me here. I make it a point to avoid public places whenever possible. I am essentially a very quiet man, a shy man. This fellow probably thought he knew me because he may have seen me in Monte Carlo, where I have my summer home. Everyone in Monte Carlo knows everyone else no matter how private one tries to be!"

Fletcher squirmed and said that he hadn't known Jeán had a home in Monte. I'd known it because Jeán had told me one night in our room when Fletcher was taking a shower. He told me that he had an apartment high on a hill in Monte Carlo, and he said the view of the palace and the bay was breathtaking. I had gasped in wonder, and he told me that it really wasn't all that great. The apartment was in terrible shape, it was a long walk-up, only one window had a view, and his wife lived there.

Rita kept looking at Jeán as though he were a giant Christmas present in Neiman-Marcus wrappings or as if he were two pounds of Godiva chocolates contained in a Fabergé egg. The unexplored package before her was so intriguing that like any eager child, she could scarcely keep her hands off it!

Jeán solved the problem. He asked her to dance! There was a schmaltzy string trio playing "Come Back to Sorrento" and "La Vie en Rose" and "Deep Purple" and stuff like that.

I had seen Rita Hayworth dance on the screen with the best of them. Fred Astaire, to mention only one, but when she melted into the arms of our boy Jeán, I had never seen her in finer form, a form in all its fineness pressing itself against the matching fineness of Jeán's form. On that day I accepted the theory that man and woman were created as one entity, one body, perfectly joined in all the right places. God's curse in Eden was their separation for all eternity. But that day on the small dance floor of the dining terrace of the Hôtel Réserve in Beaulieu, France, on the shore of the Mediterranean, God gave in, and Adam and Eve became a single word. Adameve, or Jeánríta, whichever sounded more romantic!

We ate squid and mussels and cheese and lettuce *fatigué* and wine and sweet pears, and it was wondrous. We agreed that true civilization takes money and a good digestion to make it worthwhile; otherwise, savagery is a better way, and basically more honest!

Jeán was Epicurus in person. He had a very sexy laugh and laughed a great deal, and all his courtliness was for Miss Aywort. She said she'd love it if we all drove to Monte Carlo after lunch. She had a limousine standing by, at her call. Jeán protested that nothing would please him more than the drive, but of course, we must go in his car, "in my baby carriage," he said . . . "my beautiful little baby carriage," and he laughed merrily and Rita joined in and said that she would love to ride in his baby carriage. Jeán recovered himself to say, "I knew it. I knew in my heart of hearts that you would be this kind of woman, Miss Aywort. On the dawning of this day, on this fateful day when I would meet the most magnificent woman in the world, I said to myself, I said, 'Jeán, would you dare, would you have the unbelievable temerity to drive in your ancient baby carriage machine to meet the queen?' The very thought amused me to the degree that I knew I must do it, and Miss Aywort, I knew that you would be amused as well." Then he said, "It would not have been amusing if I had arrived in a clumsy limousine. Limousines are for funerals. This is a *fête!*" Rita was overjoyed.

Jeán pressed his luck. He said, "All your life you will be escorted in limousines, but who dares to drive you to Monte Carlo in a baby carriage?"

Fletcher dared intervene by saying there wasn't room in the baby carriage for four people. Jeán studied Fletcher's face in disbelief. "My dear friend," he said, "for the right kind of people, my baby carriage has all the room in the world."

That was an overstatement on Jeán's part. It is a pleasant memory for me that I weighed less than Rita Hayworth, so I was chosen to be in the sandwich, back in my old lateral spot, where I could continue my study of Jeán's ear. This time, however, I had to put my left arm around him. It was either that or amputation. Fletcher needed the extra inches to make a sort of lap for Miss Aywort, who, in such a position, rose a full head above the top of the windshield. Her billion-dollar face that launched a thousand ships and sold a billion posters was in constant danger of decapitation as Jeán lurched and veered and sped dizzily along the Midi. Rita had a great view of everything. She liked it. Fletcher's eye level met the cleavage of her strapless dress, and what with the bouncing and jouncing, his view wasn't bad either, I guess. He liked it.

Having miraculously arrived at Monte Carlo, Jeán followed a serpentine route along narrow streets to the brow of a hill where there just happened to be another of his favorite cafés, a dreary little place with three outdoor tables, wobbly and worn. We chose the one least likely to tip over. Jeán ordered "De war's White Label" for all of us. He said it as if the White Label were the outcome of some conflict . . . of "de war."

Rita laughed at everything he said. She asked him if we could see his home there in Monte. Jeán said, "Ho ho, I am afraid you might not like to see what you would find in my home. I think, my dear Miss Aywort, it would come as something of a shock to your beautiful eyes."

Rita waited for him to clear that up. She was eating it up, and she wanted more.

Jeán told her, with perfect conviction and honesty, that in his house there was a situation at the moment that would make everyone most uncomfortable. "After all," he said, "in my wildest dreams I never could have thought that we should meet." He was holding her hand close to his lips as he talked. Rita was transfixed. He said, "I must confess to you, Miss Aywort, that I am a man of strong desires and appetites! A night without love is, for me, impossible."

Rita suddenly became the good little Mexican girl she has always been. She slowly retrieved her hand, but Jeán reached for it again. During all of this scene Jeán's drinking companions and neighborhood buddies were strolling to and fro in front of the café. A couple of old women leaned against the building and watched. That loose-living waiter from the Pyrénées was eating Rita Hayworth's hand, in public! How did he ever maneuver that? Local boy makes good, mais oui! How good can you make?

Panic seized Jeán at four-fifteen. The steeple bell had tolled the four notes of the quarter hour, and Jeán knew that the bell had tolled for he!

The levity, the joy were woefully absent on the long voyage home. Jeán's eyes were riveted to the highway. There was heavier traffic, all insane drivers. Rita fell asleep, crouched down as best she could, all over Fletcher, who held onto her for dear life, his and hers. I had to go to the bathroom, of course, but I wouldn't have dared give voice to the urge.

Back at Beaulieu, Fletcher had to jostle Rita into wakefulness. Jeán had sprung out of his side of the baby carriage and had pried open the tinny little door to facilitate the removal of the body beautiful. He ordered Fletcher to stay where he was, and with a definite urgency, he guided Rita into the lobby of the Réserve. We could see him kiss both her hands, twice each, and then he dashed for us. The motor was running and he hopped behind the wheel and we were off, as off the road as I ever care to be! Jeán made it to the kitchen entrance of the Provençal with seconds to spare!

Fletcher and I felt we had sufficiently recovered our land legs to attempt the trek to the dining room at about nine o'clock. Jeán, in his starchy white jacket and his shiny black trousers, bowed as we entered. When he came for our order, he bowed again over the table and said, "Madame, monsieur, you see why I feel it is foolish to sleep in the summertime? One has to stay awake, or there is no magic in one's life!" Then he smiled, handing us the *carte*, and said, "I am completely at your service. I await your pleasure." That night at midnight a strange waiter brought us a bottle of champagne. It was from Jeán.

15

CTUALLY THE ESCAPADES of my life, the deviltries, really don't trouble my conscience all that much. I have reservations about settling down permanently in heaven anyhow. If ever I do make it to heaven, if there IS a heaven, I don't want to spend a lot of time sitting around talking about the bad old days back on earth.

If some supercilious saint who never knew anything but sanctity even as an earthling wants to know how a nice soft old angel like me could have sunk so low as to have tried to terminate her own existence . . . how a sweet fluttery old thing like me could have so disgraced herself as to have been labeled *an alcoholic* . . . I may just spit right in that saint's eye. That saint is likely the sort who believes in the "right to life" for the fetus, and in capital punishment for everyone else, and likely belongs to the Heavenly Branch of the National Rifle Association.

This world I live in is full of such saints. Hour after hour they are televised by satellite from extravagant studios in Virginia or Pasadena or Dallas. If they end up in heaven, then heaven is far from all it is cracked up to be. These living saints who advertise themselves as the moral majority and line their pockets with millions upon millions of petitioners' pennies are revolting enough, but far worse are the meek and the humble who shall inherit the earth, and in the shape it's in, they are welcome to it. They are the thin-lipped matrons in rump-sprung slacks who nudge each other and whisper as I pass them with my cart in the supermarket.

The other night, on my own time and for free, I was on my way to talk to a group of high school students and parents and teachers about teenage alcoholism, an epidemic in our fair country. I was early, so I stopped at a roadside diner for some coffee. I sat at the counter, and over against the wall in a booth, a woman was pointing me out to her companion. He looked around, checked me out, and went back to his food. When I was leaving the place, I had to pass the pair of them, and the woman said, "Excuse me," so sweetly, such a sweet lady. She said she always loved everything she ever saw me do and it was just swell to meet me in person and wouldn't I please sign her napkin for her mother, and "thank you a lot, Miss McCambridge, thank you!" And as I turned away, she leaned across the table and hoarsely whispered, "Alcoholic, y'know."

I stepped back to a point where I could meet her eyes with mine. She giggled. I let her hang there. Then I reached over and picked up the napkin on which I had been foolish enough to sign my name. I looked at it and then said, "You won't be needing this," and I tore the paper into bits of confetti and spilled it directly onto the food in her plate. I said, "Sometimes I forget how careful one must be in the company of strangers."

The law states that alcoholism is as legitimate a disease as is diabetes. There are zillions of people who say that alcoholism is a disease, but not many of them BELIEVE it. I know many professionals in the field who don't believe it, who are, in truth, scornful of the alcoholic. I tell them they are making a living *because* of my disease, while I am making a living in *spite* of it. Alcoholism . . . "the only disease in which the patient is blamed if the treatment fails." Senator Harold E. Hughes.

A doctor who has been making his living, and quite handsomely, as an expert on alcoholism for as long as I can remember is a perfect illustration. He is in no way a careless man. Every gesture is measured; every word is well calculated; every lonely hair on his balding head is carefully placed to maintain his assiduously studied image. If he is asked the time of day, he will consider the advisability of answering such a direct question.

He was sitting next to me on a TV panel discussion show about alcoholism. I had just quoted Abraham Lincoln who said about us alcoholics, "If we take habitual drunkards as a class, their heads and hearts will bear an advantageous comparison to those of any other class. There seems ever to have been a proneness to this vice among the brilliant and warm-blooded. The demon of intemperance seems ever to delight in sucking the blood of genius and generosity." I said that four of the eight Americans who have won the Nobel Prize for Literature drank alcoholically, that the average American alcoholic is, like me, a college graduate in the top third of his class; that the higher the incidence of alcoholism, the higher the percentile of IQ.

During a break for a commercial this unctuously proper man of medicine, whose elegant automobile operates on fees collected from alcoholics, leaned toward me and said, "Don't talk that way, Mercedes. You are making them sound too good!"

I suppose it is understandable that people who have had no exposure to learning about the disease can have no acceptance of it. I cannot see that they will ever understand unless they are aware of who and what an alcoholic is. Either I am, under the law, a person with a treatable, a recoverable disease, or I am a misfit in society and should be removed from same. I am anything but anonymous, but that is far from a popular statement.

One of the cruelest, most unfair judgments sustained against me is that I have spoken out as a recovered alcoholic to stimulate my acting career. This judgment, ironically enough, comes mainly from alcoholics! Har har de har har!

The purpose of my speaking out in the first place was to help abolish the discrimination against *us* alcoholics! Why do they throw rocks at me? Why don't they join me? For every sick alcoholic who is receiving any kind of help in this country there are thirty-five sick alcoholics who aren't receiving any help whatsoever. I would like to see that figure reduced, and I believe that alcoholics who have recovered are the greatest source for community education, for openness of attitudes, for reaching out, for going out to the sick alcoholic before he has to beg for help. Why is it so terrible to call myself what I am?

Often a stranger has stopped me on a street or in an airport or department store. He or she will call me by name, usually shake my hand, and then look both ways to be sure that no one can hear, and say, oh, so softly, "I'm one, too." In the Philadelphia Airport I said loudly to such a fella, "ONE WHAT? DO YOU MEAN THAT YOU ARE AN ALCOHOLIC, LIKE ME?" What is so terrible? The law says I'm a first-class citizen with a treatable, recoverable disease, more treatable, more recoverable than asthma, and just as legal a disease.

My good friend researcher Donald Goodwin says one of the reasons people, including doctors, have difficulty viewing alcoholism as a disease "is that alcoholism is associated with having fun, and fun is not usually associated with disease. Where, then, does that leave syphilis? Is sex less fun than drinking?"

My admiration for the phenomenon of Alcoholics Anonymous is boundless. I regret I cannot claim membership among them because their traditions insist on anonymity at a public level of press or media.

During a sultry, humid spell of weather, with a dry-socket

toothache, I traveled a long and dull route to fulfill a speaking engagement for a group that had invited me repeatedly.

I entered a basement hall. The place was packed. With my pulsating jaw, I thought: Now then, most of these good people do not agree that an alcoholic should be a known and recognized commodity, and yet, thought I to myself, they came here tonight because it was *advertised* that I would be here tonight. Now then, where do we go from here?"

The woman who was the hostess of the group greeted me warmly and introduced me to a young man who was a reporter from the local newspaper. He wanted "a story." He, in turn, introduced me to his photographer. The hostess lady said, "I told him it was all right to take pictures of you, Miss McCambridge, but of course, he can only take pictures of our backs." What she said made me want to hoot with laughter, but what she hadn't said was what made me want to scream! What she hadn't said was downright insulting and deserved a hasty retreat from the place. What she hadn't said was that, God forbid, tomorrow's paper or the Sunday feature section would show any of *them* standing alongside *me!* How could they be accepted in their community if they were painted with the same brush that had smeared me with this leprosy? I had been invited to speak, have my picture taken, and go away, leaving the community as unsullied as it was before I got there!

The long ride home was unhappy, depressing.

If they think my "going public" as a recovered alcoholic has been to further my acting career, why are they being photographed from the backs of their necks? Why don't they stick those necks out and turn around and smile at the birdie and be rich and famous, too? Har har de har har!

Alcoholism can, and has, enhanced *actors'* careers! John Wayne's drunken brawls were considered part of his charm. The terribly sick John Barrymore became a spectacle for public glee as he snorted and staggered his way across the stage to his death. There have been many others, most of whom have died drunk. The comic routines about drinking have kept Dean Martin and Ed McMahon in luxury long after it was merely boring. Alcoholism in male performers is macho. But the *woman* alcoholic who is a performer has a rougher row to hoe . . . how often does anybody say, "Why can't you drink like a woman?"

I can say that the demand for my acting services fell off sharply following my testimony in July 1969 before the Senate Subcommittee on Alcoholism and Narcotics.

If I had it to do all over again, I'd sure as heck get a whole bunch of other alcoholics to do it with me. That "solitary nobility" caper leaves scars! And misery loves company.

In Hollywood one morning, in the summer of 1969, the phone rang. A friend in New York was calling to ask if it would be okay for him to give a U.S. senator my private number. I think I could count on one finger the number of U.S. senators who wanted my private number. Permission was granted in casual jaded tone . . . would these prominent people please leave me alone?

Senator Hughes of Iowa has a voice that springs from the bottom of the Grand Canyon. It thundered at me from Washington. He was chairman of a subcommittee and wanted to conduct hearings on alcoholism. He said he hoped I didn't mind if he knew that I was a recovered alcoholic since he was one, too. That relaxed the conversation. I respectfully asked him what he wanted of me. Senator Hughes wanted of me that I should come to Washington and testify that I am an alcoholic! Poor Senator Hughes, surely an Iowa chinch bug had wormed its way into his brain! The voice from the bottom of the canyon told me that he had traversed the country several times trying to enlist recovered alcoholics whose names would be recognizable in public, alcoholics who were prominent in all walks of life. There were no takers, he said. Then I said, "Why me?" and he said, "Why not you?" He said somebody had to do it and *that* somebody might be the instrument which would help to cut open closed minds, might help to accomplish the enactment of a law that would become the Emancipation Proclamation for millions of American alcoholics. He said countless lives might be saved. I asked him how soon I had to be there.

The night before the testimony I was taken to dinner by some supportive members of the senator's staff and Judge Ray Harrison from Iowa who would also testify the next morning. He, single-handedly, reversed the abominable pattern of swinging-door alcoholism among the derelicts of Iowa. He succeeded in altering the criminal code; he came down hard on all drunken drivers, not merely alcoholics but social drinkers behind the wheel. He was a great man, Judge Ray Harrison.

There was a late arrival at our dinner party. A tall, gaunt, fair-haired, pale, and obviously not-too-well man joined us. He was Bill

Wilson, co-founder of Alcoholics Anonymous. He would testify the next day too, but as "Bill W." with the TV cameras on his back. I understood then, as I understand now, why the originator of an organization must be adherent to the principles of the organization. I understood, and I came to know and love Bill Wilson deeply, but I argued with him to the end of his life about the anonymity *bête noire*. Bill wrote his own obituary for *The New York Times*. Only in that notice was his full name finally spelled out. To this day he is called Bill W. by his followers, and I understand that. And I treasure the affection Bill gave to me. He chose to remain anonymous, but he wanted *me* to speak out. He said it was important that I do it my way, openly. He knew that I claimed no affiliation with any group; I have never claimed to be a member of Alcoholics Anonymous, but he said that he knew that many people would be led to AA by being witness to my own recovery. He told me always to refer to myself as "recovered" alcoholic. Many of my alcoholic friends are dubious about this claim because they call themselves "recovering" until they die. But I have a dozen witnesses who heard Bill Wilson ask me to promise him that I would call myself "recovered" as he and his first 100 members call themselves in the original foreword to their book. They say, "We are more than 100 men and women who have RECOVERED from a seemingly hopeless disease."

I persist. I believe that if I am endlessly "recovering," it must be that I am afraid to get well! That night in the Washington restaurant (before I became the world's foremost authority on matters alcoholic), I experienced a kind of mutuality I'd never known before. Again, it was a RISK, an audacity. We were presenters of a socially unattractive proposition. We alcoholics were going to address a body of senators, imploring that their attention and action be focused on a despicable blot on the conscience of America. We warmed ourselves at our little bonfire of encouragement and joke-telling, building up our collective fortitude; it was good! I was sitting alongside Bill Wilson on the banquette of the long table. He told wonderful stories and laughed hard and long. Once in a while he slapped his thighs. And once or twice he slapped mine. I admired it. He was not a young man, but he certainly wasn't behaving like an old man. Any male animal nearing the completion of his sixth decade of life who has lost the nerve to slap at a nearby thigh from time to time has already relinquished the will to live. Bill Wilson was alive, frail as he was!

Next morning Senator Hughes called me into his office before the hearings began. He said he would understand it if I walked out. He asked me to be aware that I would be hurt by testifying. "Crucified in some quarters," he said. "Hit below the belt . . ." Despite all this, because he was strong, I caught his strength and was sustained by it. But he was right. I got hurt.

In the hearing room, like the old Joe McCarthy room and the not-yet Watergate room, there were TV cameras at both ends . . . up on platforms. The witness table was covered with microphones and a pitcher of water and two glasses. All morning I died of thirst, but there was no way I could have poured water into a glass. I have never felt such stage fright. My private stage fright is my excitement, I use it as adrenaline, it psychs me up, I *use* it; but this was shattered nerves, heart-pounding panic!

Once or twice during the earlier proceedings I saw the red light on one or two of the cameras, but only briefly, and then they were dark again. But it was "*Christmas-tree lighting time*" when Senator Hughes announced, "We will call Miss Mercedes McCambridge, the Academy Award-winning actress. Miss McCambridge, you may proceed as you desire in your statement."

Miss McCambridge: Thank you, Senator. I am honored to be here. Initially, I would state that I speak only for myself—as an individual. I am neither spokeswoman nor agent for any organization or fellowship or sect.

My qualifications, my limitations, my exhortations are my own and I am responsible for no one but myself.

I am a recovered alcoholic person, a recovered alcoholic of the protected Bel-Air type. The AMA tells me that my alcoholism is a disease. The AMA tells me that my alcoholism is the third, if not fourth, largest killer of people in this country. Therefore, with those statistics, I must be convinced that my disease can be terminal.

I am equally convinced that my disease can be arrested. My own disease is in that state now and has been for some considerably rewarding, splendid and truly awesome time.

I say "awesome" because the remarkable thing about my disease, which could be terminal, is that I, in a certain sense, hold jurisdiction over it. I can choose to accelerate my disease to one or two inevitable conclusions—an alcoholic death or incurable insanity, or I can choose to live within my thoroughly human condition. I submit that is a remarkable thing.

It has never been more remarkable to me than it is at this moment when I am aware that perhaps my own survival, when so many have died, is for this purpose, so that I can sit with you at this level with the utmost respect and talk to you about this matter of life or death—my life or my death.

As I sit here, scores of women like me are being arranged on slabs in morgues throughout this country with tickets tied to their toes that read "acute alcoholism" or if they have been protected as I was, those tags may read "liver ailment," "pneumonia," "chronic bronchitis," "massive hemorrhage," but the mother of all those veiled, protective tickets may well be alcoholism, pure and simple. . . .

I drank, like everybody else, for a while—until this structure that is my body began its rejection, its refusal to absorb physiologically the alcohol that I put into it. My body lacks certain faculties, certain vitally needed faculties that most people have, to burn off and throw off alcohol.

This delicious chemical, this social amenity, this medicine that puts people at their ease because merely being together without it makes them uncomfortable, this medicine became my poison. The insidious, diabolical evil, the viciousness of my disease, is that the poison sets up its own craving for more of itself. . . .

So I would get sick. A doctor would be summoned, as doctors are being summoned this afternoon to fine homes all over this country to minister to ladies who are crouching in corners in the master bedroom suite, and the doctor will administer to this lady by injecting her buttocks with something that will put her to sleep, and he will leave on the dressing table two or three prescriptions to get her over the rough time that will follow.

I can unequivocally state that if I had taken one-tenth of all the prescriptions prescribed for me, for me to recover, I would be long since dead. Senators, I am absolutely convinced of that. I never did take much medicine, I don't like to take medicine, thank God.

But the woman wakes up and the doctor has left a little something called a calm-downer and she has that. Then he has left something else called a psychic energizer and she has that, according to his prescription, and then she goes out into the living room and "Oh, well," says her protective family, "a martini never hurt anybody," so she has a martini.

She has two, maybe, maybe no more than two in the beginning. Dinner, desultorily done, something to make her sleep, she wakes up in the morning, she feels badly, I submit this is the onset of alcoholism in its most disastrous fashion.

The rat race has begun. . . . There is only one way for this woman to go. . . .

I had been at the University of Mississippi in Oxford, working on a production with the students. Word came that a great and brilliant woman had died tragically and alone in a bathroom in a foreign country. This woman had been very good to me at a time when I needed a friend. I was in Mississippi and she was dead. [She was Judy Garland.]

All day long I thought about two doctors who understood people like me . . . and I [telephoned] these two doctors, one a psychiatrist and one an internist.

I had to say to them, "You must feel when you read what you read this morning that you can't be doing much that is right, because in such a short recent time three of your patients, brilliantly, excitingly special people who made this planet a better place for their having been on it, are dead, tragically dead, alone. [The other two patients were Montgomery Clift and young Nicky Hilton.]

. . . I wanted the doctors to know that I realized I could have been any one of those people. I know that sitting here now. There is no question in my mind.

Nobody need die of this disease. We are eminently salvageable. We are well worth the trouble. We are eminently equipped to enrich this world. We write poetry, we paint pictures, we compose music, we build bridges, we head corporations, we win the coveted prizes for the world's greatest literature, and too often too many of us die from our disease, not our sin, not our weakness. . . .

If you think along with our Puritanical ancestors, that the alcoholic is a spineless weakling, a morally culpable wreck, I would remind you from Shakespeare's *Measure for Measure:*

Go to your bosom;
Knock there, and ask your heart what it doth know
That's like my brother's fault: if it confess
A natural guiltiness such as is his,
Let it not sound a thought upon your tongue
Against my brother's life. Go gentle, my lord.

Lastly, I would remind you, probably on your way to your office this morning you saw what has become known as a skid-row bum asleep on a park bench. That man and I are the same person.

There is a difference between us. I am sitting here addressing you with my own sense of dignity with a certain pride, an enormous gratitude and my priceless sense of self-esteem, because I know I have my right to my life. The bum need only be shown that he has his right to his.

Thank you.

Senator Hughes: Thank you very much, Miss McCambridge, for your testimony and your statement, which I think serves to illustrate the viciousness of this disease that we are looking at today. Senator Yarborough, any questions?

Senator Yarborough: Miss McCambridge, I vote you another Oscar, this time for public service.

る

I believe I had little chance of avoiding my disease. For me, caffeine, nicotine, Novocain, codeine, aspirin, Valium, Librium, and alcohol are all not the oral magic that eases pain for other people. For me the results are disastrous. I lose all control after two drinks of anything. People used to tell me that I would spend a whole evening with them, behaving no more foolishly than anyone else, but the following morning I would not remember anything that happened after the first two drinks were served. I would have gone on drinking with the rest of them, but it was a total blackout time for me. I was trying to drink like everybody else. I couldn't make it. Inevitably the terrible headaches came, the vile vomiting and cramps, the terrifying tremors, and what was the only thing that would stop them, at least for a few hours? More of the hair of the dog that bit me. Another dosage of the sedative-drug, the socially acceptable drug of alcohol, would be enough to settle me down so that I could store up another spell of sleep and, please God, wake up again . . . this time in a less calamitous state of disintegration.

I truly believe that the greatest cause of alcoholism is the hangover. If the quivering, feverish, gagging alcoholic could ever get to the place where he felt good enough to stop drinking, he would stop drinking. Nobody understands that by the time the addiction has set in the alcoholic is MANDATED to drink . . . he cannot NOT drink! Nobody wakes up in the morning and says, "Jiminy Cricket, I feel sensational! My life is really in great shape! I think I'll become an alcoholic!" I firmly believe that when a shaking-to-pieces alcoholic says he needs a drink or he will die, he means it. Far too many DO die that way. The next drink alleviates the trembling, but the respite is brief, and that kind of treatment eventually kills. The pattern must be broken. Withdrawal must be carefully supervised; nutrition is vital to recovery, as is the rehabilitative support of knowledgeable people.

That's what happened to me, and I recovered. There was enormous suffering for people dear to me, and far more suffering for myself. I have paid my dues.

The worst thing that happened to me during those bleak times was actually quite grotesque, even ridiculous in a horrible sort of way. It was the early 1960's. JFK would soon be assassinated. I was alone. I had sublet a dreamy apartment, an itty-bitty three-room apartment in the East Sixties near the river. It belonged to a decorator at Altman's. Undersized living room, a mere slot of a bedroom, a just-about turnaround foyer, and a barely-there kitchen. The bathroom was a masterpiece of space utilization, crowded but all there. It was a *small* apartment, but it was a dreamy one. There was a small English desk, two small red leather chairs, a small blue plaid love seat, three fine lamps, and matching prints on a deep rose-colored wall. Very nice. The carpet was greige. Lovely! I never wore shoes in that room. I hardly ever sat on the furniture. I sat on a towel on the floor, and admired my surroundings.

The bed was narrow and chic in its green and white striped velvet cover. And the kitchen, oh, such a kitchen! No room in it, but beautiful! Three walls were deep Dutch blue enamel. You could see yourself in them! The fourth wall and the ceiling were hot, hot orange. Gorgeous! I never cooked a meal in that kitchen. Boiled water, yes. Occasionally a TV dinner in the oven, but I could not desecrate those shining walls and that orange ceiling with soot or grime from cooking. I never really occupied that apartment, I merely appreciated it, like a wee temple, where one sits on the floor.

I had been at a party on a Saturday night. That's all I remember. Next morning at five o'clock I awoke in a cold sweat, sick unto death. I could hardly make it to the bathroom, where the heaves were dry and so painful! My God, how did it happen . . . again? They had said one drink wouldn't hurt me . . . again; I tried it . . . again; and I was dying . . . again! What kind of hopeless, no-good, spineless, idiotic, rotten person was I? Again!

I managed to get back to bed and went into a chill that made my heart pound hard. My vision was blurred, my mouth was parched, my skin was on fire, and I was freezing to death. The bed was shaking.

I knew what I had to have to keep from exploding. I wanted nothing to do with another drop of alcohol . . . I hated the terrible rotten stuff and what it had done to me, but I had to stop shaking or die. I stumbled out into the lovely little living room to the little bar. There was nothing there. Like many alcoholics, I must have thrown every ounce of alcohol into the incinerator the night before. There was nothing! I needed it . . . it was not yet six o'clock on Sunday morning in New York City. I was a staggering woman cowering in a chic apartment at the East River, sick and utterly disgusting.

I got into the kitchen, barely able to stand by this time. I searched the cupboard shelves for something that might have an alcohol content. I had never done a thing like that. I was horrified at myself, but I had to stop the shaking. I opened the refrigerator. On the shelf on the inside of the door was a half-empty bottle of vinegar left there by the apartment's owner. It was wine vinegar. I wondered if it might kill me. The last thing in the world that I wanted to do was to drink it. I tried.

The immediate insult to my system forced out a violent stream of bile that threw my head back as it shot from my mouth! I lay down on the floor, on my back, gasping. I was going into hysterics. I was naked and foul-smelling from the rancid spittle in my hair and on my chest. I looked up at the lovely hot orange wall that I had not dared stain or soil. IT WAS SPATTERED WITH DARK, UGLY GLOBS! I shouted at it, "Oh, my God, I'm sorry! Oh, great good God, I'm so sorry! *Is this me?* Oh, God, God, God, is this really me?" And of course, it was. It was me.

ᨒ

Like so many other recovered alcoholics, I am to this day bewildered that it took so long for me to understand that there was no such animal as "social drinking" for me; that it had nothing to do with my willpower or self-respect or moral fiber; that it was a simple biochemical intolerance to a drug.

Alcohol is anesthesia . . . ether and water. If a chemist subtracts the components of water from alcohol, he comes up with ether. I have a hard time with any kind of anesthesia.

After a startlingly small amount of alcohol I am truly "under the influence," and the biological, the biochemical *addiction* then craves more of the drug. I am as morally fibered, as self-respectful and as will-powered as the finest citizens you care to mention. The only thing is, I am intolerant to their drug. They get their nightly "Happy Hour" fix or drug themselves at their weekend blasts and wear lampshades on their heads and flop around, doing daring little dances and making passes at other people's mates, and they are "social drinkers." They wake up with a headache that is gone by noon.

I go to their party, and if I drink NO MORE than they do, I wake up in the early-morning hours, sick as a dog. There is NO medicine for me. There is literally nothing for me to take to stop my teeth from shaking themselves loose from the gums in my pounding head! What is alcohol? A sedative. If I can sedate myself, I will stop trembling. Ah, but that only postpones things. I will wake up in a few hours, trembling again: Yes! But I can't stand the pain *of this moment.* This terrible, helpless moment. There is nothing I can take. The Librium or the Valium or the other dandy drugs that may have straightened out my party companions will only make things worse for me. "I will never drink anything again. I don't care whose party it is, or how happy or unhappy I am, or which friend insists that one, just one won't hurt me. If I can just stop shaking and throwing up and sweating and doubling up with pain! If I can just get myself back to sleep, it is bound to be better when I wake up! And I will never drink anything again! I hate the goddamned stuff. Damn it to hell!"

Waking up was often in a hospital . . . in California, in New York, in Lima, Peru, and I had no idea how I'd gotten there or who had brought me. How could it have happened? I started out at the party doing exactly what everybody else was doing, often at everyone's endless insistence, and here I was in a strange hospital! How long had I been here? Is a big fat nurse going to come in again and lean over me and say, "Now, aren't we ashamed of ourselves?" Yes, fat lady, very ashamed and monumentally depressed, and if you will get the hell out of here, I will happily die and get this whole impossible farce of life out of the way.

Finally it was a doctor in New York, Stanley N. Gitlow, who got through to me. I was in Mount Sinai Hospital with severe bronchitis. I had it, and my chart read that I had it, but this handsome stranger stood at the foot of my bed and said he believed I was an alcoholic. He said that I was not bad, I was sick, and that I could be treated and that I could be well. He said there was no more blame attached to me and my disease than there was to a diabetic and his disease! I was very sick, but I wanted to get out of bed and kneel at his feet. Somebody finally said it: I was not bad; I was sick and I could be treated and be well!

No sentence that has ever been uttered to me has meant so much. I guess one has to be as sick as I was to appreciate that. I guess a person has to be as neurotically sick with guilt as I have always been to appreciate being told that I was not bad; I was sick and could be well!

For a long time now, I have been repeating what I was told . . . looking into the burning hell in an alcoholic's eyes. I am looking at my remembered self, at my tortured, despairing, lonely self.

I'm not sure there are any accidents. I think everything that has happened to me has had to happen.

Alcohol is a very patient drug. It will wait for the alcoholic to pick it up ONE MORE TIME. It will wait forever. I don't mean that alcohol is a threat to me; alcohol, for me, *isn't*. The way Hitler *isn't*. Or Valdosta, Georgia, or brussels sprouts. I serve alcohol to my guests; I am around alcohol a good deal. It is just that alcohol, for me, is *not*.

But I learned it the hard way. Months after Dr. Gitlow had set me right, had guided me onto a path of recovery that is well-worn and proven, I was invited on a free "junket" to South America from Hollywood. There was to be a celebration in Lima, Peru, to mark the opening of a television station. They would fly a planeful of Hollywood folk to Lima for the big bash!

Billy Rose told me, "Don't go anywhere unless somebody else pays for it." All the way to South America, Billy? That's quite a free ticket! That's for me, isn't it, Billy?

The bar opened before the plane left the ground. It never closed. For some of my companions there seemed to be a desperation about the drinking . . . never an empty glass, and it is a long, long trip! I watched and sipped soda water. I like soda water!

I have a great deal of trouble with my intolerance of drunken women who call themselves social drinkers. They get so sloppy, so piggy, so loud, so vulgar, so cheap, so ugly. I guess I can't stand them because I know that I must have been just like them. I don't like to think that.

The famous cargo was pretty soused by the time we set down in Lima . . . not everybody, certainly not old "soda water" me! We were met by blaring bands of colorfully garbed musicians. Dignitaries gave everybody a pisco . . . the native, fall-right-down-on-the-ground drink. I declined the pisco but accepted the funereal sheaf of roses. We were piled into limousines and, with motorcycles screeching our coming to the country, we sped into town. The highway cut through a vast area of mud. Thousands upon thousands of people were *living* in it. In mud! On either side of the shiny limousines laden with us fantasy people were thousands of human beings living in mud! They walked on it, their huts were made of it, and they were lined up in it watching us go by!

When we arrived at the hotel in Lima, there was a kind of "When do we all meet down here in the lobby?" session during which some of my companions were briefing each other on the best tourist "buys" in Peru . . . "Llama rugs and hangings, of course, but make them let you wet a corner of the fur to be sure it isn't synthetic." "Oh, and damask tablecloths! I have a friend who got one down here . . . with forty-eight napkins . . . divine, but don't let them fool you into having it sent to you . . . you'll never get it! Better to carry it all the way home!" "Oh, yes, and never, never pay what they ask. They expect you to 'jew' them down. They expect it."

That night we were guests at a scandalously exclusive restaurant. The owners were Swiss. The Swiss had acquired priceless museum pieces of Inca artifacts, of fabulous gold and jeweled works of art. These Peruvian treasures belonged to the Swiss! The Swiss owners hung them on the walls of their restaurant! They should have been hung on the walls of mud huts where they belonged! No bell-ringing, watch-making, yodeling ancestors fashioned these majestic things! They came from hearts and souls of passion and dignity born of centuries of hardship and struggle! The legacy rightfully belonged to people who will never have the money to get in to see it! I was getting sicker, on *soda water*. My Hollywood colleagues were unmindful of the Swiss rapists.

Back at the hotel, in the parlor of each Hollywood person's suite, the management had placed a tray of booze. A bottle of wine, of gin, and scotch . . . all imported stuff, naturally. No fruit, no after-dinner mints, no bottled water! Just assorted ether!

Patient alcohol, the "gotcha" drug!

Three days later (they told me) I opened my eyes. There was a crescent of adult Botticelli cherubim leaning over me. They were a part of the Hollywood people, come to say farewell to their obviously alcoholic traveling companion. They were on their way home. They were dear, and they hugged me and kissed my forehead and told me we would see each other back in California. They left.

I didn't know where I was. I'm not sure even now. It was a hospital room, very small . . . spartan . . . humble. I was wearing my best peignoir, a Dior peignoir that had cost a small fortune. It was creased and wrinkled, and the velvet ribbons were twisted and matted. It was ruined. And I had been so careful of it . . . until then.

I had never known anybody in Lima, Peru. I went through grade school on the South Side of Chicago with a girl who became a nun and a missionary nurse. Her name was Snookie Meyer, she became Sister Mary Arthur. I had no idea what had become of her. She was in charge of the clinic where I was taken in Lima, Peru!

 singhi

I am convinced that I was born with a predisposition to the disease. Eighty-four percent of all alcoholics come from families with a history of abnormal drinking. Researchers say that persons with such family history face odds of four to one at birth that they will become alcoholics, IF THEY DRINK AT ALL!

So I will *not* be indicted by a drug-oriented society. One in three people pop some kind of drug to alter reality.

My name is not Carry Nation. I am not anti-alcohol, but I am *anti* the abuse of alcohol. For nine out of ten social drinkers alcohol is peachy-keen, but for the tenth one . . . gonzo! Like me.

When I was well enough to make the flight, Sister Mary Arthur shipped me back to California, and I was taken to St. John's in Santa Monica, where I was treated by my own doctors for what had turned into bronchial pneumonia. That was a long time ago. Since that time, for me, alcohol *is not.*

16

W HILE THERE IS NO UNDER-standing an alcoholic's suffering unless one has lived through it, there is certainly no understanding of the suffering of an alcoholic's family unless one has survived that as well. Mothers like mine choke on the word "alcoholic." To give voice to the words "alcoholic daughter" puts the spikes under the fingernails. My poor mother and father! But they came around!

My father told me that they were in the supermarket one day in Santa Monica. He was pushing the cart, and she was choosing the items from the shelves. The silly loudspeakers were broadcasting the stultifying soporific music from a local radio station. Then there was a public service announcement. I was *it* . . . saying "I am a recovered alcoholic and help is available through the National Council on Alcoholism." My mother and father listened to my voice booming up and down the supermarket aisles, and then, my father said, my mother announced to all the customers in that section that the voice they had just heard was her daughter, who had been received at the White House for her work with alcoholics. My father said it was very impressive. Mother marched alongside him as the admiring throng made a clear path for them all the way to the check-out counter.

Oh, my God, I hate the hurt I've caused . . . to the people from whose lives I sprang and to the person who sprang from mine! What a devastating lashing out . . . what monumental rage . . . what insufferable selfishness accompany the disease of alcoholism! All those years of being Judas to my own Christ! And, incomprehensible as it seems, all of it in spite of everything I could do to avoid it! Nobody despises alcoholism more than the alcoholic who is in the throes of it. Nobody despises the alcoholic more than the alcoholic himself. He lives in his death. And there in a supermarket next to the sea was a close-to-dying woman boasting about her daughter who had managed to live through it.

The last journey each of my parents ever knew on this earth was in my company. We shared the vehicle. With each of them, I rode in the hearse from the freight office of O'Hare Airport in Chicago, down the Adlai E. Stevenson Freeway and on to Kankakee, where I laid them to rest. My father's coffin was covered with the flag strapped 'round it in the rear of the hearse. A decade later, Mother's coffin was encased in a cardboard carton back there. It is a long ride to Kankakee in such a wagon.

Each of my dead parents had been readied for burial back in California. Each time when the coffin was opened in Clancy's Funeral Home in Kankakee, Illinois, for a final "viewing" by relatives, I stood alongside the metal casket with its gathered satiny lining. Each time resting on a pillow of some kind of velvety stuff was the cosmetically metamorphosized face that had once been my parent . . . first my father, then my mother.

My father bore some slight resemblance to himself. He died at seventy-three with all the earned creases of his years etched into his Irish face. In his coffin on the sleazy pillow lay a man of forty . . . no lines, no ridges across the brow; all the erupted little veins beneath the skin covered in ivory paint, but he was recognizable, and he was very beautiful. That would have made him happy.

Just before the coffin was closed, I was left alone with him. His forehead was icy when I laid my cheek against it. From that day forward, whenever my heart and my head ache at the same time, I rest my cheek against something that is icy cold. It is a sort of mystical medicine, and it works. I whispered to my father, "Thank you for my life," and we were parted.

With my mother who had been so dreadfully ill in the last years, when the coffin was opened for final "viewing" in the same Clancy's Funeral Home two handfuls of years later, her visage was so shocking I don't know that I shall ever be able to wipe it out of my memory. She couldn't have weighed eighty-five pounds when she died. She was eighty-four and as frail as Kleenex. But in her coffin, on her own sleazy pillow, her face had been puffed up like a large woman's face. Somehow her deep-set eye sockets had been brought forward. Her face was all of a piece without much definition, and there was a sooty color to her, as though the gray pallor were at work inside her and was forcing its way through her flesh. So little resemblance was there. I kissed the face of a stranger, and the coffin was closed.

At the cemetery I asked to be left alone for a moment. I didn't find it difficult to call to my mother's spirit to tell her that I hoped she knew that I knew that the only thing that ever stood between herself and me had been a mirror!

እ

My second marriage had a lot to do with alcohol. Our neighbors in Bel-Air drank a lot. So did the people down the Yellow Brick Road. So did we. Sundays, for example.

You wake up in your custom-built platform bed alongside your own Adonis in your own built-to-order dream house at the tiptop of Bel-Air. You open the sliding door to the patio and the heated pool, into which you dive deep and slide your naked body along the side of the pool, and you surface, looking out to the Pacific Ocean and Catalina Island. Your head, just above the rim of the poolside; and there is nothing out there but the sea.

The housekeeper is off because it's Sunday. Your son is off at prep school in Arizona. There are no others around. The wonder is all there. And it is all paid for!

At one end of the forty-two-foot living room is the great vase full of giant yellow mums, brought to you each and every Saturday by your loving husband. There is great music throughout the house—Mahler, Vivaldi, Segovia. There is *The New York Times*, air edition, very expensive! My father believed there were three sources of divine wisdom—the Old and the New Testaments, and *The New York Times*. Sunday isn't Sunday without *The New York Times*. Ah, the good life! And it was. For what it was, it was good. It just wasn't real.

Along about noon I would enter our kitchen, which would turn

Julia Child green with envy. I would begin the delicate preparation of my *specialité*: Escargots Magnifiques! I could broil a chicken, not a steak. I could toss a salad, and I could make Escargots Magnifiques. That's it for me and the culinary art. I used slivered almonds in my Escargot paste. Not orthodox, but delicious!

While I was thus wifely occupied in the kitchen, my mate was busy at the bar; the bar he designed when the house was built. Beautiful bar, lavishly equipped. Sensational glasses and doodads. Precious old French cutout theater scenes recessed into the wall and theatrically lighted. A pleasant place to sit on a comfortable stool and bomb yourself.

Husband was busy with his own *Specialité* . . . Martinis Magnifiques! And they *were*. Everyone we knew agreed. They were the best ever. As with everything he did, he performed a ritual. Glasses chilled in the freezer for at least fifteen minutes ahead of time. Pitcher filled with ice to chill it, then emptied. I used to watch! The next part of the ritual seemed to be the simplest. I thought anybody could do that part. I never said so, but anybody could put some fresh ice cubes in a pitcher and throw a lot of gin on top of them. The vermouth was a whisper passing over the open mouth of the pitcher. That much anybody could do. But then came the artistry of stirring with the crystal stick; the steady rhythm of the ice against the glass, the ice against the glass, the ice against the glass! Then the rubbing of the rim of the little glasses waiting for their fill . . . the rapid rubbing of a lemon peel. It made a tone, a pretty tone against the Steuben glass! Never an olive, never a toothpick, no desecration of any sort . . . just the pristine, snow white clarity of unadulterated dynamite!

Meanwhile, back at the range in the splendid kitchen, the escargots had been removed from their can, secreted in their reusable shells, stuffed with their aromatically stupefying paste and arranged on their own special tins, and slid into the oven.

One martini's worth of salad making, and French bread slicing, good bottle of wine opening, and cheese arranging; one other martini for the last dip in the pool before lunch. Music, mums, Adonis, Pacific Ocean, escargots, martinis, good wine, *New York Times*, and the top of the world for your oyster!

It would have been so wonderful if it had been real. I think we both tried to make it real, but it never was, not really.

We chartered planes from Paris to Nice, we tangoed in Buenos Aires, so many exotic bits and pieces; eleven years of sporadic exotica. We wore out! We got tired of the game. So much of what had seemed glamorous became unlivable. The amusing things had lost their charm.

For years I continued to be amused by my husband's nightly health habits. He was ever a fastidious person, very well groomed; it was part of his attractiveness.

Not every night, but many nights, I would be aware of his movement in our enormous bed. I would open one eye to peek. He felt the need to relieve himself. He didn't know I was awake. He went through his routine because for him it was the only right way to do it. Nobody had to be watching!

He wore pajamas of balloon cloth, white with blue piping, obtainable only at Saks Fifth Avenue in Beverly Hills and too expensive.

I peeked at him from the corner of my pillow. He would sit on the edge of the bed, straighten his balloon-cloth pajamas, slip his feet into his Alexander Shields alligator slippers (eighty dollars then!), and rise to his fine full height.

Across the master bedroom in front of the huge fireplace was a custom-built-for-two chaise longue of saffron nubbiness. On it lay his saffron-colored robe, also from Alexander Shields and made in the manner of the Japanese. He would don this sensational garment, there in the dark; he would cinch its sash around his middle and free the collar of his pajamas so that it lay neatly atop the collar of the robe. Then he would cross the room to the bathroom to make water. After the flushing came the washing of hands, the trek back to the chaise longue, the disrobing of the kimono, the draping of same across the longue, the straightening of the pajama collar, back to the bed, the stepping out of alligator slippers, the final adjustment of balloon-cloth pajamas, and ultimately back to dreamland! It was a performance! And nobody saw it! For years I had a real affection for it, and then it began *to drive me crazy!* It surely wasn't his fault. The performance hadn't changed. I had!

His masseur was everybody's masseur . . . everybody who was anybody! There was even a hit movie based on that masseur and the bodies he handled. I used to come tooling up to the top of Bel-Air after a long hard day on a back lot somewhere, full of cow-dung odor, and dust and grime. I'd pull my Ford into the garage next to my husband's Cadillac and make my disheveled entrance into the beautiful house. The music was playing, the uninterrupted view of all the lights of Los Angeles was outside the windows, the pool was glistening with tiny diamonds, and in the master bedroom my tummy-down husband was lying on a table, being kneaded and rubbed with oils by a masseur who did it to everybody who WAS anybody. There would be a fire in the fireplace. Each of them had a fine scotch and soda standing by, and enter the rambling wreck from some silly TV movie or some film wherein the "ugly duckling" was her role!

I'm sure my husband would have been perfectly happy if I, too, were being handled by the masseur. I've never been able to do that, but that was not my husband's fault. He believed in that stuff. I didn't!

He tried to the best of his ability to make the marriage work. I tried, too. We tried too hard. Too long. Both of us.

Once in the south of France, on the middle-class jet-set beach in front of the Provençal, my leftover husband and I were doing our best to patch up a woefully impossible marriage. One more time. We were on a crash program. Do it or die—and we almost did! It was very foolish, and very hopeless. We pretended we were very rich. We drank all day. We had rented a mildewed villa. A slatternly cook sang prettily the first morning she worked for us and swore like a tramp for the rest of the summer. We chewed long loaves of bread and hard hunks of local cheese. At night the moonlight streamed through the windows across our bed, and the stench of the cesspool perfumed the air. We raced the Corniche and wept in the Matisse chapel and danced on Bastille Day. It was hard work—frenetic, boozy, relentless dedication to the final desolation!

One catatonic afternoon on the beach a fortune-teller from Morocco came along the sand. He wore a black bear rug and a mangy turban. He studied my hand and told me I had all the emotional maturity of a ten-year-old child! And until very recently I have lived believing he was paying me a most courtly compliment! I have thought he meant that in the midst of all those faded and jaded, bored and boring misfits, I emerged as an ever-young, never-to-wither-and-die spirit! But lately I think I am beginning to grasp what the old Moor really had in mind. I was three times ten years old when he made the discovery. I am more than twice that age now when I am discovering it for myself. I ask myself: What is a ten-year-old child doing walking around in my hide? I ask myself if she is not my worst enemy. She's the one who still believes in the tooth fairy. She's the one who insists on perfection! She makes all the demands and I suffer!

We sat one night, Fletcher and I, at a very little table in a cheap nightclub. The noise was deafening, and the music was dreadful, and I had a headache. My husband was telling me something that was obviously important to him because his forehead was full of creases and his eyes were deeply serious. I could see him thinking, choosing his words with great care and definition. But above the loud music I couldn't hear anything he was saying to me. Not a word! I sat there looking at his face, working itself like a bumpy motion picture. He didn't realize I couldn't hear him. When he stopped moving his lips long enough for me to react, I would nod or shrug or shake my head, agreeing with him, and he would roll merrily on, and I hadn't the slightest notion of what the man was saying! I thought of how stupid it was! All animation and no sound! I didn't know what in hell he was talking about! I didn't know who in hell this man was! I knew I didn't really care what he was saying, and I knew he didn't really care whether I did or not! He could have been reciting Joyce Kilmer's "Trees," and it wouldn't have made the slightest difference to either one of us! For better, for worse, until death do us! The end was beginning . . . the end of the marriage that the Church said was never a marriage . . . the marriage that was a mortal sin even before it began. In the eyes of the Church I am still and always will be married to my Tolstoy in far-off Cádiz de La Frontera. He is my husband, the Church says. That might be hard to explain to his two later wives.

One day long ago at the old Pierre's restaurant on Fifty-second Street, Sister Mary Leola Oliver, who treasured me in spite of my sins, leaned across the luncheon table and took my hand. She said she had been so saddened by the news of my divorce from young Tolstoy (whose real name, of course, was Bill). Sister had great black eyes that looked like wet ripe olives, very beautiful. She said she had prayed so hard that Bill and I could "ford together the troubled stream." I agreed with her. It was indeed a great shame. But we were too young for each other, and we didn't understand each other very well, I told her. I said that we had prayed, too, but it just made things worse. I asked Sister if she thought God could forgive me, and she said it wasn't for her to say. I asked her if she wanted another cup of coffee, and she said she didn't think she'd better. I didn't think there was much else that could be said, and I looked for the waiter to get the check. Sister's ripe-olive eyes were very misty. She loved me, Sister did. She held my hand again and said that I knew what the Church felt about divorce. I shook my head yes. Then she sighed, and her voice quavered as she said she didn't think that God meant for me to live the rest of my life all alone. I was not every thirty yet. I told her it must be the rotten luck of the Irish. She didn't even smile. Then she took my other hand in her other hand and said, "Well, Mercy, dear, don't be too unhappy because God in His infinite wisdom, takes care of such things, and maybe Bill will die!" Sister looked positively saintly as she said it. If God would just do away with a perfectly healthy marvelous young Tolstoy of a man, I'd be all set . . . consecrated ground to be buried in . . . new marriage bed to lie in . . . all bets are off if Bill would just die! Incredible!

With *two* leftover husbands to account for, my wicked soul has just about shriveled and died. Their souls, on the other hand, are just as frisky as they ever were, because neither of them was born in the True Faith. They've each been married three times, determined to do it until they get it right, and I say whatever they get they deserve and I don't care how that is interpreted. By anybody.

A funny thing happened a little while ago on my way from Alaska to San Diego. It had been a long, hard flight, but I really couldn't complain. All the way from Seattle I had been bumped up into first class because the captain liked me in the movies.

We were flying over Los Angeles at dusk, and my patron, the captain, was telling us over the speakers that we were looking down on the famous Universal Studios and beautiful downtown Burbank. I knew he was going to say, "And right down there is Pasadena." Pasadena is the place where my second leftover sinless husband lives locked in the arms of his third wife. I peered down through 33,000 feet of night sky and sneered at the glowing lights and said, "You son of a bitch." To the night air, I said it. I like to think he heard me.

But I don't like to fail . . . at anything. It isn't that I've succeeded so often that failure is the rare exception, it is just that I don't like to fail. Period!

❧

Kingsley wrote that there comes a time when "all the sport is stale, lad,/ . . . And all the wheels run down." And Emerson wrote, "Your destiny is busy seeking after you. Therefore, be at rest from seeking after it."

There came a night when all my sport was stale—at the end of my second marriage, after my second stillborn child and the near-fatal accident of my one beloved son—when my wheels had run down, and my destiny came very close to losing me altogether. Too many things had happened too fast. It was my birthday eve, 1963.

I was fresh out of lifeness. That's all there was, there wasn't any more!

I had enough to drink to get the courage to make the move to the medicine chest. I swallowed everything in it. I was still under medication prescribed to see me through the trauma of my son's critical accident. I took all there was of that bottle of pills. I swallowed fifty gelatin capsules . . . it makes your nails grow strong. I took aspirin, vitamin C, everything . . . plus a bunch of sleeping pills that I had never bothered to use.

I had written a note, left the insurance policies and bankbooks on the table, put on my nicest nightgown, brushed my hair, and lay down on my bed to die. I remember saying out loud, "Thank God, thank God it is over."

I knew I was going under. I knew I was losing consciousness. Slowly. Peacefully. Then I thought of one more thing I would like to do. I got up and staggered to the bookcases in the hallway. I chose Plato's *Dialogues* and *The Wind in the Willows* and Montaigne's *Essays* and Shakespeare's *Sonnets*. I carried the bundle back to the bedroom and made room for it on my bedside table. Better I should be remembered as someone who read good stuff right up to the very end. I lay down, amused in a pleasant hazy way. I chuckled myself to sleep . . . into the grand *Peut-Être*. I had wanted to go!

I was crushed when I woke up . . . in Santa Monica Hospital.

I only know that if my head and heart were in exactly that same despairing spot this very day, I would have to do the exactly same despairing thing, and anybody who doesn't understand that is, as William James wrote, "not worth knowing anyhow."

So many famous people, so many nonfamous people have shared with me their own "emotional bankruptcy." So many many people have really wanted to die. They seem ashamed to say so. I think it would help if they said so. If we find that we are alike in our despair, we can surely handle it more successfully.

And I find it next to impossible to remain politely silent when people prate to me about the glory of being given another chance to live happily ever after! I don't know where these people are coming from! What glory? What happily ever after? There is no such foolishness! *Believing that* was what got me in all my trouble.

Life is a bitch! And if I have more good days than bad, I am a lucky person! I believe in joy, but I believe in its flip-side, agony. I believe in roaring laughter which almost follows on the heels of copious tears. I believe in black and I believe in white and I believe in all the shades of gray in between. And I believe that human happiness is a flutter-by.

My only true harmony lies deep within my soul, wherever that is. I know that somehow I am in tune with the universe. I see it in my heart's beat in the soft side of my wrist. In spite of everything I did to stop that pulse it repeats itself, unceasingly, insisting upon me. Me, as I am. All the monstrous things that I am . . . all the marvelous things that I am. The conglomerate that is me is sustained by the inexplicable force of that beat. It looks so small, inflating itself in faithful rhythm there under my skin. Each tiny pressure saying, "Yes, yes, yes, yes, yes, yes, yes."

Any day that I take time to watch my heart beat for a few minutes is a day worth living. There may be no glory nor much happiness in such a day but my heart beats in faithful support . . . of me, all day, all the livelong day of my life . . . and I wrestle with my angels, one at a time.

ҙ҉

I have loved playing the part of feisty Annie Sullivan in the play *The Miracle Worker*. I have always felt that Annie, the teacher, and Helen Keller, the student, waged one of the greatest, if unbloodiest, battles in history! And they both won! Two volcanic women determined to best one another ended by bringing out the best *in* one another.

Annie has a speech about Jacob in the Bible, who said to his angel, with whom he was wrestling, "I will not let thee go until thou bless me." Annie Sullivan, epitome of all that an Irishwoman is or ever shall be, wrestled with Helen until both of them were brought to their knees in mutual blessing!

In my quieter moments (when I am not currently seething over everything in general or nothing in particular; merely seething out of lifelong habit) I think of my alcoholism as the "angel" with whom I have had to wrestle. Maybe this angel in devil's garb chose *me* as a wrestling mate because it was the only way to stop me; the only way to halt the headlong retreat I had begun to race as soon as I was lowered from Santa Claus's phony lap in Marshall Field's store back in Chicago when I was five years old! Hell-bent as I was for infinity, I doubt that a force less mighty than alcoholism could have stopped me. The enraged small child was too frightened to halt on her own. She had been a fugitive from what she understood was gross injustice.

She felt she had been laughed at, betrayed, and she would never stop running . . . ever! But . . .

She was running out of steam as she ran into alcoholism country. She didn't see the booby trap, the ha-ha fence. The fall bruised her considerably, even broke a couple of ribs, but it probably saved her life, and she knows it!

I can think of no enemy more formidable, more cunning in its battle plan, and yet—there are times when I think that the fray has ended in a blessing. Not at all times, by any means. I harbor resentment for the people who write "hate mail" to me; I viciously resent cheap magazine and newspaper stories about my "rise from the gutter" (a direct quote from one such story that appeared in a great Philadelphia newspaper). When these things happen, I threaten to resign from all activities in alcoholism; I limp away like a beaten pup, and I hurt.

This is a letter I treasure and reread each time the uglies put on their gorilla suits and chase after me. This letter, from the public relations director of the National Council on Alcoholism has helped me so much, so very much, as an effective antidote to the poison darts:

Dear Mercy:

. . . Like any other person who has embraced an unpopular cause, you have been criticized and ridiculed by some thoughtless, uninformed, useless, selfish and just plain stupid people who have never achieved one good thing in their drab lives. Waking up in the morning and getting dressed exhausts their resourcefulness. However, the trouble with these negative jerks is that they are very vocal and all of us have a tendency to accept what they say as representative of the general population. That's human. And that's why you now hurt so much.

However, it is also human (and I don't understand it) for people who are grateful for what you are doing to remain silent—like my friend . . . who said seeing you on TV put his entire world back together but never wrote to you because he felt you received so much mail that his letter would never reach you.

And then there are those who have worked in the field of alcoholism for so many years. Consider the positive impact you have had on them, think of the doors you have opened, think of the large number of alcoholics they have been able to help as a result of your walk.

You *have changed public attitudes* in a significant way. Mercy, strong evidence of this is the response we're getting to the May 8 event in Washington, D.C. To date, 36 public figures have agreed to participate. These are not only actors, but an astronaut, a famous surgeon, a network president, a congressman, industrialists, etc. Such people were unapproachable a few years ago. *You have made the difference.*

I guess what I'm saying all adds up to a plea that you not become defeated at the hand of an awful person like the writer of the Philadelphia story. Please, if you can find it in your heart to do so, take strength and encouragement and justifiable pride from all the good things you have caused to happen. I am not articulate enough to enumerate them all but they are monumental in quality and scope.

In your letter, you asked that I remove your name from all lists and committees, I will do this when you show me how to remove John Hancock's name from the Declaration of Independence.

Please, Mercy, call me after you have read these words.

> Much love,
> Walter Murphy
> National Council on Alcoholism

Usually re-reading this letter dries the salt from my wounds, and I sidle back into the middle of life's parade, where I rightfully belong. It's rough on my constitution, but it's the only place to meet interesting people.

17

HE GREAT PEOPLE I'VE MET always have time for the niceties. Pint-sized people never have time, just the big ones. I met Marlene Dietrich when she was still the reigning beauty of the screen and the international nightclub circuit. Life was beginning to catch up with her, and some of the tread was worn off her tires, but she was still racing pell-mell, as only Marlene could.

My second husband was the creator of the program *Studio One*. It was a magnificent show, first on radio and then into live television. He was responsible for its success, and he brought fine style and distinction to the programs. Every worthwhile actor liked doing *Studio One* . . . for little money; it was simply a great show for a fine showman. And that's enough about Fletcher's excellence. I don't see any reason at this late date for me to blow his horn. There's a new wife now, let her blow it!

One long-anticipated week the scheduled star of the show on *Studio One* was the great Marlene. All of us "accompanying" actors were very excited indeed. How often did we get to share a microphone with such a legend? The men in our company were particularly natty that day, and I had attempted crystal blue eye shadow, but it made me look like an anemic owl, so I removed it. We sat around the big rehearsal table down in the basement of the old Forty-fifth Street theater, scripts in front of us, pencils poised. We waited. Marlene was late. Someone said that being Germanic, she was a stickler for discipline. The gifted director, who was not yet my husband . . . well, not really . . . said he would go upstairs and phone her agent. As he started up the stairs, she started down. He backed away the way actors have to do in films where English kings make entrances. The men around the table stood up. I found it difficult not to join them. She was among us! A taffy-colored vision—shining, cream-and-honey vision. Massive nutria wrap-around coat with a tightly cinched belt and huge rumpled collar, a beret of the same fur, covering nearly one-half of that *face*, the cigarette precariously held between vivid lips. The one eyebrow that was visible, thinly arched in a state of eternal indignation. She flung her zillion-dollar coat on the table. Not over a chair, but flung on the table! Her honey-colored leather purse with the Hermès mark was flung on top of the flung coat, and then the beret was flung, too! We beheld an untidy mess of very expensive stuff in the middle of the table we had previously used for paper bags containing sandwiches and coffee from the Stage Delicatessen.

Beneath her now-discarded outer finery, she was another layer of creamy taffy . . . all cashmere now . . . sweater, slacks, even her hair was taffy-colored. No jewelry, glorious low-heeled Belgian moccasins, taffy, too . . . only that whorl of red outlining her mouth, everything else a monotone. This was an all-blond person, with a sensational figure, her face made up to look as though she had never used makeup in her life. And the *gold* . . . the cigarette case, the lighter, the pencil, the clasp on her handbag . . . all right out of Fort Knox.

And the woman herself . . . the woman Marlene, talking rapidly in that effectively calculated accent . . . was telling us breathlessly how sorry she was that she was late, and why! She said it was because of her daughter, Maria. She said:

"Day take nutting from me, I can get dem to take nutting! Dat's goot, I admire dat, but you should see de place vhere dey liff! You should see it! Cood you belief it, on Turd Avenue dey liff. Turd Avenue! In a valk-up yet. You valk und valk, up and up to a plaze you vouldn't belief. Dat's vhere dey brink my grandson, into such a place dey brink dis beaudifull boy!" She had taken over the entire rehearsal room now, striding around the table like an angry taffy-colored Lorelei, leaning into our faces to emphasize a point. She said:

"I coodn't stant it. I had to get my hants on dat plaze und fix it up somevay, somevay Gott knows how! I said to my daughta und her hussban, I said, 'Go. Go to a plaze for a few dayz vhere you cood be avay from dis plaze, from da baby, you neet a chainch, you neet to get avay, bot of you . . . I vill treat you to a few dayz. Go! Go to da mountainz, go to Canada, I don't care, juss *go!* I tolt dem I vood take care of da baby, und ven I had to come to dis rehearsl, I vood get an honest-to-Gott nurse to relief me. So! Dey vent, und oh, my Gott, vas I happy! But (und this izz da reezon dat I am late, und I am zooo sorry. I am never late, never!)

"*But* the reezon izz my daughta's fault. She gave to me instructionz, orderz, dey vere about da baby's formula, vat he drinks from his boddle. A soufflé is not so hard to make as dis formula stuff. She wrote it all down; four ounces of dis, ten drops of dat, blend wit a haff cup of dat, add sixteen ounces of dis, put it all in a pot, und varm it. Take it out, und add two spoons of dis and something of dat and more of somezzing elze, und den da baby shood drink it. Isn't dat terrible? Did you ever hear so terrible?"

She was *asking* us. None of us said anything. She was getting a little Wagnerian now and had put one of her cashmere-sheathed legs on one of the chairs. She was leaning on her knee—very impressive, certainly compelling gesture. She said:

"Vell, it *vas* terrible, it certainly *vas,* I can tell you, because *my daughta tolt me* dat da only vay I cood be certain dat I had mixt da formula in da right vay vas to examine da baby's poo-poo!" She held her hand across her forehead and said, "Can you imagine dat? She tolt me ven da baby poo-poos, I am to take da diapa full of da poo-poo and *examine it!* She tolt me if da poo-poo vas too light, I haff put into da formula too much of dis or too liddle of dat! She told me if da poo-poo izz too dark, I haff not put into da formula enuff of dis or dat! Now, da reezon I am late, ladiez und gentlemen, und I am never late, never, da reezon izz becauzz I don't know how to tell vat is too light und vat is too dark! I take da diapa over to da vindow. I examine da poo-poo. Izz it too light, I don't know . . . izz it too dark, I don't know. Da honest-to-Gott nurse und I bot examined it. She doesn't know eider, und dat izz vy I am late, und I am sooo sorry, I am never late."

Only a woman recognized as the world's most glamorous lady would dare tell such a story.

During Marlene's nightclub years she always wore incredible gowns, iridescent mermaid-sheaths which were executed by Jean Louis but which surely were effected by Marlene herself. The glitter of the pailettes and sequins was a hand-sewn masterpiece of precise placement. No Hollywood star ever had his front teeth capped with more attention than Marlene gave to each of those gleaming flakes of glass!

The deliberate sparseness of the sparkles in the chest area made the most of her two best points, the flesh-dyed elastic body stocking uplifting and all but revealing all that really mattered in that area.

It was in the middle of her torso that the visual light-show began its masterful camouflage. Cascading past her belly and around to her backside and down her thighs to the floor below were the multi-faceted glistening streams of gold and silver, magnificently providing what nature had left wanting. Nobody but Marlene thought there was anything wrong with her figure, even Marlene didn't think there was much need for improvement—but in later years she mourned the loss of her once plump and firm behind. Marlene knew exactly how many pailettes and sequins were necessary to create the derrière that wasn't there. Her audiences innocently observed two discreetly firm little bumps, that were really two carefully massed piles of shining deceivers . . . "now you see it, now you don't." Jean Louis got the credit for the gowns. He deserved it, certainly, but just as certainly, I feel it should have been shared. Marlene gave a lot of people credit, but the Dietrich distinction was always her own invention. Marlene knew better than anybody what to do with what she had to do with.

One day she and I were looking at some stunning large photographs that John Engstead had made of her. She indicated with the end of a pencil her faulty features. It was fascinating. The famous high cheekbones were nothing more than a suggestion, as God had made them. Marlene knew how to shade and light them. Marlene knew that by constantly disciplining herself, she would not allow her lips to close fully. She said it gave the impression of fuller lips, it made her mouth look characteristically sexy. I tried it in my bathroom mirror. It would take practice.

One night at a party at our house a couple of years before fate began shooting us all to smithereens, Marlene told the story of her funeral . . . the narration in the form of a movie-shooting script. Judy Garland and Sid Luft and Michael Wilding and Rita Hayworth and Nicholas Ray . . . all the lonely lovely people were there. Marlene held court for more than an hour, describing her Last Hurrah! The funeral service was to be held, of course, in Notre Dame Cathedral, following a procession along the Champs-d'Élysées past the somber throngs of people lining the avenue. There would be a pause in the march as the coffin was carried through what Marlene called "my arch!" She said it with such conviction that one could believe that a plaque had been struck and put in place: "This Arc de Triomphe is the exclusive property of M. Dietrich!"

Of course, Notre Dame would be jammed with mourners, all present by special invitation; but, she said, the film would cut to a wide airplane shot of the Île de la Cité, slowly coming in over the Left Bank and the Seine, first focusing on the preciously graceful steeple of Ste.-Chapelle and then closing in slowly, slowly to pick up a lone figure, far beneath the flying buttresses. It is a man in a rumpled suit, a fawn felt hat pulled far down on his face; he is leaning against the wall in an insolent manner, one foot braced against the stone. Several times during the film the camera comes back to this fellow with the thin column of smoke from his cigarette making its own Turkish incense to honor the glamorous corpse inside. Unmoved by the tolling bells, the booming organ, he stands alone, puffing contemplatively as a non-participant . . . "He is Jean Gabin!" In telling the story, Marlene might as well have announced, "Napoleon Bonaparte" . . . her voice had that kind of force!

Earlier on in this screenplay of Marlene's dealing with her own demise, there is a scene of her newly dead body lying on a slab in the Paris morgue. Leaning over the sheet-covered form, still unmistakably Dietrich's shape, are two worried American women. Marlene says, "Dey are vhispering to each udder! Somezzing izz wrong. Dey are very upset. Da camera comes around to a close-up on der faces. . . . Ve see who dey are! Oh, my Gott, oh my Gott, look who!" Marlene held us, her rapt audience, in suspension, then told us sotto voce that the two women were her hairdresser and makeup woman from her films. They had been sent for from Hollywood to "prepare" the corpse! Marlene said that the trouble was that she herself had always directed her own hair styling, and particularly her own makeup, but she has never said anything. The professionals always got full screen credit for making her look so photogenic! And all those years she faithfully demanded that they be engaged by the producer because she wouldn't dream of doing a picture without them! "Now," she told us, "dey are in real trouble. Now dey don't know vat to do. I am lying der, looking like hell, and vat are dey going to do? It izz very sad for dem. Dey should haff paid attention. Dey shood have watched me more clozzely all doze years. Dey could haff learned!"

Once when Marlene was appearing in London, her press people asked her if there were any special Britishers she would like to meet. She loftily declared she knew them all. Then she thought of one who, she said, was worth all the others put together . . . Sir Alexander Fleming, the discoverer of penicillin. Sir Alexander Fleming was delighted and arranged a small dinner party in her honor at his residence. Before dining, he presented her with a gift she treasured as if it were "A Diamond as Big as the Ritz." It was a wee casket containing three small pieces of the moldy bread from which he had derived his magic drug!

At his table, when dessert had been cleared, Sir Alexander offered Marlene some delicate mints from a crystal bowl on a silver stem. He asked her if she didn't think the dish was beautiful. Marlene must have said it was very nice, and Sir Alexander told her it was one of a pair, the twin being at the opposite end of the table. He said they had been presented to him by the Queen in honor of his discovery of penicillin. Marlene exploded. "She vat? Da Kveen, vat did she do? You vork for your lifetime, and you find a miracle dat vill last forever and saffes millions of lives, and she giffs to you *two lousy candy dishes?* Two knickknacks to put on your table, for Gott's sake? How could a Kveen do dat, such a ting? Da crown jewels from da Tower of London she should giff to you, da castles in Scotland, da whole British navy . . . somezzing! But two lousy candy dishes? Vat izz dat?"

Once when I was driving Marlene to the Los Angeles Airport (she never learned to drive), she said, "Der izz alvays somebotty to drive, alvays. So much trouble, da car, da gazzoline, da vinshield vipers, vhy should I be boddered with dat? Sombotty else cood do it bedder dan me. So let dem do it." So I was doing it. We were talking about the upcoming Academy Awards show. I was to present one of the Oscars (Frank Sinatra turned out to be the winner), and Marlene asked me what I was going to wear, and I told her I hadn't even thought about it, that I would find something and it would be okay. She said, "No, it von't be okay; not if *you* get it, it von't. Don't buy anyting. I vill send you zome tings of mine from New York . . . you cood choozze a nice vun und vear it; den it vill be okay." I protested . . . a useless endeavor with Marlene. She said, "You zee, da trouble wit you, I am going to tell you. Only somebotty who luffs you vill tell you such a ting." I always worry when people start out with that "only someone who loves you" stuff; I know I am about to be zapped with a real jolt. Marlene actually patted my hand on the steering wheel as she told me sorrowfully, "Darlink, I haff to say it because I luff you and I vant you to be happy. Darlink, belief me, you don't haff to look azz *bad* azz you do!" Only Marlene could do *that.*

At about ten o'clock the following night a handsome American Airlines pilot arrived at our door with a large package full of very expensive Dietrich gowns. The pilot said Marlene knew him personally and had asked him to deliver the package himself. What had Marlene done? Did she pack all those fantastic things as soon as she got back to New York and run over to her friend the pilot's house, and did he just happen to be flying to Los Angeles the next day, and did he think nothing of taking the package all the way up to the top of Bel-Air to a person who doesn't have to look as bad as she does? I'll never know. When I asked Marlene, she said, "Please, shudd up, darlink. Don't vorry about it."

I didn't want to wear Marlene's dresses, and in those days I could, I mean size-wise. I spread them out—four of them—on our bed and over the chaise longue. Gorgeous! Absolutely gorgeous! Even before I tried them on, I knew they were all wrong for me! All of them! I knew it! One was a long misty gray crepe de chine, a Dior dream of a gown, simple, simple, sheath with long tight sleeves. (All Marlene's clothes had long sleeves. She said, "Any voman over tventy-fife who shows her upper armz in publick izz a fool. Already da turkey vattle haz started. Already dere izz da hanging loose skin bouncing back und fort, und ven singers on da stage or in da moofies raise dere bare arms, it makes me sick to look at it, seasick it makes me, all dat ugly looze skin vaving back and fort . . . terrible . . . ugly . . . makes me sick, all dat.")

Another of her gowns on my bed was a chocolate-brown silk evening suit. Marlene was made for it. I wasn't. The third glorious garment was black, as was the fourth. One of them was backless—no back at all. Marlene may have had a puritan's protection of upper arms, but this dress displayed the sacroiliac, and mine is not all that attractive. So it had to be the fourth dress. It had to be one of the four because Marlene would be watching the awards show on TV in New York, and when I was introduced, I had better appear in one of her gowns! The only one left was a black chiffon. It was made by Galanos, probably cost a billion dollars, a starkly simple bodice with a skirt of hundreds of tiny stitch pleats. A gown for Marlene to wear in Vegas, or in London, or Monte Carlo . . . I didn't think it was a gown for me to wear anyplace, but I had to wear it. I thought about breaking my leg or catching pneumonia, but the great night came, and I wore the dress knowing I would have to enter a convent the next day or disappear into Mexico because the whole world would have seen how goofy I looked.

The next day the whole world, or my part of it, said that I never looked lovelier. They kept saying it, everywhere I went, digging it in. Some of them seemed surprised that I could look like that.

I returned all four gowns to Marlene, but she sent back the one I wore, saying, "Darlink, it neffer looked dat marffelous on me. Pleaze, I vant you to haff it, vear it all da time. Don't vear anyting elze!"

The thing about Marlene Dietrich is this: If the gown she let me wear had been the only gown she owned, she would have given it to me. I have never known a more giving person than Marlene, and for so much of her life, so few have given to her. They know who they are, and I wonder how they can live with their success, knowing that much of it was achieved by standing on the shoulders of a great and beautiful woman who nurtured them, supported them, made love to them, and from whom they walked away, the luggage she had given them crammed with the gifts she had bought for them. Marlene never walked away from anybody. The shoe was always on the other's foot, likely a very expensive shoe that Marlene had paid for.

It wasn't merely the giving of *things*; she gave of herself to people she felt deserved it. Sometimes her judgment wasn't all that good. I've been with her when she held back the tears. I've been with her when she couldn't hold them back.

In the period of my own Gethsemane there were three years of cumulative disaster. Most difficult was the emptiness at the end of two full-term pregnancies. Out of thirty-six months I was pregnant for eighteen, and both babies, both sons, were stillborn . . . placenta previa . . . volatile hemorrhaging . . . wild ambulance rides . . . emergency Cesareans . . . transfusions . . . both boys removed surgically from their previous living quarters . . . both dead.

When Marlene heard of the first misfortune, she was devastated. She made us promise that we would telephone her in New York as soon as the second baby arrived, this time well and strong! We called to tell her the bad news, and she hung up . . . she slammed down the telephone. I thought that was terrible. Of course, she was shocked, but her feelings should have been for me and my husband!

About fifteen hours later, having flown from New York, Marlene was sitting next to my hospital bed in Hollywood. She sat day after day, as my mother had done when the first baby died. When I went home, Marlene moved in with us for two weeks, usurped the housekeeper's role, cooked German pancakes and chicken paprika and bought me some black leather slacks!

Another famous lonely lady sat with me late at night, at the time of the second baby's lifelessness. My doctors had removed me from the maternity floor for obvious reasons, and I was moved downstairs with the gallbladders and hernias . . . where I couldn't hear crying infants being delivered to their mothers for nursing.

One late night, under sedation, I became hysterical, sobbing and carrying on quite noisily. My door was closed, but the other patients must have heard me because I opened my eyes at one point, and seated in a chair (which she had pulled close enough to the side rails of my bed for her to pat my shoulder) was a little blond person enveloped in a black mink coat. It was Marilyn Monroe. She was in the hospital for minor female-type treatment. She said she couldn't stand hearing me cry, so she got out of her bed to come and sit with me . . . there was just the night-light in the room, and a tousled-haired wondrous waif was comforting the troubled.

18

A NOTHER GREAT WOMAN reached out to me, except in her case, I reached first. It was Mrs. Rose Fitzgerald Kennedy. I was appearing at the Royal Poinciana Playhouse in Palm Beach, something no actor should experience more than once. It is the only theater I've known where the center spread of the *Playbill* is a wide-lens picture of the *audience!* The picture tells the story of the theater. The Palm Beach people consider their theater an accouterment to their affluence, the theater is window-dressing for their sables and rubies and emeralds, which are paraded to the performance in varying degrees of Rolls-Royces. What is happening on-stage becomes something of an intrusion with which they are quite bored by the end of Act One—these people Scott Fitzgerald said were "different from you and me." They wander out into the lovely night to be carried in their lovely autos to their lovely clubs, the lovely Jewish people to their lovely club which admits no lovely Gentiles, and the lovely Gentiles to their lovely club which admits no lovely Jews.

On opening night I approached the façade of the Royal Poinciana Playhouse, where my name was displayed, presumably as an attraction. There was a red carpet, great Hollywood-type arc lamps, TV crews, eager masters of ceremony, and news persons . . . the works! Curtain time was a full hour away, but the glistening Rolls-Royces and the occasional Maserati were lined up for a full block, waiting to deposit the bejeweled, both the Jew and the non-Jew. They would saunter languidly across the red carpet to the waiting cameras, say a few words between carefully capped teeth, and, laughing and frolicking in the lap of luxury, they would disappear into the restaurant which adjoins the theater to sip nectar on the rocks and nibble on hummingbirds' wings.

It was Christians and Lions time again. "Actors are the puppets who prance for the public pleasure." I huddled against the shrubbery and skirted the edge of the gaudy spectacle and made my way to the rear of the building, to the service entrance, ironically marked "STAGE DOOR!" I felt like part of an animal act in the circus . . . waiting in my cage to go out there and show off; but a tiger or a lion has an advantage. It can roar and scare hell out of the people. If I ever play the Palm Beach Royal Poinciana Playhouse again, it will have to be as a tiger!

The time away from the theater was worse. In the rarefied and privileged air of Palm Beach there is not a lot to do if you're not parking your Rolls in front of a boutique, or having a Chinese pedicure, or getting an evaluation about another face peel from another, absolutely marvelous new doctor. "There are no poor in Palm," as the saying goes, and the rich are not given to mixing with strangers, so I was filling in a sultry morning by reading (for lack of anything else readable) the Shiny Sheet. That's what they call the "in" paper in Palm. It is, indeed, very shiny, and like M & M's candies, it doesn't melt in your hands the way tawdry papers like the New York and Los Angeles *Times* do.

The "Social Notes from All Over" column mentioned that the elder Kennedys had arrived for the season. It was the year in which Ambassador Kennedy would die, and he and his nurse and Mrs. Kennedy had journeyed down by train from Massachusetts.

I looked out of my hotel window at the ocean lying beyond the fringe of tossed green salad of palm and magnolia trees, and I realized that I might be within shouting distance of Rose Fitzgerald Kennedy, for whom I had a deep reverence and admiration. I thought how much I would like to tell her that . . . just tell her . . . *that!*

So I wrote on a piece of the hotel stationery. I wrote that there were many areas in which I was fed from the well of her courage . . . that like her, I was an Irish Catholic Democrat who had lost two sons; like her, I knew the heartache of being unable to help someone near and very dear who is incapable of coping with life's normalcies. I thanked her for being so available to the world, for participating with such great spirit through so much tragedy. As a postscript to my letter I wrote, "There is one way in which I feel I can never successfully emulate you, and that is in your glorious figure." Mrs. Kennedy was seventy-eight that year. I really liked writing such a girlie kind of compliment to such a venerable lady! So now the letter was finished. I folded it, put it into a hotel envelope, wrote "Mrs. Rose Fitzgerald Kennedy" on the face of it, and stopped. How was I going to find out, in this intensely private sanctuary of Palm Beach, where the Kennedys live? The phone book in Palm is for people like plumbers, not people like Kennedys. Nobody is listed in the phone book. It is superfluous, except for the Yellow Pages.

I slipped into something minimal, as a defense against the humid, dank day (if Chloé is still lost in the swamplands, they might try searching in Florida any morning before the mold dries up). I drove my little rented heap over to Worth Avenue and asked a man where all the rich people lived. He directed me to Ocean Avenue.

There was nothing between me and the sea but billions of dollars worth of part-time residences, all of them carefully protected from my prying eyes by great fences, with feudal spikes on top to impale any invading tribes. There were no people, just fences or impenetrable jungles of tropical horticulture. I tooled along in my noisy little rig, envelope for Mrs. Kennedy on the seat beside me, on the street paved with gold that had no addresses.

I *did* see a woman 'way down the road. She might have been waiting for a bus. A bus? Well, why not a bus? Maids ride buses, even in Palm! I descended on this must-be-a-maid figure and asked her if she might possibly know where the Kennedy house was. I tried to ask it in that molar-locked way rich people talk. I didn't look rich, the car didn't look rich, but I saw Jackie Onassis coming out of her Fifth Avenue building one day in an old black coat and a brown scarf around her head . . . I looked richer than she looked. The woman DID know, and I turned the car around, and in less time than it takes to say Marjorie Meriwether Post (who lived on that street, too) I was parked in front of the Kennedy place. Beautiful fence they have . . . a wall of adobe, cascading bougainvillea vines, magenta, purple and deep pink. A seamed and cracked and exquisite old monastery-type door led into a lush courtyard with fat geraniums and great graceful ferns. The door was securely locked, but a crack was big enough for me to see into that wonderful patio palace! There was an iron thing to pull. It must have rung a bell somewhere inside. The only sound I could hear was the surf. I felt like a fool, but I stuck the letter under the heavy old door and ran back to my tin lizzie and tore down Ocean Avenue and wove my way back into the mainstream of Palm Beach traffic. My secret was safe. I had pulled off the job! I had successfully penetrated the most exclusive residential avenue in the world. I didn't put my own return address on the envelope because I didn't think there would ever be an answer. I had paid homage, in a sneaky little pilgrimage, to a great lady.

No more than ten days later I was back in California and in the accumulation of mail was a Wedgwood-blue envelope engraved on its outer flap with the name *Rose Fitzgerald Kennedy* and stamped on its inner flap with the name CARTIER.

It was a letter, not a note, and I shall leave it to my grand-daughters along with my hand-made shingle from William Faulkner's gazebo in Oxford, Mississippi, and my marble fragment from the temple of Zeus in Athens.

Apparently, Mrs. Kennedy had to learn from her secretary who I was, and that has special significance for me. If she had known me, or known *of* me, a letter might have been expected. The point is, she DIDN'T know me and wrote that she thought my letter came straight from the heart. She wanted me to know that she had thought about me while she was at Mass that morning and she prayed that what she could write would have meaning for me. She told me that her feelings about my letter to her were of humility and affection. She believed that life is a challenge (and who should know better than she?) and that each of us has a particular task and that since her secretary had told her I was an actress she felt I could influence others for good, and peace, and understanding. She gave me three suggestions to live by: To pray a little, to enjoy life as much as I can, and to refuse to surrender to age, or weariness, or defeat. She wished me well, always, and identified me as her dear Miss McCambridge.

Beneath her signature was a postscript. She told me I must WALK three and one-half miles a day through all the weather of the year if I would keep my figure.

I marvel that this trim and vigorously vain little woman braved the rain and sun and sleet and snow and heat and humidity and smog for three and one-half miles every day! I marvel at the extra half-mile!

I marvel, too, that she considered second in importance, only to praying a little, the admonition to "enjoy life as much as you can." I make a mental list of all the "enjoy" areas in the Kennedys' lives. It's not easy. Yet their matriarch lists "enjoy" right under prayers, as a *modus* of successful *vivendi*. "Spunk" would be my grandfather's word for Rose Fitzgerald Kennedy. She is one spunky lady!

Obviously my impertinent mash notes dare to rush in where angels fear to tread. When Henry Kissinger was secretary of state, he was the cover story in *Time* magazine in the first week of February 1972.

I was rehearsing and about to open in an ill-fated Broadway play rather unfortunately titled *Love-Suicide at Schofield Barracks*. My own fate was not so "ill" as the play's, which closed at the Anta Theater after only four performances. I got a nomination for a Tony Award . . . not very much exposure, a total of four performances in a role. I was crushed about the play but over-inflated about my nomination.

One of the American Theater's treasures, dear great Cheryl Crawford, produced the play, and one day during final rehearsals she and I were sitting in my dressing room and she was reminiscing about all the other actors and actresses who had used this ugly, high-vaulted, paint-chipped beaten-up old room. She was saying that we "latter-day saints" were lucky because there is now a bathroom with working fixtures. She could remember when there was nothing but a chamber pot behind a screen. She walked over to the place where the pot and screen had been. She stood there in silence. This was a hallowed spot for her. As though she were placing the nation's wreath on the Tomb of the Unknown Soldier, she proclaimed in her clipped New England accent: "Lynn Fontanne used that pot, and so did Alfred Lunt. They dressed together in this room, and many's the time I sat over there on that couch and carried on a conversation with both of them while one of them was busy over here behind the screen."

While I am rehearsing a play, I try to read nothing that might distract my concentration from the work in progress. I find I have to "marry the part." (All the while I played *Who's Afraid of Virginia Woolf?* there might as well have been a tunnel between my place on East Sixty-fourth and the Billy Rose Theater on West Fortieth). So on a Sunday morning before rehearsal I got into the bathtub with Henry Kissinger. I had no intention of becoming more than mildly interested. He had been appointed by Richard Nixon after all. Ho-hum, Henry, I'll just read about you until it is time to go to the theater.

If I'd been wearing a hat, it would have been knocked off and drowned. The final paragraphs of the story dealt with Dr. Kissinger's address to the Washington Press Club, which was, according to *Time*, "visibly moved" by Dr. Kissinger's remarks. I have had some exchange with the Washington press. To see them "visibly moved" by anything other than the quaking of the earth beneath them would be a sight of some significance. On the other hand, had the Washington Press Club been privy to my privy that Sunday morning, they would have seen me in the bathtub, where I, too, was "visibly moved" by Dr. Kissinger's words.

He had said that we were inclined, as a nation, to blame the Vietnam debacle, or the shaky economy, or the crime in our cities, or the race question et al. for our unrest. He said that we have been trained to believe that if we fulfill all the right conditions, we will be guaranteed the right results. However, he said, "Ours is the first generation to realize that the road we travel is endless and, that in traveling it we will find not Utopia, but only ourselves, and," Dr. Kissinger said to the Washington press, "it is this awareness of our essential loneliness that accounts for so much of the rage and frustration of our time."

Hallelujah, Henry, whoever you are! Nixon or no, you are for me!

All my life, all my livelong life I had been fulfilling right conditions and expecting good results. And burning up with rage and frustration when the good results never arrived. I did the right things for what I thought were the right reasons, and I know that I am and always will be essentially alone, and no wonder I am enraged and frustrated! Hooray for you, Henry! You tell it like it is!

I got out of the bathtub, drip-dried by striding up and down looking for some sort of truly impressive stationery. None such. So, with what there was, plain typing paper, I wrote:

Dear Dr. Kissinger:

I don't usually divert my attention to anything but the play while I am "into it," and while I am not the kind of actress with whom you are likely to spend a glamorous evening [this was during Dr. Kissinger's Casanova period when he was running in and out of chic places with Jill St. John and everybody like that], I am nonetheless your newest ardent admirer. I thank you, sir, for being vulnerable at your level. Your statement about loneliness is the song my heart sings, too. I am deeply grateful to you, sir.

I addressed the envelope "Dr. Henry A. Kissinger" and stopped. Then with a flourish I wrote: "State Department, Washington, D.C., Private." No return address.

More than a year later, in March 1973, while I was artist-in-residence at Catholic University in Washington, I was invited to a lavish reception at the Indian Embassy. I was escorted by one Morris Appelbaum, a gentle man who liked my Medea. Neither he nor I knew very many East Indians, and the other elegant people in the ornate ballroom were fascinated by their own closed circles, so Morris and I wandered from hors d'oeuvres tray to potted palm where toothpicks and small doilies can be disposed of handily.

In the far corner of the vast room full of saris and sequins there was a cluster of camera people and microphone people. Somebody was there in the middle saying something significant, we thought. Suddenly, like the Red Sea, the cluster fell back, and the Moses of that era came forth. It was Dr. Kissinger. He had seen me. I was fully sixty feet away from him, and he was coming toward me, his arms outstretched, palms up. I've worked with some very foxy actors in my time, and when an un-rehearsed gesture is utilized by one of them, you can bet I will do the same thing. It is the only insurance I have against what might happen next, you never know; and there was a huge group of Washington notables watching this action. I let him cover the full distance, but my hands were ready for his, palms up. He closed my hands between his own and said in that low-gear growl wrapped in gossamer wings: "You wrote me a note which I have kept.

It touched me very deeply. I am so happy to be able to tell you this."

I told him that I was happy, too. That I had never dreamed anything like this meeting would take place.

The Washington press was stretching its antennae toward us. I told Dr. Kissinger that I had read his remarks about loneliness to at least 150,000 students across the country and that their response was remarkable. I told him they would come to me afterward and hold me in their arms for telling them that he thought about what they thought. Dr. Kissinger kissed my hand. His eyes were misty, and he said: "This touches me more than all the tactical things." He turned away and went immediately to his car.

The press corps descended on me and Morris Appelbaum like those blackbird crones in *Zorba the Greek*. The reporters said that Kissinger didn't spend that much time with Nixon. They wanted to know what we were talking about. I told them it was loneliness. They scoffed! But the next day their papers carried the story.

I have an elegant color photo on my library table. It is lavishly inscribed. Dr. Kissinger is smiling. I let people draw their own conclusions. What the heck!

19

THE MASH NOTE THAT SPAR- ked one of the finest segments of my life wasn't in the form of a letter. It was a telegram . . . sent to a voice I had never heard until one summer's night on the beach in San Diego. It was 1952, and we had brought a radio down to the sand to listen to the Democratic Convention.

What was that strange name? The last name was Stevenson, but the first name was strange! He was governor of Illinois, they said, but I hadn't paid much attention to Illinois since I had moved to California and removed myself from mundane Middle West goings-on. If I *had* heard the name of Adlai E. Stevenson II, I'm not sure I would have cared very much, but on that rare California night when there was no fog, no damp chill, when the beach was sleek and glistening, my husband and I and our best friend heard the voice. Heard the speech. Heard the language of civilization as it should be. We were stunned. We had no idea what the man looked like. He spoke *to us!* At long last, somebody on the political scene spoke *to us!* With wit and graciousness, and concern, and hope, and courage, and respect—respect *for us* . . . the people!

I sent a telegram that night to the Governor's Mansion in Springfield, Illinois. I informed the man behind the voice that I wanted to help him become President. I asked him to put my name on the volunteer list, and I thanked him for the finest speech I had ever heard.

On a sporadic but continuing basis I realize how poor my life would have been if I had never known Adlai Stevenson. *Time* magazine quoted me as saying that "as far as I was concerned, there were only two kinds of people in the world—everybody else and Adlai Stevenson."

I have never been able to clarify my feelings about Governor Stevenson. I am a person who needs heroes and heroines, from Shakespeare to Mrs. Siddons, to Emerson to Mrs. Kennedy, to my dog . . . to any number of breathing things who resuscitate me when I am overcome with an attack of emotional or spiritual asthma. But because I came to *know* the hero that was Stevenson, he means the most. I never had dinner with Shakespeare, my dog never did say that he loved me, and on the morning after I tried to do myself in, there did not appear from Ralph Waldo Emerson at Santa Monica Hospital a telegram which read: "Courage, my dear, dear Mercy. Remember the words of St. Luke: 'It is only through our endurance that we gain possession of our souls.' Adlai."

Aside from my son, no person has ever shown for me the gentle concern I knew from Governor Stevenson. He always endeavored to understand and give logical reason to the dumb things I did. He even carried my cause to others.

On one of the baker's dozen of great nights in my life, two men watched me perform, together. It was the off-Broadway *Cages*, two one-act Carlino plays. In the first piece I played a prostitute; in the second, a Gloria Steinem-type Park Avenue snob.

Sitting in the eighth row center were two balding gods in Brooks Brothers suits. One was Harold Clurman, undisputed genius of the theater, who had written in his book *The Fervent Years*: "To Mercy McC., who revived the fervent years for me." Seated next to Clurman was Governor Stevenson. Harold Clurman told me later that when the curtain came down on the first play (the prostitute one), Governor Stevenson turned to the woman sitting on his other side and said, "I understand in the next play she is a lady." Poor Governor Stevenson . . . he was always trying to clean up my act.

While he was our Ambassador to the United Nations, he would introduce me to members of foreign delegations as "America's Finest Public Speaker . . . female." I think the word "actress" was not altogether comfortable for him, and he wanted to leave no doubt in my mind that America's *Truly* Finest Public Speaker was hardly female.

The governor cared enough about me to say that I was a puzzlement, like an errant colt whose will must not be broken but who needed to be reined in from time to time.

One night during the run of *Virginia Woolf* in 1964 I was having some soup and a custard with him in his apartment in the Waldorf Towers. The long, long play had an eight o'clock curtain, so I had to "eat light" and be there by seven. Adlai skipped the soup, but over the custard I told him that an old friend whom I'd met on a boat in South America had phoned the theater that day. He was Al Sheen, brother to Bishop Fulton J. . . . . He wanted two house seats for the evening's performance for his brother, the Bishop. I phoned Al after I'd received this alarming message and explained to him that the language of the play was not taken from the Baltimore Catechism, and I would find it most difficult to deliver my lines knowing that Bishop Sheen was sitting on the aisle or more likely falling into it, prostrate from prurience! I begged Al to discourage His Excellency, but Al said that there was nothing I could say on that stage that would shock his brother, that he had heard it all. Maybe, but not from *me*! But Al insisted, so I had the tickets set aside in the Bishop's name.

Over the yummy custard in Adlai's lovely dining room (looking out smack-dab at the Pan Am Building, which Adlai called his Berlin Wall because it hid his view of the Statue of Liberty), I told him how nervous I was about the Bishop. I said, "You know very well that when he hears the opening line of the play coming out of my throat, I will be burned at the stake in Times Square tomorrow at high noon."

The opening line of the play is shouted . . . by me . . . in darkness. It sets the mood, you might say. The curtain rises; the stage is dark; the loud and raucous laughter of a man and woman are heard offstage. There is the sound of a key in a lock, a door opens, letting in a shaft of light, and I say—I say, with feeling—I say, with full volume—I say, with unmistakable definition, "JESUS H. CHRIST!"

And good evening to you, Bishop Sheen!

Adlai said he really saw no need for my concern, that the solution was simple. Then his head tilted in the quizzical way he had of letting you know that what he was about to tell you would, in fact, have a germ of rationality, but it was actually meant to be clever . . . and it always was! He said, "When you arrive at the theater tonight, send a note out front to be delivered to the Bishop when he picks up his tickets. Write that you are exceedingly flattered that he wanted to see the play, and you would like him to bear in mind that the opening line, rather than an obscenity, is actually a fervent prayer that the rest of the performance will go well." We laughed. We laughed so hard. So often.

The Governor had a favorite line of mine from *Virginia Woolf:* "I have no sense of humor. I have a fine sense of the ridiculous, but I have no sense of humor." We used to talk about which was more important, or if you must have one to the exclusion of the other, or if they might not be, in the end, a blend, indistinguishable from each other. We decided it would be best to have both . . . that unless you have both, it is impossible to laugh until you cry, or even better, cry until you laugh.

Adlai enjoyed laughing at himself, never bitterly, but with a tolerant acceptance of his own stuffiness. He was amused, entertained. We had great fun remembering "the time when . . ."

My favorite was the first time I ever spent any time in his company. It was on the first campaign in '52.

So many were smitten by this small giant from Illinois, so many of us jumped on his bandwagon. In this case, it was a plane . . . the forward section gutted to accommodate the machines of the press. He and his staff sat aft, behind a drawn curtain. He had spoken in San Francisco and was flying, I think, to Kansas City or maybe it was Denver. (I traveled thousands and thousands of miles on both of Governor Stevenson's campaigns. He said to me at the tail end of the second try, in '56, "Dear girl, you are going to kill yourself working for me." I told him I couldn't think of a better way to go).

Anyhow, Humphrey Bogart and Lauren Bacall and Robert Ryan and I had been the Hollywood "potboilers" at the San Francisco appearance and would function in the same way at the next stop and the next and the one after that, *ad infinitum*, up to and including the night in Springfield, Illinois, when we sat with the Governor and his sister and his sons in the Lincoln house and listened to the dreadful election returns giving proof to the sorry fact that Americans could not accept the challenge offered by a man who was Democracy personified. Americans chose, instead, a kindly General who said he would go to Korea.

Oh, that sorry night! When the defeat was excruciatingly clear, we all piled into the cars in front of the Governor's Mansion and followed him back to the musty old Leland Hotel Ballroom for his concession speech. John L. Lewis with his black mink eyebrows stood next to me with a leaking dixie cup, emptying its bourbon contents onto his belly. He was weeping. We were all weeping. We looked up at Adlai Ewing Stevenson II and heard him quote from Lincoln: "I am too old to cry and it hurts too much to laugh." And then he went home to bed, and we fell back into the mediocrity to which we had been accustomed before this bright candle had appeared to burn away the gloom.

It seemed inconceivable that American history would repeat itself four years later. I sat with Governor Stevenson and his family, this time in what was ironically labeled the Presidential Suite of Chicago's Blackstone Hotel. Once more Americans chose the kindly old fellow in the soldier suit.

"A prophet is [indeed] not without honor, save in his own country." But back to the first time I ever sat with Adlai, in flight from San Francisco to Denver or Kansas City or wherever . . .

He sent an aide forward in the plane to invite "the actors" to join him for lunch back in his section behind the drawn curtain. I had shaken his hand and had my picture taken with him and had exchanged the politest of conversation bits, but this was to be lunch . . . an entire meal period. Aye, and there was the rub, for me. I do not conduct myself decorously whilst eating on airplanes. Something always remains, on my person, in liquid or gooey form. God knows I've tried, but it seems to be something I cannot avoid. I told myself that if I thought I was going to make a mess of myself in front of the great man, I had another think coming to myself. I ordered myself not to eat. Not to eat. Not to touch a thing. Just to say, "Not hungry, thank you."

The Bogarts, Bob Ryan, and I moved back to join the Governor. He was sitting in a window seat, riding backwards. He asked the Bogarts to sit opposite him, facing him, and indicated that Bob Ryan should sit across from the Bogarts, on the aisle. There were some papers and folders on the seat next to him, and he gathered them up and handed them to an aide and said, "Now, my Illinois girl, this is where you belong. Right next to an Illinois boy!"

I was thinking that Lauren Bacall was probably born in New York, but I'd bet she was sorry that day that she wasn't begat in Joliet, the way I was! There is nothing in life that I like better than being teacher's pet.

The Governor was having his "bourbon and water with a little sugar"; the others were offered and accepted a drink. I didn't even want water. I was taking no chances. I would merely sit there the entire time with my hands folded in my lap, as the nuns said.

The food came. The Governor insisted; I protested. He won. The tray was placed in front of me. I was glad I wasn't going to touch it. It looked awful. That loosely-woven slab of Weimaraner-colored stuff airlines call roast beef was lying there, infringed upon by a blob of cubes that probably began as potatoes. They were now smothered in staphylococcus syrup, yellow and getting yellower. I didn't touch anything. I didn't even play the game of "let's try to free the cutlery from the plastic." I sat with my hands folded under the tray in my lap. Just as I'd told myself to do.

I was wearing a favorite dress, deep slate-purple wool. I had bought it in Paris, not in a shop of haute couture but in a shop of haute enough couture for my pocketbook. It had sleeves with little points on the ends . . . held snugly to my wrists by the daintiest zippers I had ever seen. It was a humdinger of a dress.

The Governor was telling us, with great verve, about the vast historical significance of the state of Illinois, about how little of its history was known and how much attention it merited. I was captivated by his narrative and had foolishly dared to raise my left arm . . . the one nearest him, to support my elbow on the armrest between us. This allowed me to cup my chin in my hand, showing off my pointed French sleeve with its dainty French zipper. It worked! He saw the zipper and was obviously impressed because the sight broke his concentration ever so briefly. He began the sentence again, something about Father Marquette coming down the river with the fellow my hometown was named for . . . Old Joliet himself. While the Governor was now, once again, absorbed in his story, he dipped the tip of the napkin into his water glass, dampened it well, and without interrupting his phraseology, he proceeded to remove with the dampened cloth the nasty little display of abscessed potato sauce that had somehow found its way along the full length of my dainty French zipper and my pointed French sleeve.

He cleaned me up, put my hand back in my lap, and went right on talking. The Bogarts and Bob Ryan remained stonily oblivious. It was just an unfortunate happenstance that never happened, that's all.

Years later Adlai would ask me to tell someone the story . . . someone like Senator Bill Benton, who thought it was mildly amusing but wasn't altogether undone by it. Adlai and I were . . . every time! We reenacted it, pantomiming the action and laughing ourselves silly.

When the Governor first moved into the Waldorf Towers apartment, which was the official residence for the United States Ambassador to the United Nations, I told him I didn't think it was his kind of place. I was trying to cover up my fury at his having been so horribly treated by young Jack Kennedy. *Stevenson should have been President.* At least, he should have been Secretary of State.

I told him he really needed somebody like me to do the little things around that fancy place. He told me to mind my tongue, that the United States would hardly domicile an Ambassador in a fancy house.

I said he needed someone to take care of Q-tips, egg timers, bathtub pillows . . . that sort of thing.

Sometime later, while I was in California, he wrote, ". . . and there has been so much to thank you for, even if you didn't send the Q-tips, bathtub pillow and egg timer!"

This letter, written in pencil on Waldorf Towers stationery, is particularly interesting. I had said on the phone from California that he should go right on saving our crumbling world. In this letter he writes, "Do not expect me to save 'our crumbling world,' especially since they played that Cuba trick on me. x x x Adlai." The letter is dated the day following the Bay of Pigs fiasco, during which Kennedy sacrificed Ambassador Stevenson to cover himself. Adlai Stevenson cast no aspersions, but he wrote about his feelings, in pencil, to a friend in California.

As soon as I received that letter from the Governor, I called Hammacher-Schlemmer in New York and told them to get a special messenger over to the Waldorf with two boxes of Q-tips, an egg timer, and a bathtub pillow. They didn't have the Q-tips. I asked them to have the messenger pick some up at a drugstore on the way. The important thing was that all those articles had to be delivered to Ambassador Stevenson's apartment that afternoon before he came home from the UN. Hammacher-Schlemmer can do anything.

Macy's can do almost anything, but Hammacher-Schlemmer is the champ!

His next letter was a typical Adlai Thank-you. He said the egg timer had served a great purpose. He was using it to real advantage. He allowed one running of the sand per diplomatic telephone call. As the final grains fell, the conversation was terminated. He said he had no previous idea of the myriad uses to which Q-tips can be put. As for the bathtub pillow, he felt he should wait until I got back to New York to explain it in terms he could understand. Next time I went to New York, the pillow was in place. He said he had put it there "for show," but it looked "used" to me.

As I knew Governor Stevenson was the only right way for me to have known him. It should never have been more than it was. We talked about it only twice, once when I was staying at the Hay-Adams Hotel. My lovely corner room looked out on Lafayette Park and beyond it to the White House. We pulled two blue damask chairs over to the opened french doors and sat together. It was a warm but not muggy Washington night. The illuminated White House was exquisite with golden light spilling from its windows. I said there was a line in Noel Coward's *Private Lives* about the Taj Mahal "in the moonlight . . . unbelievable." We agreed that it couldn't have been more beautiful than what we were seeing, and besides, the Taj Mahal doesn't have the majestic Washington Monument in the background, piercing the night sky.

Adlai told me about a night when he was a guest in that house across the street. He was to occupy the Lincoln bedroom. He knew he could never bring himself to sleep in Lincoln's bed. He felt nobody had a right to sleep in Lincoln's bed. And he *didn't!* He slept the whole night on the hard couch in the bedroom. Later he learned that Lincoln had never slept in that bed, but Lincoln *had* slept on that couch!

Adlai Stevenson knew that I worshiped the ground on which he trod with his small clay feet. I told him so, often. A lot of women worshiped him, in one way or another. Adlai was easy to love, and so many did love him.

At one of his last birthday parties a smattering of his favorite people were gathered once more in the white-on-white drawing room of his quarters in the Waldorf Towers. Oh, the women! Oh, my goodness, the women! Senator Benton called them (including me, I guess) "Adlai's seraglio of middle-aged ladies."

There were rich women, oh, very rich women, widowed or barely husbanded, brilliant women, philanthropists, scientists, diplomats, actresses, writers, women with titles of lesser nobility, and me, I guess. It was fascinating to watch Adlai make his way around the room, being gracious and charming to each little cluster. I swear every female eye in that handsome salon knew where he was every minute of the evening, including me, I guess. I felt closest to Adlai whenever his eyes found mine across a crowded room: the great Assembly chamber at the UN; the stage of the Cow Palace in San Francisco, in a salon full of his seraglio, from the convention floor at the '60 convention during the half-hour demonstration in his honor, and especially from the great altar at the Cathedral of St. John the Divine when he delivered the eulogy at Eleanor Roosevelt's memorial service.

It was a chilling and dark Saturday in November 1962. All through lunch that day the Governor had been testy. I was on his left, his sister on his right, and his middle son, Borden, was with us, and so were the John Steinbecks. I asked the Governor what was wrong, he seemed so cranky. He said he had little appetite for the task before him at five o'clock that afternoon. The Steinbecks would not be joining us for the memorial service, they had previous plans; it would just be the family and me.

I asked Adlai what Mrs. Roosevelt would have expected him to feel about the afternoon's observance. He said she would have told them to do without it. He was cranky. He said all the newly purchased wine should be thrown out of the forty-second-story window. He said the upkeep of the building was beginning to lack its earlier excellence. He said it wouldn't be so unpleasant to bear if the rent were reduced accordingly. It was too damned high for what it was not worth. Pretty testy there, Governor.

He looked at me sternly and said, as though I were to blame for his bad humor, "I don't even know which robe to wear. The instructions to the participants in the procession indicate that full academic regalia is in order for those who are not members of the clergy!"

I wasn't about to say "boo." He waited for me to say "boo," and since when he waited for me to do something, I always did it, I said I had a wonderful idea. He obviously didn't believe me. I said he should wear the robe and hat from Oxford, when he was made a Don. He was aghast! The robe and hat are brilliant rosy red. He reminded me that it was to be a funeral service. I reminded him that I knew that. We were both speaking staccato now. I said that all the prelates and potentates from every nation in the world would be garbed in vivid velvets and brocades, carrying staffs of jeweled ornaments, and there would be acolytes in purple and red and white, a kaleidoscopic array of colors throughout the procession. Had the Governor been in any other mood, I don't think he would have agreed. But he did! Testily!

We rode through Central Park in the nearly dark of New York on the wintry afternoon. Adlai held the folded crimson robe on his lap, and I held the hat . . . a lopsided something between a tam-o' shanter and a floppy bonnet, full of distinction and tradition, but actually a foolish hat.

When we arrived at the cathedral, we entered by the stage door, an entrance on the side just off the main altar area. The sudden brightness of the room after the gloom outside was all the more startling because there was almost no sound. Perhaps a hundred people, mostly men, men in business suits and topcoats, were greeting and introducing each other in low, respectful tones. They made a quiet fuss over the Governor, who was immediately ushered into a small dressing room to "robe up." Adlai motioned me to follow him into the severe little room. He said that since the choice of robe was mine, I should have the honored duty of assisting him. It was like investing a Pope! I held the crimson robe for him; I fastened it; I placed the silly red tam on his dear egg-head. It was medieval! I wished him luck and withdrew to join his sister and his son in our first-row seats on the main altar.

Looking out at the lateral pews, I could see the Roosevelt family, in the first row. Behind them sat 11,000 people.

The sheer might of a cathedral organ has always been the voice of God for me, and God was present at Mrs. Roosevelt's memorial service. St. John the Divine is a Grand Canyon of a cathedral, and the roaring opening chords of God's voice in that place stilled time. A heavy pounding, commanding dirge preceded the opening action from the south door of the sacristy. BOOM, BOOM, BOOM, BOOM . . . and then: a deep-purple-shrouded crucifix held above the head of a black-robed deacon! BOOM, BOOM, BOOM, BOOM . . . and then: scores of black-robed figures bearing unlighted tapers and draped staffs of mourning! BOOM, BOOM, BOOM, BOOM . . . and then: grizzly bearded Orthodox holy men in dismal black hoods and garments! BOOM, BOOM, BOOM, BOOM . . . and then: brown-skinned, yellow-skinned, red-skinned, and white-skinned faces covered with yards and yards and yards of dead black vestments! Occasionally there was a glint of gold from a decoration around someone's neck; there may have been a border of purple here and there, but mostly BOOM,

BOOM, BOOM, BOOM and *all* black . . . and then: marching alone, and not very tall, a cranberry red little mass. I wanted to die. That is not an overstatement.

The Crimson Tide would have to pass by where I was standing. The oncoming Scarlet Streak would momentarily appear before me. He looked at me! Only for a second. I don't think that what I saw was pain, exactly: incredulity, perhaps, or sheer disbelief. It was only for a second.

Adlai's eulogy that afternoon, spoken from his heart, in honor of the woman he admired before all others, should be required reading for all students of English and drama and ethics and truth. The Governor, from our vantage point, seemed suspended in the pulpit, no longer bound to the earth but soaring on the wings of Mrs. Roosevelt's spirit.

God Himself must have been moved because His voice was gentler during the recessional. As Adlai approached our section, he saw me again. Again only for a second. But this time he winked! No smile, no hint of recognition, just a wink . . . a little one! My heart sang.

As we got into the car for the trip down through the park in the now rainy night, he tossed the lovely red gown and the silly hat into my lap and told me to take care of them since it was my idea in the first place.

It is said that people learn to hate each other because of little things . . . not big ones.

I know I have always learned to *love* because of little things . . . I'm not at all sure that there *are* any big ones.

I can only know what love is insofar as I can *feel* it. The only way I can *feel* it is in the specialness which marks it mine. If who and what I am matters to who and what somebody else is, that awareness is my feeling of love, and when that somebody winks at me for my foolishness, and I am aware that it was my foolishness, and what the wink represents is marked *mine* . . . the word is "love." And it can be intimately expressed and intimately received, surrounded by 11,000 people gathered in one of the world's largest cathedrals. Intimacies I have known in darkened *chambres de nuit* are as nothing in comparison.

One night Adlai asked me, because he was feeling joyously festive, to recite for his birthday party guests in his apartment in the Towers. I would sometimes read to him when we were alone. Sometimes I would spontaneously break into a Shakespeare soliloquy to impress him with what he thought was my amazing memory storehouse of worthwhile things. But to recite! To this crowd? "Oh, no, oh, no no no." From Adlai: "Oh, yes, oh, yes yes yes." He ushered me to the east side of the room and announced that his guests were about to enjoy the great good fortune of hearing an Illinois girl recite birthday poetry for an Illinois boy. Oh, dear, oh, dear, dear dear.

Governor Stevenson was born on February 5, 1900, in Los Angeles, of all places. He always gave his birthday party on the Friday night nearest his natal day . . . midweek late-night parties were not his dish. This Friday night was not far from Valentine's Day and the only Valentine poem I knew was *Blue Valentine,* Joyce Kilmer's tribute to the Virgin Mary, the poem which had won for me my college education! Such an incongruous exercise . . . the recitation of a simple plaintive prayer addressed to the Queen of Heaven in gratitude for her incandescent light that shines on us below, even on those of us at a birthday party on the forty-second floor of the Waldorf!

Kilmer says, "It is like the light coming through blue-stained glass, yet not quite like it, for the blueness is not transparent, only translucent. Her soul's light shines through but her soul cannot be seen. It is something elusive, tender, wanton; infantile, wise and noble." The lyricism is Stevensonian, and he was pleased. So was Senator Benton, who was, at that time, the chairman of the *Encyclopaedia Britannica.* He was a bit tiddly, and my recitation obviously got to him. As the polite applause of the others died away, and after Adlai had thanked me and kissed my cheek, Senator Benton came forth and told me that I had a real talent for poetry. It had been a long time, he said, since he had heard such an unspoiled gift for expression. I tried to tell him about Joyce Kilmer, but he wasn't buying it. It was my poem, nobody else's, and he wanted me to know I had a great future as a poetess of some stature. Each attempt of mine to tell him otherwise was understood by him to be a protestation of undue modesty.

I found Adlai and told him. He said to forget it. The senator wouldn't remember it in the morning.

The Senator *did* remember, for many mornings. I had gone back to California, but he was in hot pursuit of his newly discovered genius . . . he wrote to my agents, not once, but twice! Impressive letters arrived in Beverly Hills on *Encyclopaedia Britannica,* Office of the Chairman, stationery. The need was for a copy of my lovely poem about the Valentine and the blue light. Hollywood agents don't give much of a damn about encyclopedia stuff; they would tell you it is a "hard sell." They told me it was a personal matter I could handle, but if it ever came to a point of publication, I should remember that our contract held me exclusively bound to them. I assured them that I wasn't about to publish any poetry. I explained that it was a misunderstanding—that Joyce Kilmer had written the poem. One of my agents said, "Oh, yeah. 'Trees.' " I said, "Yeah, 'Trees.' "

I never answered Senator Benton's letter. I think it would have caused him considerable chagrin. Adlai thought so, too.

During the evening when I sat looking across Lafayette Square at the shimmering White House with this twice-refused candidate for its occupancy, we talked about the word *emotiva*. The previous year I had been in Spain and was given the mounted ear of a bull killed by El Cordobés, *numero uno de toreros!* It was said that on the day this bull was slain, El Cordobés fought with *emotiva*. Adlai said it was a magnificent word, like the word *chutzpah* in Yiddish, or the word *filótimo* in Greek. *Emotiva* is impossible to translate in all its meaning. El Cordobés fights with *emotiva* on his greatest afternoons; Toscanini was the embodiment of *emotiva;* the unmatched grace of an elephant in a circus bowing on one knee to receive the applause of the audience is *emotiva;* a Persian cat washing its face is *emotiva*. When two people, whose times together are necessarily sporadic, can resume a conversation left unresolved two months before, when the enrichment results from the simple no-strings sharing of experiences covering a dozen years, that is *emotiva*. When Governor Stevenson said, "I do love you so," there was no category into which such a sweet declaration could fit and be comfortable. We knew. "Those who know don't say. Those who say don't know." *Emotiva* is inexplicable. You can know it only by having it, and there is no way of acquiring it. It derives from nothing; it cannot be transferred. We talked about it for a long time that night at the Hay-Adams Hotel. We talked about it until the floodlights were no longer calling attention to the House of the Great White Father behind the fence across the park.

In one of his letters to me, Adlai wrote, "I am eating each word from you for nourishment these days. Thanks for feeding me . . . Emotiva."

His last letter to me was mailed from Geneva. I received it in New York the morning after he had died on a London street. Once again I was living on the East Side of New York, not even a stone's throw from the river. I walked over to look at the water a while, and then, with care, I hand-shredded the letter and flung its small bits to the breeze. I have since been sorry I didn't keep the letter. He had written, "I write to you with a very full and tired heart." Adlai Stevenson's heart was never one to "tire." The last line of the last letter was: "Emotiva—dear Mercy—Emotiva forever. Adlai." Why did he write "forever"? What was he sensing when he wrote it? Why did I tear it up, leaving no record of it?

My mother called from the coast to say that Governor Stevenson's sister was trying to reach me. It was an invitation to the funeral service to be held in the National Cathedral. I took the train down to Washington. I didn't want to stay at the Hay-Adams, so I checked into the Madison. I had a light supper in my room in front of a silent TV set. When it grew dark, I went downstairs and told the desk I might be out most of the night, but they were not to be concerned. (Better hotels fuss over solitary women guests.)

I told the cabdriver to take me to the side of the National Cathedral, to the entrance of the Bethlehem Chapel. He said there wasn't anything open at the Cathedral; "it was locked tighter than a drum at sundown; otherwise the lousy bastard kids of D.C. would get in there and draw dirty pictures on all the walls and steal the candlesticks from the altar." I interrupted his diatribe to say that he was wrong this time; the chapel would be open all night for a vigil. He said, "This ain't a town where a lady oughta be wanderin' around by herself in the middle of the night." I asked him please to be quiet . . . please.

At the door of the Bethlehem Chapel, which is tucked into the cavernous underpinnings of the National Cathedral, there was a security guard who recognized me. I asked him if it would be all right if I stayed awhile once I was inside. He said his orders were to keep the public moving, but he suggested that I sit along the wall on one of the marble window seats. He said he didn't think anybody would bother me. Nobody did.

The files of weary people shuffled in through the door, relieved from the heavy, humid night outside. They were told to keep moving along to the exit.

There is little to see, little to look at in such a scene . . . the tableau of a metal box covered with the flag, a single wreath at its foot; four young men from the armed forces standing guard at the four corners of the coffin.

As they were relieved from their sentry, shuffling backwards, their feet did not lift from the floor; they gazed steadily over the coffin as they moved into position to be replaced by their relief team who scraped their heavy soles along the marbled floor to lock themselves into rigidity as *they* now guarded the bier. Sedate and silent transfer, save for the slow scrape scrape of booted feet. There were several shuffling changes of the guard during the long night.

The thinning out of the crowds who had come to pay homage was gradual. The humanity for which Adlai Stevenson gave his life slowly removed itself from him . . . little spurts of people . . . then more and more empty intervals, and finally the relentless reality of the last day. It was dawn. "Emotiva . . . Emotiva forever, Adlai."

So many people, I'm sure so many women must have known Adlai Stevenson longer or more completely than I knew him. They were, therefore, perhaps to him more dear. I have no way of knowing, and neither have they. To me, at least, it doesn't matter. They can't have known or shared the sweet attentions he paid to me. A rich man can afford to be generous to many, and Adlai Stevenson was a truly rich man who gave of himself until his "very full and tired heart" ran out of funds. Thanks to him I am a wealthy woman, indeed. I am sustained by my lion's share of his legacy. He loved me so . . . he told me so.

20

I AM RICH FROM THE BEQUESTS other gifted people have seen fit to leave to me as I walked alongside them, or tagged along after them, or worked at my trade with them. Young Jimmy Dean, gifted blazing comet who came speeding across the sky and, in fiery light, fell off the world as suddenly as he had come.

We worked together in 1955 in the filming of *Giant,* Edna Ferber's saga of Texas and its cattle and its oil and its men and its women. Elizabeth Taylor, Rock Hudson, Chill Wills, Jane Withers, Sal Mineo, Dennis Hopper, Alexander Scourby . . . and Jimmy Dean. George Stevens, master editor, director, and not-always-benevolent dictator, had a lot of problems with Jimmy. Everybody seemed to have a lot of problems with Jimmy. Nobody had more problems with Jimmy than Jimmy had.

When Jimmy Dean died he was twenty-four years old. He was no more than laid to rest "back home in Indiana" than the thousands of his closest friends came forth to talk or write about him. They made certain that the good was not "interred with his bones," but they featured the evil as well. The truth was somewhere *East of Eden.* I saw one opportunistic entertainer cry real tears on the *Tonight* show for Jimmy. This fellow spoke of Jimmy as his "buddy." He wept for the great personal loss he had sustained. Garbage! Reams of rotten pap were written about Jimmy. Also garbage!

Jimmy Dean was one of the most cautious persons I have ever known. There was no chance of knowing Jimmy any better than Jimmy wanted you to know Jimmy.

I have refused to line up as part of the legion who lay claim to knowing the workings of a young man's mind that has been disintegrating into dust for a quarter of a century.

He was a private person who has been public property for as long in his death as he lived in his life. American students and students in London and Madrid and Rome and Munich all want to know what James Dean was like. There are Jimmy Dean posters and T-shirts. In the 1980's young girls swoon at the mention of a name that was erased in 1955!

"What was he like?" they ask. I ask them, in return, to think what he might be like if he had lived. He might look like Marlon Brando. He surely would have lost most of his hair . . . he was having trouble with it at twenty-four. He might look like George C. Scott. He didn't eat regularly, but when he did eat, it was something to see! In Texas one disgustingly hot night, during the filming of *Giant,* he and I ate a full jar of peanut butter, a box of crackers, and six Milky Ways and drank twelve Coca-Colas! We were both mad at George Stevens, and we ate ourselves sick at him. Jimmy might have grown into a grumpy, sour-faced, paunchy middle-aged man; or he might have survived, Paul Newman fashion. The point is that none of his cult will accept the futility of preserving forever the image of a rumple-haired, blue-eyed bird of a man whose spectacular flight ended with his being splattered against a lousy pick-up truck that made a too-soon turn onto a dreary highway above Bakersfield, California.

Then there are the older ones who have a cult that is even sicker than the young. These are the psychological experts who say that

Jimmy was doomed to die; that his death wish was the paramount thing in his life. Garbage! They say that his sexual personality was ill-defined, blatantly psychotic, or traumatically arrested . . . take your pick!

Few few few few people, I think, were privy to Jimmy Dean's "self." I certainly was not one of them, nor were the voluble Dean experts.

It is a terrible thing to die young and famous. The vultures never get their fill.

Location films, when the entire company is off somewhere away from home can be great fun; *if* it is London or Rome, for instance. In my case, when it was London, I had a lot of free time to enjoy the great city because the film was taking forever to shoot. Folk like Katharine Hepburn can be very demanding. I don't say she hasn't the right, I merely say she IS! That was *Suddenly Last Summer.*

In my case, when it was Rome, it was the unfortunate remake of *A Farewell to Arms* . . . and again it was taking forever. Folk like David O. Selznick can be very demanding. I don't say he hadn't the right, I merely say he WAS! In spades, he was! So I had Rome to wander in and wonder at, whilst being handsomely paid for not working, just "standing by" at Doney's or in the Grand Hotel or being pinched on the Via Veneto. Locations can be dandy, and locations can be hell!

Giant was filmed, in large part, in a large part of a large place called Texas . . . in a large part of the ugliest landscape on the face of the earth. Sheer nothing! No hills, no water, no trees, no grass, just vast acres of creepy-crawlies and dive-bombing bugs and biddy towns thousands of miles apart.

One such town is Marfa, Texas! Marfa! Even the name evokes magic! It is located somewhere south and east of El Paso in a region of the damned. The Marfans or Marfites or whatever they call themselves may be terrific individuals, but if they are, why don't they move?

There *was* a hotel where our company was quartered . . . except for Elizabeth Taylor and Rock Hudson. Houses had been found for them to live in. The rest of us were corralled in the old hotel, by Gawd! The kitchen gave off a scent of frying fat, twenty-four hours a day. Everything edible is fried in Texas! Or it is buried in the ground to cook before it is eaten. There is a scene in *Giant* at the big barbecue where my brother, ol' Texan Rock Hudson, introduces Elizabeth, his beautiful bride from ol' Virginny to all his ol' friends and neighbors, come to celebrate and drink and eat and Yahoo! Boy, Howdy!

I had to stand over a steaming pot and be photographed as enjoying it while two cowboys lifted a scorched bundle of cheesecloth-wrapped something onto the table in front of me. I had to slit it open with a huge knife, being photographed as enjoying it, and I had to lay bare for the camera a complete calf's head . . . ears, tongue . . . everything. Burned eye sockets, hell-black, in front of me . . . little stiff hairs peeking out from the ears, the roasted tongue drooping out of the juicy mouth!

Neiman-Marcus is one thing, and the Dallas Cowboys are another, but Texas food should be forbidden!

"The steaks at night are big and bright, deep in the heart of Texas!" And they are always afloat in grease. Next morning you are served a smaller steak, which serves as a platform for two fried eggs . . . all of this afloat in the same grease! "Chicken, you say? You bet! Comin' up!" Same grease! They are right. Comin' up! For hours afterwards. I couldn't believe the crust of an apple pie! Same grease!

There was nothing to do in good old Marfa. No points of scenic interest. Nothing! There was the mash-feed store downtown, and a couple of real hot-spot storefronts called gin mills. A few tired places where you could buy groceries to take home and fry in grease . . . that was about it for Marfa.

Jimmy Dean and I, and too many other actors, were all languishing at Warner Brothers' expense out there in the Panhandle, where we would likely be kept until our brains burned up and our bones turned to chalk.

The people in the company who were lucky enough to be shooting would leave the hotel at dawn to drive out to the stark grandeur of the mirage-house Warner's had erected in the center of five million acres of nowhere. The house had been assembled in Hollywood, taken apart, each section marked and shipped down to Marfa by rail and reconstructed on its incongruous site for filming. There were three high walls and an open back and no roof.

Anyhow, the lucky ones who were working out in the brutal sun at the location would leave us unlucky, non-working ones in town. Day after day after day! It drove us crazy!

Jimmy Dean and I would say to each other, "If you weren't here, I'd kill myself." We got along, maybe because we had to, rattling around out there in the land that God forgot. One day he said, "Listen, Madama!" "Madama" was what he called me in the film. "Listen, Madama, you and me together are more than sixty years old. Twenty-four are mine, the rest are yours. What I mean is, any two people who are as old as we are should be smart enough to figure a way to beat this Marfa rap! They got us nailed in here, Madama! We gotta kick our way out, I am tellin' YOU." He clapped his hands, let out a Texas whoop, and threw his holey straw hat on the dirt and jumped on it. . . . hard! "Hooooeeeeeee!"

Before either of us was officially on film in Giant, Jimmy tried several times to steal my Stetson hat. He knew that if he switched my hat with his and was photographed wearing it, I couldn't be photographed wearing it! Mine was the perfect Texas hat! I had to watch it like a hawk until after the first scene in which I wore it, making it forever identified as my hat!

It was originally Gary Cooper's hat. The sweatband inside the brim was taped "G. Cooper."

Back in Hollywood when I was doing wig and make-up tests at Warner Brothers, G. Cooper wandered into the make-up department. The hairdresser was placing on my head the never-touched-by-human-hands brand-new Stetson hat.

G. Cooper hooted!

"Where in hell did you come up with that silly-looking headgear?"

We explained that it was my character's hat for Giant.

G. Cooper stomped and said, "You mean to sit there and tell me that a Texan woman who spends most of her waking hours in the middle of hundreds of head of cattle would be caught dead in that stupid store hat?"

He was upset, G. Cooper was. He went to the phone and called his wardrobe man. A hat was brought! G. Cooper placed it on my head. He was right! The hat was Texas! Giant! Right!

The hat was also a good bit the worse for wear. There were indications that it had been doused from time to time. I said it must have been rained on quite a bit. G. Cooper said, "Nope. Peed on a lot! That's what makes it such a fine Texas hat. No self-respecting rancher wears a hat that his horse hasn't peed on!"

The hat had surely lost all of its stiffness. It rolled into shape easily at the slightest touch. The discoloration gave it a certain added interest—dark golden streaks, wavering blots of bleach . . . interesting.

Jimmy Dean wanted that hat!

Sometimes as I stood in the blister of the Texas sun, G. Cooper's peed-on hat on my hot, wigged, and perspiring head, the air around me became recognizably ammoniated, but it was a great hat, and I managed to survive the malodorousness.

Jimmy Dean wanted that hat.

Jimmy Dean didn't get it!

Warner's gave us Chevies to drive. Pitted Chevies, stripped raw from sand and wind. Jimmy, on a day of near-to-bursting frustration, drove his little Chevy out of town and, with his BB gun, shot all the windows out of it. The company manager took his car away. Besides, the highway patrol had mentioned several times the indelicate topic of Jimmy's speeding. They found him indelicate on another score. They claimed that he relieved himself against a post in the middle of Main Street. I asked Jimmy about it. He said he did it because nothing else was happening. I told him the story that Alan Moorehead, the Australian author, had told me about Winston Churchill. Sir Winston was on holiday at Maugham's villa on the French Riviera at St.-Jean-Cap-Ferrat. Each morning the chauffeur would drive Sir Winston along the seawall until a particular scape caught the great man's fancy. There he would set up his easel, palette, paints and brushes and cigars and brandy and soda. He would sit on his stool, hat pulled down to keep the sun's glare from his eyes, and he would paint. Paint and smoke and drink. The villagers of the Midi would stand apart at a respectful distance and observe the Greatest Briton at work.

One morning he felt the need to relieve himself. He put down his palette, his brandy glass, and his cigar, and walked over to the seawall and let spray . . . at great length! When he had finished, the villagers applauded! As he walked back to his easel, they shouted, *"Magnifique!"* and *"Formidable!"* Sir Winston stopped, took off his hat, and bowed!

Jimmy Dean couldn't wait to get back to Marfa's Main Street. He said he would drink a whole tank full of beer, and he would stand there and flood the street. I told him Americans don't know enough to applaud outstanding performances the way French people do.

One morning, after the working actors had abandoned us for still another day, we felt our fuses were getting very short.

We often got up with the working group and waved good-bye to them as the trucks and cars disappeared in all that dry dust. It was likely to be the most excitement we would see until they all streamed in at night: filthy and sore and burned, and ravenously hungry, even for the same old steaks fried in the same old grease.

On the morning we were more than usually jangled, we sat in the coffee shop. At least it was cool. Marfa, in itself, is not a stimulant for good conversation. Porcine grunts will do. I watched Jimmy take a pecan roll from the basket on the table. It was stale, and all the sticky stuff was dried up. Jimmy unrolled it slowly, until it lay stretched out on the table like a brown, bumpy snake. We sat there, looking at it. Then Jimmy took another pecan roll from the basket and did the same thing to it. He laid it down next to its twin on the table. Then he said, "Wanna see a good trick?" I nodded. "Watch this one," he said.

He lifted one of the unrolled rolls and began stuffing one end of it into his left nostril. He packed it in until it held. Several inches of brown, bumpy snake dangled from the nostril. He matched the operation in his right nostril. Then he said, "Shall we go?" He took my arm, and we walked out into the lobby, where three ranchers dropped what was left of their eyeeteeth as we passed. Jimmy said, "If anybody asks you, just say I am so rich I got dough coming out of my nose." Nobody asked me.

Upstairs he sat on the floor and I lay on my belly on the bed. Best thing to do after a Marfa meal is to lie on one's belly for a while. I told Jimmy about a waiter in a sleazy seaside hotel in Alicante, Spain. He was my waiter. He served me every day. I was his princess. His jacket was frayed at the cuff; his black trousers were as shiny as a waxed Mercedes-Benz; his shoes might not last out the day.

His ministrations which accompanied my breakfast could not have been equaled by any maître d' in the world. It was like my second husband's martini routine, a spiffy performance!

He brought a deep glass bowl full of hot water and placed it on the small serving table. He selected from a fruit tray the finest Valencian orange he could find and speared it with a long-tined fork. In an *arena de toros* he would have been granted both ears and the tail of the bull for such a thrust . . . and he never missed! Then, standing in front of me, holding the speared orange, he dipped it into hot water, swirled it furiously, and lifted it high, as if it were rising from the Rhine. Then he shot his poor frayed cuffs and, holding the fork at eye height, he pierced, as if in surgery, the rind of the fruit. The knife was Toledo sharp. The peeling of the orange was executed in such a way as to keep it in one perfect piece. At the end of the cutting he held the curlycue over a small plate in front of me and let it fall in formation. It stood on its own, a perfect hollow orange! He never missed! ¡Ole! Emotiva!

The Marfa oranges were thin-skinned and not well ripened, but Jimmy Dean bought a bowie knife in town and tried. Jimmy Dean tried anything, sometimes at my expense.

He made me promise to drive him in my Chevy, since his had been taken from him, out into the wasteland to see the jackrabbits jump. He said they jumped the highest at dusk. Out on the pot-holed road, he made me stop the car, and he got out and straddled the hood like it was a horse. He had his BB gun. He told me to drive nice and easy, "like a slow gallop," and he popped off the jackrabbits. I got very cross and turned the car around and headed back to town. That damned kid up there pow-powing away at the leaping lapins.

There hadn't been any other cars on the road . . . there never were . . . but somebody saw us and the company manager took my Chevy away. Jimmy pleaded our case on the grounds that he was killing the rabbits to save the crops. It was pointed out to him that there were no crops. Also for Jimmy and me there were now no cars. It was good that there was no place to go because if there were, we couldn't go to it.

Another great idea of Jimmy's has marked me for life. On one of the rare days when I actually was called to perform before the camera, the Texas sun melted my make-up, which sank into my open pores and blossomed into serious infection. My face was bad, but my neck and throat were deeply burned. I still have the scars.

The company doctor ordered me to bed, with drawn shades . . . my eyelids were burned, too. He prescribed antibiotics and healing salve and said if it didn't get better, I would have to be shipped back to California. I wanted it to get better because it was hugely painful, but I wouldn't have minded being shipped—anywhere!

My room was, to say the least, air-conditioned. Frigid is a better word. Great gusts of iceberg wind stormed through the grid. The cheesy, sleazy cover on my bed waved back and forth as in a storm on the North Atlantic. Jimmy fixed it.

He sat with me every day. He sat on the floor and practiced his guitar. He was teaching himself how to play it. I kept wishing he had had the opportunity of learning somewhere else than in my dark and icy sickroom in Marfa-for-God's-sake-Texas. He said we would both die of pneumonia in that room, so he went into town and bought a roll of heavy packing tape, and he begged or stole a large piece of cardboard to seal off the wintry blasts. Now there was no breathing in the place. No air at all! Just the guitar plunking away on my nerve ends. Just the burning hide of me.

Jimmy announced that I would never get well in that hellhole with that "crappy medicine." He went downtown again, and this time he came back with some ointment that he knew would turn my hide's tide. It not only would take the heat away, but would shrink the pores, and I would be as good as new. He told me all these lovely things while he smoothed the cool cream onto my parched skin. I whimpered in gratitude. He said he would leave the rest of the tube for me to use up that night. He said not to worry, he could get some more tomorrow; he would bring half a dozen tubes with him, and we would clear this danged thing up in nothing flat! I watched him putting the top back on the tube. Curious thing it was, the top, and small wonder. It was Preparation H. I wanted to tell him his sense of direction was severely impaired, but I waited unti he had left, and then I washed, with great pain, the hemorrhoidal remedy from my face and throat. Next day I told Jimmy that the doctor said it was bad for my Irish kind of skin. Jimmy was miffed.

James Dean was a dedicated, perfectionist actor. I watched him develop bits of business until they seemed a part of his nature. He asked cowboys to teach him intricate tricks with a rope. He worked himself bleary-eyed with that rope, but if you watch him as Jett Rink doing tricks with that rope in *Giant,* you will see a Texas boy who has been working with a rope all his cotton-pickin' life! I watched him learn how to let his hat fall from his head, watched it do a complete somersault and land, top side up, on the ground in front of him . . . just the way he wanted it! Every time he did it.

While he was playing Jett Rink, he was inseparable from Jett Rink; he did NOT become Jett Rink, but Jett Rink was his constant companion! I know what it means. You measure everything you do in terms of how the character you are playing would do those things. It's a good game. I know of none better!

I have worked with another master of "the actor's game," on the opposite side of life's stage from Jimmy Dean. Jimmy Dean was twenty-four. Joseph Buloff was sixty-five! Anybody who claims to know American theater and doesn't know Joseph Buloff is a dunderhead.

We were rehearsing a company of Arthur Miller's play *The Price.* There was a fuel strike in New York, and the rehearsal hall on East Seventy-fourth Street was freezing. We worked in our coats and mittens and boots and mufflers. Mr. Buloff was sitting, center stage, in an old beaten-up wooden chair. Rehearsal had stopped for a point of discussion which took nearly an hour's time. Joseph had been sitting, huddled in his overcoat, legs crossed, shoulders hunched. When, finally, rehearsal was resumed, he made as though he would rise from the chair. I watched it happen. His right leg, which had been held crossed over his left leg in the cold room for so long a time, had fallen asleep. He knew that it would not move under its own power. He looked down at it for a minute, and then with the palm of his left hand he pressed against the inner side of his right leg just above the knee. He pushed. The dead weight of the leg slid heavily off its support and plopped its foot on the floor. A thud! Joseph was still pressing his hand against the lower inner thigh. He studied his own pose in that position. Studied it. Then he lifted his head and smiled his impish Hebraic smile, and it was the portrait of the artist as an old man.

Joseph was caught in the moment of discovery . . . the only way to artistic truth. You have to be *caught* at it. Shakespeare says it: "An honest clown cannot make a jest unless by chance, as a blind man catcheth a hare." Joseph stayed in his chair and rehearsed that same piece of business as carefully as a magician perfecting an elaborate illusion, except there was no trickery here. It was faithful to truth. Joseph knew that the bones and muscles of the old man he was playing had lost their spring, their ready mobility. When an old man sits for too long in one spot, his legs are likely to go dead on him.

Joseph Buloff's lifeless leg improved my own performance in *The Price*. I watched each time Joseph tried to get up from his chair or sank back into it. His timing never varied. He didn't call attention to the action; he went on smoothly with his lines as he applied the pressure necessary to move the dead leg. Sometimes he did it impatiently, sometimes in pain, doing it only because it was something that had to be done. I was working with an actor fully practicing his craft, and it prompted me to better practice mine!

One afternoon at the Coconut Grove Playhouse in Florida, we had done a matinee for college students. They remained in their seats after the performance to "ask questions" of the cast . . . Gary Merrill, Ralph Meeker, Joseph Buloff, and myself. One of the braver students raised his hand and addressed his question to Joseph: "Mr. Buloff, how do you get to be . . . I mean, what is the best way to, you know, what do you have to do to get to be a really great actor?"

Joseph Buloff has a way of making you wait until he decides what is the best possible answer, since you were considerate enough to ask the question in the first place. Using this technique, Joseph can make "the correct time" sound like a statement of significance. In this instance he drew his head down into his shoulders like a turtle in retreat, and holding his arms in an attitude of mass benediction, he said, "The answer to your question is simple. There is only one way to become a great actor . . . first, you do four hundred plays!"

There is nothing derisive about Joseph Buloff. He merely knows that artistic truth has little tolerance for anything that falls short of its mark. I wish every student actor could have been in the wings with me night after night and observed from that special darkness the splendor of Buloff out there in the bright glare.

An old and brilliantly gifted, professionally meticulous, and uncompromising actor was my friend Joseph Buloff.

A young and brilliantly gifted, professionally meticulous, and uncompromising actor was my friend Jimmy Dean.

Edna Ferber sat in my California kitchen one rainy afternoon and autographed several books for me. Such a pile of books, almost as tall as the wee "Giant" herself. She wrote that I could have played the heroine in most of her novels. I liked that. I like authors to like me. Robert Penn Warren does, and Tennessee Williams, and James Michener, and Archibald MacLeish, and Dylan Thomas did. Miss Ferber wrote in my copy of *Giant*:

> In Texas, dear Mercedes McCambridge, when they want someone to move they say, "Come alive!"
>
> No one had to say that to you. You came alive as Luz the moment I saw you. And thank you, Ma'am.
>
> Edna Ferber Aug. 1955 *

When Jimmy died, Edna wrote me:

> Perhaps it is strange, dear Mercedes, that when I first learned of Jimmy's death I thought immediately of you. I opened the morning paper at breakfast, saw the photograph and read of the hideous accident. And after the first shock it was like the solution of a puzzle. Later Henry Ginsberg [the film's producer] telephoned me. He had very thoughtfully decided not to call me at midnight.
>
> You understood the boy, tried to help him and did not resent him. I regret a letter I wrote him and which he must have received two days before his death. He had surprised me by sending me his photograph in costume as Jett Rink. I wrote him:

---

*Publication of excerpt from previously unpublished correspondence and inscription is with the permission of Harriet F. Pilpel, Executrix of the Estate of Edna Ferber. No quoting or copying is permitted without the permission of Harriet F. Pilpel, Executrix of the Estate of Edna Ferber.

"I loved getting the picture. Your profile is startlingly like John Barrymore's, but then I know your motorcycle racing or one thing or another will fix that."

How are you, my dear? I think of you often.

Yours,
Edna*

I wrote back and told her how I had learned of Jimmy's death:

Dear Edna:

Having miraculously survived Marfa, we were all safely back in Hollywood and had been shooting for about two weeks. Last Wednesday, September 27, at 5:30 in the afternoon, Jimmy officially ended his "major photography" in the film. At the insistence of Warner Brothers, he had signed a promise not to race his new Porsche until he would no longer be needed in front of the camera. He kept that pact, and on that last day of his work—Wednesday the 27th—he had the gleaming new Porsche delivered to the studio. I had "the first ride." He drove me back to my dressing room on the lot—over the "SLOW" bumps on the studio streets. We bounced like a yo-yo—Jimmy gunning the motor like he was riding a Texas bull!

He asked me what I was going to do to celebrate the end of the picture. I told him my husband and I were going to drive north.

"Hooooeeee," he yipped. "Whyncha come to Salinas and watch me race this baby on Saturday?"

I told him I wouldn't go into the next block to watch him race in anything.

Good-bye, Jimmy.

My husband and I started out for San Francisco where we had reserved the Fairmont's fanciest suite overlooking the bay. We were off for a week of rest and riches. The first night we stopped over in Terra Bella (about forty miles from Bakersfield) with our dear friends the Howard Bakers: Next morning, Saturday, we started out on a shortcut route for Pebble Beach, where we would spend the night. We had gone about sixty miles, I guess, on this isolated highway—straight and solid and deserted. I told Fletcher the country was very like the *Giant* country in Texas. Fletcher said we should watch for a gas station

---

*Publication of excerpt from previously unpublished correspondence and inscription is with the permission of Harriet F. Pilpel, Executrix of the Estate of Edna Ferber. No quoting or copying is permitted without the permission of Harriet F. Pilpel, Executrix of the Estate of Edna Ferber.

because the tank was low, and pretty soon, on our right, there it was—a beaten-up old station with a lean-to tin-roofed garage—nothing else— just hot space.

A great slovenly peasant girl came out to fill the tank, and while Fletcher was with her, I went inside to the grubby little cigarette stand for a couple of Cokes. Then the fat lady said to Fletcher, "We have James Dean's sports car in the garage." And Fletcher, knowing that Jimmy was always racing up in that area, said rather calmly, "Oh, is that so?," thinking Jimmy was having it repaired there. Then he heard me call, "Oh, my God," and he thought I had seen Jimmy coming out of the men's room and we were wildly glad to see each other. But what had happened was this—another cow-like lady inside the station told me that Jimmy's car was there and then pointed to it through the open door leading to the garage. I shrieked, "Oh, my God," when I saw it because it was a crumpled mechano-set and the blood was everywhere. By that time Fletcher had come inside and they told us. It had happened one-half mile down the road we had just traveled.

I will never understand what devilish fate made us stop at that particular place—of all the stations in central California. The lady said she had never seen any body so limp and broken, and she kept saying things like that, in the morbid way strangers do—she didn't know who we were—or Jimmy. They had told her, "the kid was some kind of movie star." We drove—stunned—on into Paso Robles to the funeral home, but there were so many cars there, and we didn't want to be in the way, so we circled the block a few times and then went on. We spent three days in San Francisco, and I broke out in a fever, so they flew me home and off to St. John's Hospital.

As you said, in your thoughtful letter which I have just re-read, it IS like the solution of a puzzle. Jimmy could never have died in any other way. The people up there seem to think it was a local boy's fault, because that turn-off has always been a dangerous corner, and in the dusk, with its deceptive light, he may not have seen Jimmy's streaking low gray bullet. The boy's name is Turnupseed.

If Jimmy knows, I'm sure it would make him laugh to know it was a man named Turnupseed who did it.

I didn't write to Edna that I carried a monumental rage in my own heart! Mr. Turnupseed may have been entirely blameless, but I might still be paying my debt to society for what I wanted to do to him.

21

ON A CONTINUING BASIS, more than anything, I am grateful for not being in prison. I will make detours to avoid passing by a prison. I avoided going by the old Joliet, Illinois, prison. When I have been lucky enough to have a balcony room on the bay side of the old wing of the Fairmont Hotel in San Francisco, I look left toward the Golden Gate Bridge rather than right toward Alcatraz. At the side of a highway on the outskirts of Philadelphia is an abomination of a place called Holmesburgh Prison. I close my eyes . . . it is the American replica, I think, of as ugly a place in London, called Wormwood Scrubs Prison. I find the very names offensive. Holmesburgh and Wormwood Scrubs. Acres of high stone fences with guard posts in corner turrets, muddy gray stone, black iron window bars, barbed wire atop the walls, giant searchlight lamps . . . ugly, dank places for rotting mankind! I try to avoid the Triborough Bridge coming in from the airports in New York. The taxi swings around Rikers Island, and I am hypnotically drawn to look to the left. Always there are silhouettes of heads in many of the windows on many of the floors of the tall buildings which hold human beings who have done no more than I am capable of doing. "There is no man so good, who, were he to submit all his thoughts and actions to the law, would not deserve hanging ten times in his life." Montaigne.

Poor dead Montgomery Clift felt the same way. Many dreary dawnings in London Monty and I shared a Rolls limousine the studio provided to drive us out to Shepperton. We were filming *Suddenly Last Summer*, in 1959. The lovely car would pick me up first . . . I lived in Hampstead near the Heath . . . and then we picked up Monty at his hotel. Monty was already dying . . . wasted from too many pills, too much booze, too many injections of speed prescribed by his criminal New York doctor (Monty wanted to give me part of his supply of hypodermics containing the junk he swore was megavitamins); I believe to this day that Monty thought what he was pumping into his belly with those needles was *good* for him!

En route to Shepperton Studios we passed Wormwood Scrubs Prison in the early misty mornings. Many mornings Monty was too hung-over to stay awake for the trip, but times when he was awake and at all lucid, he would ask the driver to stop for a minute in front of Wormwood Scrubs. We just sat in the back seat of the Rolls-Royce and looked out at the hulk of gray stone hell. Monty swore a lot in his everyday conversation, but from his sore, swollen mouth on the Wormwood Scrubs mornings his profanities had a terrifying obscenity.

It is my most vivid memory of Monty Clift. Milky-eyed, sweating from all his pores the sweetly-sickly odor of vodka, fetid and foul. He was haggard; the once-so-beautiful face scarred and hollowed into deep grooves where the stubble of beard grew, already gray. Through the closed windows of the Rolls, he shouted fiercely at the wet fortress of Wormwood Scrubs. He called feebly, drunkenly, this doped-up genius of a man. He called to the "poor locked-in bastards, sons of bloody bitches." He wanted them to know that he belonged in there with them . . . that the real criminals are on the outside . . . that the insane ones are not in the crazy houses. Monty had a cackle laugh, flat and cruel when he wanted it to be. As the driver pulled away from the ugly façade of Wormwood Scrubs, Monty's snide, giddy giggles would diminish until his head fell back against the elegant buff upholstery and he was back into heavy drugged sleep . . . on his way to his day's work! An international superstar of the silver screen.

If I had been able to use any kind of weapon powerful enough to inflict fatal damage, I very likely would be in prison myself. I have been angry enough to kill. Given the same circumstances, I could be just as angry, just as murderously intent in the next ten minutes. The best friend I ever had in my life, Sir Malcolm Percy, was brutally kicked by a man two dozen times his size. Sir Malcolm Percy was a West Highland White Terrier who was given to me by Adlai Stevenson. The brute who did the kicking was an actor in El Rancho Park in Los Angeles, across from 20th Century-Fox Studios. I didn't know he was an actor . . . strangers in the park who were witness to the horror said his name was Bruce Bennett and he had been Joan Crawford's husband in some film-or-other (wouldn't you know it would be *Joan's* husband?). All I knew of him was what I saw, and I didn't care for it. He was a very big man, and Sir Malcolm weighed . . . tops—fifteen pounds!

This giant-person was wearing a gray sweat suit that said "UCLA" on it . . . I should hate to have been hanging from a tree for the years it had been since he had been any part of UCLA. To say he was of an age to play character roles is putting it kindly. On the screen, with a good make-up job and a lot of diffusion in the lighting, he might have looked marginally manly, but in the harsh Los Angeles sun in a collarless, out-of-shape gray sweat suit with "UCLA" on its front, he looked silly. And he had with him as silly a looking dog. She was a miniature gray poodle . . . he and she were a fuzzy gray set! And she, the strumpet, was in heat, and off her leash!

Frankly Sir Malcolm Percy was off his leash as well, but he was, if you don't mind, NOT in heat. He and I were far across the meadow playing ball, and suddenly Sir Malcolm, at full run, skidded to a stop. He dropped the ball, which was unlike him, and up-periscoped his short white tail, and then he took off like a whippet. The wind had shifted, and he had picked up the scent and plunged pell-mell over the mall to make love to the Little French Princess! White Knight in pursuit of Fair Maiden!

When Fair Maiden saw wild-eyed White Knight dashing toward her, she suddenly became all virginal. She flew into the outstretched arms of her master . . . literally flew. He was a tall man and she was a little dog and I saw her fly from the ground into his arms! Natural modesty is one thing, but that poodle belonged in a nunnery!

Meantime, my little White Knight, unmindful of her morals, had covered the greensward and was trying to get at her behind, which was hidden in the folds of her master's great sweat shirt.

Instinctively my virile little dog was determined to perform magnificently, but he was thwarted by the shivering, overbred, lop-eared, nearly mangy high-rise-apartment-dwelling poodle, snuggled in sweaty-shirted arms of the fading leading man. Sir Malcolm, on his stubby little legs, was trying to jump high enough to make some kind of contact. Then Joan Crawford's tinsel-town husband began to kick my Sir Malcom Percy. (During all this I was running across the meadow to intervene.) Sir Malcolm, being noble, was stunned by the kicks. He barked heartily in protest and then did the only thing he felt would give him any kind of advantage. He lifted his leg and peed on Bruce Bennett's sweat suit! Bruce Bennett yipped! His flagrantly fragrant poodle had been yipping, and now so was he . . . yipping and flagrantly fragrant!

I had reached the battle scene at this point and was infuriated to see the yipping man really attacking my dog, kicking with his enormous peed-on feet. The terrible things he was calling Sir Malcolm only made me madder. I tried to claw at the man's face. His poodle tried to bite me. I tried to bite the man. So did Sir Malcolm. If I had been presented at that moment with a cudgel, whip, a machine gun, I would have killed Bruce Bennett. *Do not kick my dog!* Particularly when your own dog is running free in such a condition as to arouse the normal appetites of any self-respecting male . . . of whom there seem to be very few left . . . of any species! Sir Malcolm Percy had a very healthy attitude toward sex. I was not about to have it distorted by the likes of that teasing French snip of a poodle and her yipping master!

Of course, had I been in compliance with the leash law, Sir Malcolm Percy would not have been kicked . . . frustrated perhaps by the scent of sex in the air, but not kicked! It was, essentially, my fault, as it was once before in Central Park in New York City, on which occasion brutality, in all its ugliness, was directed against my small white dog! Had I not unhooked his leash from his collar, it would not have happened. I disregarded a city ordinance designed to protect both man and beast, and I am chastened by my commission of the crime, but again, if I had been presented at that moment with a cudgel, whip, or machine gun, I would have killed! This time a New York cop!

It was the first of February, but not cold in the park. We were a tiny band of regulars . . . "dog walkers" of the East and West Sixties and Seventies. Sometimes an interloper from Eighty-fourth Street would make an attempt to join our ranks, but our clique of animals had a chilling indifference to outsiders. My own dog, Sir Malcolm, was a special problem. I tried to keep it from being known, but he WAS a bigot. Perhaps because he was so white a white (except when he needed a bath), he may have felt there was something sinister or dangerous about any dog that was black; or Sir Malcolm, being a Scot, may have been concerned for the property values of our neighborhood. Whatever he felt, he made it embarrassingly clear that he did not want to go to the same park with black dogs! At sight of one, he always came to me first. He would nudge himself against my calf with his snout, making little jabs at me, and he would mutter, complainingly. I had a feeling that, deep inside, he was trying to suppress what he must have known were First Amendment infractions. Sir Malcolm was nothing if not reasonable, but he did have strong emotions. I felt very sorry for him during an interlude he almost had with a Labrador retriever. She was black as the ace of spades, but she was gorgeous. Sleek and shiny and svelte and BIG! Like a lot of small males, Sir Malcolm loved big females! This midnight Labrador was named Nefertiti, and the sound of that name made Sir Malcolm's nose twitch like Chaplin's mustache. Because of Nefertiti's color, Sir Malcolm tried to keep up appearances as a bigot, but it was painfully obvious that "he lusted for her in his heart." One day in the park he suddenly went to pieces and behaved as badly as I had ever seen him . . . worse! Nefertiti was off her leash, was gamboling on the green. Sir Malcolm was grumbling halfheartedly, and in a flash he was gone. The small white body, maddened with depravity, had clearly decided to hell with everything and was speeding toward his black woman, who, sensing the questionable threat such a small rapist might offer, decided to give him a run for his money. One of her legs was as long as all four of Sir Malcolm's. She towered over him to the degree that as she ran across the meadow with her long, lustrous tail held high, little Sir Malcolm was canopied beneath it. At full speed, not being able to see where he was going, he was hardly a formidable sex maniac. Of course, he didn't catch her, and as I watched his solitary walk back to me, I grieved for his tormented heart. He had behaved like an animal, and he knew it. I asked him once when I was trying to trim his beard *if*, given the chance, in a quiet corner of the park, *if* the time was ripe and the lady was willing, *if* he and Nefertiti might make beautiful music together. It was a dirty trick on my part. His nose twitched, and my clipping shears came close to cutting it off.

Anyway, on the first of February, a not-too-cold-day in the park, Sir Malcolm, off his leash, was mingling with two of his friends who were also horticultural scientists and who were also off their leashes. They were Pepe, a schnauzer who lived with Hungarians, and Poco, a dachshund who lived with my good friend Miss Eric. The three small dogs, heads together, were investigating a frozen portion of the earth's outer crust. Pepe and Poco were older dogs, and I think Pepe had been fixed, but they seemed to be above mundane matters like sex. For Sir Malcolm, science was fine, but celibacy was for the birds. So, when a fancy lady sashayed by with a fancy lady beagle, Sir Malcolm excused himself from his associates and began his sexy saunter behind the new attraction. I let him go because I felt that sort of thing was good for his ego, and usually nothing ever came of it . . . one look at the beagle told me she wouldn't hold his interest for long . . . too underslung . . . no hips at all. One moment trotting playfully along behind a beagle, and the next moment, a true *cause célèbre!* Front page of the New York *Post!* "Jackie K.'s Tapes . . ." "The State Lottery . . ." "The Long Island RR Strike . . ." *and* a picture of Sir Malcolm Percy above the caption "DOG FIGHT . . . (Story on page 3)."

The picture is the only one on the front page . . . one-sixth of the total page in size. I am holding Sir M., kissing his nose. The caption reads: "Actress Mercedes McCambridge complained bitterly today that a policeman in a jeep chased her beloved 'Sir Malcolm' across Central Park in a display of cruelty." On page three:

MERCEDES TAKES A CASE TO CANINE REVIEW BOARD
by Bill Burrus

Actress Mercedes McCambridge charged today that a policeman in a jeep chased her dog across Central Park so fast that he came within inches of running the terrier down.

"It was terrifying to watch," she said. "The dog's white tail was just inches in front of the jeep. If he'd panicked, he would have been killed."

The Academy-Award winning actress called it "the worst kind of Storm Trooper action; it was cruel; it was like a scene from a very bad movie of Hitler's day."

The actress, who won her award for a role in "All the King's Men," complained to Mayor Lindsay's office and said she planned to present the case to the Police Civilian Complaint Review Board.

She said the chase started at 8:40 A.M. after she had unleashed the 21-month old West Highland White Terrier—named "Sir Malcolm" by the late Adlai Stevenson—in the park near her apartment at 16 E. 80th St.

"I know I was wrong to unleash him, and I plan to pay the $5, but this is the most blatant example of cruelty I've ever seen," she said.

"When the dog would swerve the jeep would swerve and bear down on this little bitty dog," said Miss McCambridge, adding that "Sir Malcolm" weighs 12 pounds. [He gained a little . . . he liked noodles and cheap paté de foie gras.]

She said that after the dog was caught the officer's manner was "officious."

"I said, 'Look, buddy, just because you're in a jeep and wearing a uniform, you don't exercise whatever repressions you've got going on this little dog," Miss McCambridge said.

She first called the 22nd Precinct station house and they asked her "Well, what would happen if there had been a small child in the park with that dog unleashed?"

"That's beside the point," said Miss McCambridge. "The dog wasn't chasing a child, the policeman was chasing the dog all the way across the park—and cruelly."

Miss McCambridge, leaving for an extended trip to California today, watched "Sir Malcolm" several hours after the incident. "Look at him," she said. "He's still shaking."

Miss McCambridge, 49 [why do they always have to DO that?], was one of the nation's best-known radio actresses. She won her Oscar as the best supporting actress in 1950. Later, she had the role of "Martha" in the Broadway production of Edward Albee's "Who's Afraid of Virginia Woolf?"

I think it may be true that "greater love no man hath than this, that a man lay down his life for his friend," and since a dog is man's best friend, I deem it only right that the two times in my life when I might have taken a life it was because I was trying to save my dog's. I like to think it will make a difference on my heavenly report card; all I know was I had no control over what I was doing. *I will kill you if you hurt my dog!*

Sir Malcolm's life and limb mattered so much because he was the only thing I ever felt was mine . . . the only being, place, or thing that I felt belonged to me. In a life of flight, one is not apt to stake claims as one flits. There is nothing in the world that is my PRIVATE PROPERTY. I somehow felt, rightly or wrongly, that Sir Malcolm Percy was. He was a present, to *me*, a gift from a man I adored, who held his noble hand over Sir Malcolm's eight-week-old head and said, "I hereby dub thee Sir Malcolm Percy." (Adlai Stevenson could say things like that and get away with it.)

I've watched others claim parts of the earth and its peoples as they journey through life. Some of them do it gracefully; some of them do it as their right; some do it shamefully. I, however, apologize to a chair if I bump into it; sometimes I apologize lengthily, explaining to the chair that it wouldn't have happened except that I was in a hurry to get to the door to catch the mailman. By this time, of course, the mailman has gone! But I must feel that the chair has prior and rightful claim to the space it occupies, even if I am paying rent on the space and indeed am responsible for giving the chair a good home away from the warehouse! Why do I tell a chair that I am sorry?

I have reached a state in life where I can buy a whole house full of chairs and can bump into them until they are black and blue. But as with chairs, everything intimidates me merely because whatever it is got there first and belongs to somebody else. But not Sir Malcolm Percy. He was MY DOG!

There is a marvelous man whom I call son, but I never thought of him as *mine*. I had the privilege of sharing the same house with this child as he grew, and grow he did, handsome and extremely kind and notably Ph.D.'d, and splendidly wedded, and blessedly fruitful with two wee women with whom he is now privileged to share the same house as they grow, and grow they will, to be lovely and kind. No person belongs to another person. But Sir Malcolm Percy was different. MINE! MY DOG!

Has a *Homo sapiens* ever lived who would spend every night of his life on the rug next to my bed waiting for me to wake up the next morning? Watching from some undetermined hour in the middle of the night for the first flutter of my skimpy little eyelashes? Ready to jump onto the bed to lick my nose? Excited beyond belief just because I woke up . . . one more time? Happy to run all the way down to the kitchen and back just to bring me his favorite rubber mouse? Show me the *Homo* who would be *sapiens* enough to do that.

22

&

THE WINTER BEFORE I WAS blessed with Sir Malcolm Percy, I was blessed with the part of Martha in *Who's Afraid of Virginia Woolf?* at the Billy Rose Theater. It was 1964. I took over the part from Uta Hagen, and while I was in no way obligated to reflect her interpretation of the role, there were certain established technical details which I had to accept. I couldn't believe one of them. When I began rehearsals, the wardrobe mistress, Sophie Field, said she would keep me supplied with appropriately cut disposable diapers! I was stunned, and I said so! Sophie's smile made the Mona Lisa look like Phyllis Diller—Sophie's attitude was one of rueful tolerance of mankind in general and actors especially. Throughout the play there is a great deal of drinking (watered-down tea), and in Act Two there is a great deal of fighting and screaming and jumping around. It's the baboon hour. A normal bladder can stand just so much, and at capacity level (and if you are wearing tight-fitting slacks, *on-stage*) you had better be wearing a diaper, too! It has nothing to do with common decency; it is purely physiological logic! One's cup runneth over!

Sophie always told it like it was, even if she didn't have any idea of what she was talking about. One night I wanted to cut her tongue out. Later she admitted she deserved it.

I'd been performing in the play for only a few weeks, and I was loving it. The part of Martha is a privilege, a challenge, and a great ego trip. I was a hit in a hit! There's no business like that kind of show business!

Sophie and I had worked out a careful little routine at which we became quite adept. By the time the curtain falls on that play any actress who has truly "played" the part of Martha from the rise of the curtain, a lifetime ago, must be drenched with sweat and thoroughly disheveled. Martha ends up on the stage floor for her closing line. The curtain would barely touch the floor . . . I would jump up and dart off-stage, where Sophie was waiting with a damp towel (dry towels don't absorb sweat the way damp towels do). I would blot my face and neck while Sophie smoothed my hair and costume. I threw the towel at her, she caught it, and I was back on-stage for the curtain calls, serene and unruffled. The audience had to think that the whole grueling performance didn't bother me a whit! Complete collapse was imminent, but not until I was safely back in my dressing room.

On the night of Sophie's near murder, everything went smoothly until I dashed off-stage and reached for the damp towel. A hand tossed it, and I used it and threw it back. As always! *Sophie wasn't there!* Her husband, Max, had had another attack, and she was on the telephone. The towel hit a small dapper man in a velvet-collared Chesterfield. My damp, sweaty towel hit him, plop! My practiced aim would have hit Sophie's middle, but Sophie was tall. The little gentleman was shorter than I was, and he got it right between the eyes. I said, "Oh God," and rushed back on-stage for the curtain calls. As soon as they were over, I ran off into the murk of back-stage and asked the stagehands to find the little man I hit because I wanted to apologize. They said they thought that was a good idea because his name was Billy Rose and he owned the theater.

But that wasn't why I wanted to kill Sophie. That came later when Billy Rose was sitting in my dressing room, captivating me as he well could. When Billy wanted to be charming, you might just as well give in without a struggle. He said he'd like to take me to Sardi's for something to eat. I told him I couldn't do that because I'd have to wear old corduroy pants and a sweater. He said when a person walked into Sardi's with Billy Rose, that person could be wearing a potato sack! I *wanted* to walk into Sardi's with Billy Rose! Such head turning, such buzzing it would cause. *I wanted it!*

Just then good old Sophie stuck her head in the doorway and said, "Honey, I've got to run to get the last express! Max is bad again."

Billy Rose and I said we were sorry, and Sophie almost left, but then she *did* it! As an afterthought she said, "Oh, and, honey, you are all out of diapers, but I'll pick some up in time for you to wear tomorrow night." And she left!

The largest single stockholder in the telephone company, the prime example of a self-made tycoon, a noted producer, songwriter, art collector, theater-owner, and lady-killer—alone in a room at midnight with a Broadway actress who wets her pants.

Later, when Billy and I got to know each other far too well, he sent me, on a weekly basis, huge packages of disposable diapers. I gave them to the Salvation Army.

A lot of people despised Billy Rose. They called him a "ruthlessly mean little bastard." Every great man I've known has a "ruthlessly mean little bastard" streak in him. I think its standard equipment on that model. I loved Billy. Not enough, I guess, but quite a bit. I'll ever be grateful to him for many things. One night, in the Algonquin, where he never understood why I wanted to pay my own rent, he was sitting in a red plush Victorian chair that was too big for him and I was curled up on the floor beside him, patting his knee. Billy needed a lot of patting. Some people think I pat too much. Harold Clurman told me to stop it because it made him nervous, but Billy Rose liked it.

We were just talking. Those were the best times with Billy. I loved to hear the man talk, and so did he. That night I asked him if there had been a continuing motivation that had persisted throughout his life from the time he was determined to become the world's best typist and shorthand writer (because secretarial school was all he could afford, and he knew he had to be the world's best something), and Billy said he'd always been guided by this: "When you find yourself in a tunnel, don't turn back. Keep going until you see a steady gleam of light at the other end, and then go for it with all your might, knocking down everything that stands in your way."

I told him that sounded like the route of Attila the Hun, and Billy said that I had asked the question and he had given me the answer. He said success carried its own malevolence.

I had heard at least three versions of Billy Rose's winning the prize for being the world's champion typist and shorthand writer before I ever met him. Each version varied from the others. I like Billy's version best. It may not be the truest version, but I like it best.

Billy had no money for college. Education would end with high school. But Billy was already looking for that single gleam of light at the end of the tunnel, and he was determined to go for it. He told me that he made the rounds of his friends and his families' friends on the Lower East Side and up in the Bronx and asked them if they would be willing to invest in him . . . at five dollars apiece! He guaranteed them that if they took this small flyer, he would return them a high profit. He would use their collected fivers to buy a course in business college, and they wouldn't set eyes on him again until he came back with documents proclaiming him world's champion typist and shorthand writer. He got the money! They got the document! Billy Rose DID become the Champ. Bernard Baruch, the Wall Street Wizard, heard about the little guy who pulled off such an unlikely feat. He met Billy, was beguiled by him, and Billy had found his master. He never called him anything but MR. Baruch!

Billy was funny, too. We had a terrible fight, and I flew off to Los Angeles and hid. I got an unlisted number, and it hadn't been in service more than two hours when Billy called from New York. I was furious. I asked him how he got my number, and he said, "My dear girl, you forget, I own the telephone company." I said he didn't own *that* telephone company, and I shall never forget his soothingly patient tone when he said, "Mercy, don't you know when you own one telephone company, you own them all?" And he roared with laughter. I have been revived so many times from the tawdriness of life by the exquisite arrogance of that one remark. To have heard a man say that is a great medicine!

When I'm waiting my turn in the check-out line at the super-market or watching the swarms of humanity bulging out of a subway, or noting my paycheck, after the taxes withheld, I can hear Billy saying that wonderful line!

I used to talk to Billy about how much radio meant to me. It didn't really excite him, but he said if I wanted my own radio station, he would buy me one. The only thing I ever let Billy buy for me was a lynx coat. He said I couldn't refuse it because he'd already had my name embroidered in the lining. He gave it to me one night in his silver Rolls-Royce. He had brought me home to the Algonquin, and the chauffeur parked right in front. The doorman, the bellboys, the desk clerks, even the switchboard operator frowned on my friendship with Billy Rose. They were always trying to keep me away from him. The switchboard lady used to lie when Billy phoned me. She would tell him there was no answer in my room. She never even rang my room. So, Billy and I were saying good-night in the back seat of the Rolls, and then he said: "Please remove that ugly coat." It wasn't ugly, I said, and besides, it was winter. But Billy insisted, so I took the darned thing off. He lowered the window and threw the coat into Forty-fourth Street. I started after it, and he held me back. Then he spoke to the chauffeur, on the intercom (because the partition glass was always closed), and asked that the package on the front seat be delivered to the rear seat. The chauffeur got out of the front seat, carrying a huge white box, and opened the back-seat door on Billy's side of the car to deliver it. I thought it interesting that it never occurred to the chauffeur to lower the glass and toss the package over his shoulder! It was the softest, most beautiful natural Canadian wild lynx coat, and it had my name in it. I wore it, holding onto Billy's arm, as we sashayed into the Algonquin lobby. Eyes bugged out, great gasps were heard, and Billy kissed me on the cheek (he couldn't reach my forehead) and ushered me into the waiting elevator. I waved regally to the staff as the doors closed. I was tempted, but only slightly, to go back and retrieve my old coat from the middle of the street, but I resisted. I'm glad. I don't know what ever happened to my old coat, and frankly, Billy, I don't give a damn!

My only child, now an impressive Doctor of Economics, and a fine success in a prestigious financial house, was just beginning his graduate work at UCLA when he read in some gossip column that his mother and Billy Rose were an "item" in New York. He phoned me and gave me hell! What was I doing with that infamous, notorious little man? I said he should hold on just a gosh-darn minute . . . that Billy Rose was a marvelous person, a brilliant and terribly lonely man. My son said that Billy Rose had been married twenty-five times! I told my son that Billy Rose was a "loner," no children, and one of the richest men in America. There was a long pause, and then my financially oriented son said, "Mom, you mean he has no children at all?" I said no, and wasn't that sad? My son said, "Well, sh—, Mom, what that man needs is a son!" Even *today*, when Billy's name is mentioned, my son takes on "a lean and hungry look."

ॐ

A lot of people think I missed the boat with Billy, but I knew, and I think he knew, too, that any boat we embarked on together would be a rerun of the *Titanic*.

In the sizable fleet I have let sail away without me, one of the boats I surely missed was the ark of evangelism. Billy thought so, too. He was sadly certain, as was I, that I could have founded a church that would scare hell out of people . . . the kind of church that grows very rich from the mites of widows and all other frightened folk who are willing to pay for anything which promises to punish them in God's Holy Name. They need to be assured on a continuing basis that they are no damned good, never were and never will be . . . mostly never will be. And they happily pay for the privilege, and pay and pay and pay. It is the solid guarantee of success in the God business, and Billy and I just knew I could have pulled it off. 'Tis a pity 'tis too late!

The closest I came was in a film that I thought was pretty good. It was 1961. I think if *Elmer Gantry* hadn't been released in the same year with all its lavish exploitation, our little picture, *Angel Baby*, might have made a bigger splash! There was barely enough money to develop the negative, much less advertise it. But it was a raucously roaring picture about terrible people . . . dumb, red-necked crummy gospel nuts!

Joan Blondell and Henry Jones were my favorites . . . grand performers. They played broken-down wrecks on the evangelist trail . . . both drunk, reeling, spouting hellfire and brimstone, through the soggy South in an old mess of a car with a leaking roof and four smooth-as-silk tires. Joan played the piano, and Henry gave 'em "what-for" . . . growling, spewing, scarlet-faced, spittle-spraying Jesus man! In the script, as in reality, came offering time, and the poor misbegotten Dixieland Christians, with their minds grown mushy from mildew, gave what they could . . . which was usually enough to keep Joan and Henry good and soused on the next lurching leg of their crazy crusade. They worked so splendidly together.

George Hamilton and Salome Jens and I were an unlikely *ménage à trois*! George and all his blindingly white teeth and patent leather hair was my young husband whom I forced to make love to me in our rickety trailer while I quoted verses from the Old Testament about the evils of fornication and lust. It was so sick it was swell! Salome Jens, handsome pony of a person, was the simple-minded good girl who believed that miracles were "a piece of cake." My George had the "hots" for her, so I demolished their tent in the middle of a packed revival meeting! Wonderful! We shot it on the campus of Miami University in Coral Gables. We hired hundreds of Florida cracker people as extras, and they played it for real! People got trampled, there was much wailing and imploring the Almighty to have mercy . . . the whole thing was faked, we told them that; they didn't care; it was a ring-a-ding debacle, and they loved it! There was a local boy who had a bit part. He was kinda cute, but he was always disappearing into the bushes with a scantily clad Florida dollie. I didn't catch his name, the crew called him "hot pants," but his paycheck, meager though it was, was paid to the order of Burt Reynolds . . . cute but girl-crazy! Probably never amount to much.

I liked best the scenes wherein I evangelized. It was exactly the excitement I got from doing the Demon in *The Exorcist.* When you can tremble with fury, shouting ominous pronouncements, it doesn't much matter what side you are on, heaven's or hell's. The rafters ring, the people are terrified, bestiality might as well be beatification . . . it is all the same insanity, and it is a romp of an acting exercise, AND when you are being paid for it, I can't imagine a more beneficial cathartic!

I thought, almost seriously, about taking on such shenanigans as a lifework, one night in Chicago. Lyndon Johnson was President and had just referred to himself as a deeply religious man, and I was sorry. I didn't think it was fitting for a President or anybody else to so speak. A deeply religious person has no need to say such things. Maybe a Republican President might, but no card-carrying self-serving Democrat would be pompous enough to say such a thing! Thus it was that the pompous pundit of the Pederales pointed the way to what might have become my earthly road to glory. The thing that stopped me was Fat Jack Leonard.

In Chicago, where I was doing a play at a now-defunct dinner theater on the mid-North Side of town, I was billeted at the Hotel Ambassador East. During his short life-span my dog became a pet patron of a few swank hostelries. At the Ambassador East it was not unusual for us to come home from the theater and find a large covered tray full of pre-bedtime goodies for Sir Malcolm Percy . . . a hunk of beef, assorted scraps, but best of all, the great rib bones from luscious roasts, all crisp and peppery, and not yet jelled. How do I know they were crisp and peppery? Because Sir Malcolm shared his wealth. Many a night we arranged ourselves atop the spread-out want-ad section of the *Tribune* and enjoyed together all that was left of several gourmet dinners. It is a great way to wind up an evening. I wouldn't advise it with just any old dog, but with Sir Malcolm it had a panache all its own!

One night, when Billy Rose had flown out from New York to see me, we found, once more, under the lid of the chafing dish, the great platter of prime rib bones, at least a dozen of mastadon size. I think Billy was shocked as he watched me preparing our picnic in the middle of the celery green carpet. The thing about Billy was that he would have gone along with the proceedings if Sir Malcolm and I were about to feast on raw tarantulas.

The phone rang, and it was Fat Jack Leonard (Jack E. Leonard), ascerbic, foul-mouthed nightclub comic who became a gentle cream-puff person as soon as he left the stage. He was stopping at the same hotel. Many a night we had walked Sir Malcolm for health purposes, his and ours. Not everybody is well suited to late-at-night big-city dog walking. Show people do it best. The dog owner has relaxed; the performing is over, the make-up removed; the stinging, light-burned eyes are beginning to cool off; the adrenalin is almost drained dry. Soon it will be safe enough to sleep. The walk is usually made in old shoes, gratefully changed into. If the weather is harsh, the old slouch coat and hat will do. If a morning paper is available, it is picked up at the corner newsstand. It's a lazy, slowing-down time for show people.

Dogs who are sensitive (and Sir Malcolm Percy was more sensitive than anybody) know what their walker is feeling. There is no tugging at the leash, no growling at the tigers and elephants lurking in the shadows. The sensitive dog does what has to be done as soon as it becomes possible to do it, and then it is back to the hotel, and so to bed!

One can't always count on the serenity of a city at midnight, however, and even a dignified dog like Sir Malcolm becomes street-wise through experience and necessity.

He and I were living at the St. Moritz on Central Park South in New York one year. I had abandoned the Algonquin. NO DOGS, they said! HRUMMPH, said I.

Sir Malcolm approved of the St. Moritz, and the hotel returned the compliment. We walked in a regular pattern during our midnights. Out of the hotel, avoiding the revolving doors (Sir Malcolm didn't trust them . . . I don't think I would if I had to be responsible for a tail). We turned right and sauntered down to the Plaza Hotel, where Sir Malcolm could bark halfheartedly at the disreputable old nags of horses who were tethered to the few remaining carriages that will take you for a ride around the park for a half hour for the small fee of four hundred dollars. The bushes around the Plaza fountain, bordering Fifth Avenue, were just Sir Malcolm's size. That spot was his first call to duty each night. Then we moved on into Fifty-eighth Street, and west to Sixth Avenue, the street that has never made it as Avenue of the Americas . . . everybody knows it is plain old Sixth Avenue putting on airs. There is a luggage store on the corner for which Sir Malcolm had the utmost contempt. He always saved the last lifting of his leg for the doorway of the luggage store. After that there was only the short block between Fifty-eighth and Fifty-ninth Streets and we were home.

Sir Malcolm could always count on being greeted several times each night by the prostitute ladies. They patrolled our walking block in pairs, figuring, I suppose, that with all the hotels in the area there must be enough work for everybody. There must have been. These were very fancy ladies! They all knew Sir Malcolm and fussed over him. He reveled in his late-night meetings with them. They might have done worse. They would call out, "Hey, Sir Malcolm," "Hello, little fella," "You sweetheart, you," "You're my lover-boy, aren't you, Sir Malcolm?" Canine Casanova.

One hot summer night he had just finished staining the steps of the luggage store one more time when a great hullabaloo broke out ahead of us in front of the little delicatessen. Several bodies seemed to be engaged in fierce combat. All of a sudden on the quiet street all hell broke loose. That's the way it happens late at night in big cities.

A hulking Minnesota-Viking-type man was lurching against the window of the deli. He was shouting filth at a little drunken derelict who had been on his way to sleep it off for another hot night on a bench in Central Park. Apparently he had collided with the great Norse god, who was also drunk, but not derelict. He had been exiting from the deli with some cold beer to take back to his expensive hotel room for another air-conditioned night on his company's expense account. In the collision the little drunk was knocked to the sidewalk. He was crying because his glass eye had fallen out from the force of the impact. He was crawling on his hands and knees, weeping and cursing and feeling around the sidewalk for his lost eye. The stupidly intoxicated bear of a man towering over him was yelling dirty names at him. Just then two of Sir Malcolm's harem ladies ran around the corner and joined in the war. Two more ladies approached from across the street, which meant Sir Malcolm had to get into it, to protect his own. The whore-ladies were kicking at the giant bully, hammering their spiked heels into his legs. They were beating on his head with their handbags. Sir Malcolm barked commands at them, straining at his leash to be let loose so that he could spring for the jugular. Everybody was cursing now . . . Sir Malcolm, too.

The little drunk, in all the grub and grime of the pavement, had found his eye and happily popped it back into its socket: the dirty sightless orb from the dirty unsightly street. He picked himself up, and as though he were ignoring everything that had taken place, he staggered off toward the park to his bed on the bench. The prostitutes decided to waste no more of their night's energy on the big blond slob. They straightened themselves and resumed their cruising, and the brute of a behemoth slunk off with his sack full of cold beer, and as suddenly as the uproar had erupted, it died away, and New York on a hot midnight became quiet and sinister once more . . . Late-at-night city dog-walkers—a breed apart.

The night in Chicago at the Ambassador East, Fat Jack Leonard had phoned because he wanted to join us on our walk after our shows. I told him that he was too late. I told him I had company, but he was welcome. Fat Jack said, "Is it dog company or human company?" I told him it was Billy Rose. Fat Jack said, "Is it the real Billy Rose?" I said it was; at least I thought it was. Fat Jack said, "I'll come. The real Billy Rose is a real dog, and I get along good with dogs."

Fat Jack declined the offer to sit on the floor on the spread-out *Tribune* with Billy and Sir Malcolm and me because, he pouted, he was wearing his fancy best gray slacks and didn't want right-wing newsprint all over his backside. He said he'd never be able to show his tushie in public again. Billy allowed that it might be the kindest thing Fat Jack could ever do for the public.

Fat Jack grumbled further because we didn't have any napkins and our hands would be all-over greasy from the messy beef bones. He was making Billy edgy. Billy got up and went into the bathroom and came back trailing an unbroken ribbon of toilet tissue. He wrapped it once around Fat Jack's walrus neck and told him to keep pulling on the paper until he ran out. It would serve as a never-ending napkin, and would he please shut up?

Fat Jack said the narrow toilet tissue would not protect his slacks, so I spread a hand towel across his vast thighs, and we four fell upon the table scraps left over from "effete snobs'" banquets. Sir Malcolm sensed that he was host to the occasion and waited until we had served ourselves before he chose with his nose his own bone. Fat Jack wanted to fling denuded ribs out the window in Elizabethan abandon, but Billy indicated the leather wastebasket as a suitable substitute for such tasteless impetuosity. Billy could be very sarcastic, like all short guys.

Having been amply fed on our upper-crust leftovers, we arranged ourselves in appropriately comfortable slouchings and embarked on an exercise in good discourse. Sir Malcolm Percy excused himself and retired to the bedroom for the night. Should he have been needed for any reason, he could have been found lying diagonally across the king-sized bed, all limbs extended as far as possible in all directions so as to occupy with his small body as much space as he could reach. Sleeping on a floor, he compacted himself into a neat little white crescent. Sleeping on my bed, he became Ichabod Crane!

I opened the Socratic endeavor by offering as a topic the opinion that our President, LBJ, was using poor old God as a smoke-screen when he called himself a "deeply religious man." Billy said everybody who has ever lived has used poor old God as a smoke-screen. I objected to that, more for argument's sake than from conviction. I said that in my own experience I had known at least a handful of fervent people who never used poor old God for anything other than the supreme object of their adoration and love. I said there was a time, long before I had met either of these present evil companions, when even I was that saintly.

Fat Jack sputtered behind the huge bone he was working on and said: "You realize, of course, that you have just described yourself as a deeply religious person."

And Billy snorted: "And one who has always used poor old God as a sure-fire smoke-screen."

They were both right.

Billy said: "Mercy talks about Jacob and his angel! It's boring! When Jacob wrestled with *his* angel, it was a one-time shot. Mercy wrestles with her angel twenty-four hours a day, and when the poor tired son of a bitch cries 'Uncle,' she grabs him by the throat and makes him put up his dukes and his broken wings. She'll fight that damn fool angel until she drops down dead on top of him."

Fat Jack said: "Looks like we got us another Joan of Arc, right here on Chicago's Near North Side. Downstairs on the street there are loose women selling themselves for carnal pleasure. Halfway up in the next block Hugh Hefner is sloshing around in his indoor swimming pool with his private collection of Kewpie dolls, and I'm sitting up here with two nuts who are eating dog bones in the middle of the floor. I see before me a sawed-off little Jewish promoter and an Irish mick of a dame who wants to talk about deeply religious fanatics . . . like the President of the United States. I have to be a very crazy person to put up with this."

Billy agreed that Fat Jack was, indeed, a very crazy person who was fortunate enough to be making a living out of his craziness and therefore had no room for complaint.

Then Billy rolled over on his back, and said to the ceiling: "How would you like to start a church?"

Fat Jack said: "Who, me?"

Billy said: "No Tiny Tim, not you."

I wasn't about to pick up that hot potato, so I said nothing.

Billy said: "I could do it for you in six months. By this time next year you could be back here in the Windy City for a gigantic revival meeting. The main event would be your walk from Navy Pier to the Planetarium on the surface of the lake!"

Fat Jack said: "Oh, Jesus Christ Almighty."

"Precisely," Billy said, and he wasn't even smiling!

I said I thought maybe it was time to clean up the bones and call it a night.

Fat Jack said: "It's only a quarter to three." Billy and Fat Jack simultaneously burst into a round of "One for My Baby."

Fat Jack asked Billy if he'd like to dance. Billy told him to go to hell.

Fat Jack said: "Speaking of hell, tell us more about the cockamamie church you're going to open up in the middle of Lake Michigan."

Billy said: "Clear a couple of million the first year, easy."

Fat Jack said: "Yeah, easy, no taxes on any of those God routines, y'know."

Billy said, yeah, he knew.

I cautioned Billy that whenever he took off on some loony idea like that, it always lasted for hours before he ran it into the ground. Tonight it was too late. He didn't even hear me. He said: "We can do a variation of the Aimee Semple McPherson thing. First we'll have you kidnapped."

I said: "Thanks a lot. That's my favorite all-time dream . . . to be kidnapped.

Billy said: "I know some guys who will do it for next to nothing."

I said that would be just fine. I asked how soon they could make it.

Billy wasn't listening.

He said: "We'll hide you out on a boat someplace. Maybe off-shore from my Jamaica place."

Fat Jack said: "What about off-shore from your island in Connecticut; it's closer."

Billy said: "No, it's too close. Somebody might find her."

I said that would surely be a dirty rotten shame . . . if anybody ever found me.

Billy sat up and looked right through me. He said: "We could start with a bunch of stories about how you have been acting kinda funny lately. People have been noticing that you aren't quite yourself . . . that you were heard to say you were listening to vibrations from Virgo, pulsations from Pluto."

Fat Jack said: "And bells ringing at Bellevue."

Billy said: "Then we could have a New York cabdriver tell the *Daily News* that you sat in the back seat of his cab and introduced him to Saint Peter, who told him not to worry, that his place in heaven was assured because of his holy mother's prayers of intercession all these years. We can have the cabdriver swear that Saint Peter materialized in his vehicle on Eighth Avenue between Forty-first and Forty-second streets . . . right around the corner from the beautiful Billy Rose Theater."

Fat Jack said: "Opportunistic son of a bitch. Horning in on Saint Peter's publicity."

Billy said: "Why the hell not? What did Saint Peter ever do for me . . . so far?" He told Fat Jack to keep his remarks under his hat. Fat Jack said that only little Jew bastards wore hats in the house. Billy said that was wrong . . . that only *good* little Jew bastards wore hats in the house, and Fat Jack said nobody could possibly ever call Billy Rose a *good* anything, that he was all bad, all b-a-d!

Billy agreed. He said he was all bad, all Jew, and all bastard, and would Fat Jack please shut up so he could think? There was silence.

Sir Malcolm sneezed a couple of times from his purloined bed in the next room. Fat Jack called out: "God bless you."

Billy said: "Look who's the religious fanatic now. God-blessing a dog, for chrissake."

Fat Jack said: "Listen, if you want to be such a smart-ass about it. The story goes that the night before Christmas, when there weren't any vacancies at any of the motels along the main drag in Bethlehem, the expectant mother had to give birth in a barn with a couple of cows and chickens. I'd like to lay you fifty to one that whenever Christ hears an animal sneeze, He blesses them, just for old times' sake."

Billy had taken off his shoes and was rubbing his stockinged feet.

He said: "I can cook up a couple of other sure-fire miracles! With eyewitnesses! Then we'll have you mysteriously disappear. We can have you snatched in front of the studio where they do the *Today* program. You had just been a guest on the show, and suddenly you were spirited away. We'll get you down to the Battery and over to Jersey on a tugboat, and from there it should be a lead-pipe cinch."

Fat Jack said: "Oh, sure, once you land in Jersey everything is a lead-pipe cinch."

Billy said: "I can remodel my old Aquacade out in Flushing for maybe half a million bucks. I can put a dome over it with wires and pulleys. We can fly in real angels. We'll keep the pool. It's big enough for you to baptize thousands at one dunk."

Fat Jack said: "Oh, God, not *dunk!*"

Billy threw his shoe at him. Then he said: "We can have you found again by having you suddenly appear at the Sunday afternoon tea dance at Roseland Ballroom. We'll have you waltz onto the floor all by yourself in white satin robes and strew Easter lilies as you glide across the floor. I'll have giant spotlights rigged up to celestial intensity, the orchestra will stop, and a single harp will play something really beautiful."

Fat Jack said: "How about 'Lulu's Back in Town'?"

Billy said: "All the papers will be full of it."

Fat Jack said: "All the papers are always full of it."

Billy said: "Not as full as you are of it."

Fat Jack said: "Takes one to know one, Billy boy."

Billy kicked my foot with his and said: "How would you like to take a course in hypnotism?"

Fat Jack said: "Why not send her to Haiti to voodoo school?"

Billy asked me how long it would take me to memorize the Bible. I told him I was a very quick study.

Fat Jack said: "You are also a very quick candidate for the funny farm if you listen to this little jerk any further. Do yourself a favor, throw him out the window."

Billy said: "The difference between a big fat dumb fella and a little skinny smart fella is what makes the world go 'round." He waited for it to sink in.

Fat Jack said: "I wish I had my notebook with me. I always write down pithy little gems I hear from the lips of the great ones. And I gotta tell you, my little friend, that that last line you laid on us was probably the pithiest little gem in a big world full of pith."

I said Fat Jack was right.

Billy lay back on the floor and stretched himself. He lifted his feisty little legs into the air and pedaled a make-believe inverted bicycle. While pumping vigorously, he said: "It's actually a hell of a good idea. I'm going to give it some serious thought as soon as I get back to New York."

Fat Jack stood up, folded his bathroom towel napkin, and placed the toilet tissue on Billy's belly. He said: "I gotta go down to my room and seriously think about getting some sleep."

Nobody tried to stop him.

I told Billy I thought Jewish guys insulted each other too much. Billy said that was how they showed their love for one another. I said I thought that was dumb. Billy said it was because I was a Gentile. Sometimes Billy was terribly anti-Gentile. I could usually calm him down by telling him how it was with me when I was growing up in Hyde Park in Chicago, a district "over-run with Jews," my people said. I was taught to be as anti-Jewish as Billy was taught to be anti-Gentile. I said I thought that we were too much alike . . . that's why we were taught to stay mad at each other. I could remember terrible things I was taught about the Jews.

There was a Jewish family across the hall from us on Kimbark Avenue . . . they cooked kosher. The odor of their food was likely no more offensive to us than our corned beef and cabbage was to them. I didn't exactly like the smell that came from their apartment but I didn't pay much attention to it. It made my aunt Noonie sick. She said: "Once the Jews move in you never get the smell out!"

The old Jewish lady and her old Jewish husband lived alone in their big dark apartment. Mack, the black janitor, said that all they did was eat and sleep because the old man was retired and they had nothing better to do.

"Leave it to the Jews," my mother said. "You don't catch any of them working until they drop dead on the spot. All the rest of us have to scrape like geese in gravel right up to the day they carry us out feet first, but the Jews are all retired nice as you please and sitting on the sand in Florida and driving their big Cadillacs right down the middle of the road!"

Aunt Noonie said: "Well, you know it is born right in them. They learn it at the mother's breast. Squeeze a dime until it hollers for help! And that's where they've got it all over the rest of us. They've all got the first dollar they ever made because they never let it out of their fists, and that's how the wind blows with your fancy Sears, Roebuck Jews, kiddo."

Then she said: "That smell in the hallway out there is enough to knock you right off your feet."

"Well, that's what you're smelling," my mother said. "Cooked feet. That's how they make soup over there, for God's sake, with feet! Cooked chicken feet! They just throw in the whole wrinkled foot— toenails and all! How would you like that staring you in the face when you sit down to supper? How much more can you get out of a chicken by boiling its filthy feet? Honest to God, I wouldn't care if I was starving to death, they'd have to force it down my gullet before I'd swallow a turd-covered chicken foot!"

My uncle Leo said: "Listen here, there's no two ways about it. The Jews own this whole town of Chicago, believe it or not by Mr. Ripley. Right up this very street, in the very next block, is the biggest Jewish hangout in the whole US of A! The University of Chicago! I swear I never laid eyes on a Jew until we moved up here from down home. Just look in the phone book . . . more Cohens than all the Smiths and Joneses put together."

My well-to-do aunt Dee Dee said: "Oh, don't blow a gasket, Leo. It isn't only out here on the South Side. There are just as many of them on the Near North Side, and out where I am in Rogers Park it is even worse. And we're the horses' asses in the ball game. Nobody but us, you know that, don't you? And I happen to know what I'm talking about." Aunt Dee owned 480 acres of fine down-state farmland in her name. Aunt Dee Dee didn't have to know what she was talking about. Everybody in the family treated her as if she did because everybody wanted to be remembered in her will.

She said: "I watch it happen, week after week, all of us playing right into their hands. Just like Pied Piper rats we are, the lot of us. Every single Sunday, rain or shine, I come out of Mass, and it is the same old story. Every Catholic in St. Polycarp's parish . . . all of them, Irish, Polacks, Eyetalians, all the foreigners, it doesn't matter. And all the holy Catholics hightailing it, the minute the priest has left the high altar, there they go right down the block to the Jewish delicatessen to get the newspaper and all the smoked fish and dill pickles in that smelly hole-in-the-wall, and the prices they charge in there! All the nice Catholics who maybe put a quarter in the poor box in church are shelling out a king's ransom to carry home all that junk to give themselves duodenal ulcers from a Jew delicatessen on a Catholic God's Sabbath Day!' Aunt Dee Dee had gotten going as she always did, and she ran out of breath and had to stop because she would start to swallow too much air, and it gave her "that awful gas again."

Uncle Leo piped in: "Yes, and you can bet your sweet life that the rich old Jewish bird who owns the delicatessen doesn't work on *his* holy day. No sirree! On Friday, when the sun goes down, he puts the padlock on his door and stays home and counts his shekels until Sunday morning, when he opens up for business, right after first Mass, shining up his cash register, waiting for all the Catholic fools to break their necks stumbling over each other, rushing out of holy Mass to fling their money around for greasy corned beef and black cement bread." He started to leave, but when he opened the door, he inhaled deeply and said: "I don't think I could stand it, living in a place like this. I just want to say one more thing, and then I'll have to go." He peered out into the hallway, then closed the door cautiously and said in a hoarse whisper: "What do you girls think is behind the fact that every Jewish boy in that university across the street is studying to be a lawyer? They already got the nation's economy right where they want it, in their back pockets, but if we think that's bad, wait until they get control of the *courts* in our country. Watch out, that's all I got to say, just watch out, I tell you."

Aunt Dee Dee said she wasn't born yesterday, and nobody could tell her anything about Jews that she didn't already know. As usually happened with my family, they had all run out of steam, and it was time to rest for a while.

Billy Rose used to tell me that his Jewish family believed they were being abused by the Irish people. My Irish people felt they were abused by Billy's people. Billy and I used to laugh because both sides were right, yet Billy and I knew that we both carried remnants of that dirty kind of garment around our own shoulders.

I used to say to Billy that I didn't know what two nice people like us were doing in this terrible world, and then Billy would say that he didn't know what two terrible people like us were doing in this nice world.

23

BILLY NEVER DID FIND OUT what he was doing here, and I don't suppose I will either, but whatever I find from here on in, I think I must continue the search on my own. It isn't altogether a matter of choice at this point.

Emerson says when you go solitary into your own chamber, you are not alone. He says God is there. He says that "God is very shy. He waits outside 'til all your company is gone and then enters into the lonely heart without ringing the bell." One of the few times in my life when I might accept what Emerson said happened to me in Dubuque, Iowa. I think fondly of Dubuque, no matter what. My own "lonely heart" spends a lot of time in solitary rooms waiting for a sign that God has slipped in unnoticed. I usually have to give it up because the old unhappiness comes back. I get God mixed up with my Guardian Angel, and the depressed little girl of long, long ago is back, guilt-ridden and fearful.

I never wanted a Guardian Angel. I didn't ask for one. One was assigned to me. Women can't be Guardian Angels . . . only men need apply! When you are six years old and a girl and you want to go to the bathroom, please remember that your Guardian Angel never leaves your side. Please do as I did . . . address the empty space outside the bathroom and explain to HIM that you would rather he hang around out here for a minute. Assure him, as I did, that you will not be in danger of sin in there, but you can't do what you have to do if HE is in there, and if you wet your panties, will HE explain it to your mother?

I opened doors and stepped aside and waited for what I thought was sufficient time for HIM to pass in front of me, wings and all. I never knew how big he was, how old he was, or whether he had a long beard . . . all I knew was that he was wherever I was all all all the time! There are so many things one needs to do in private. It is awful to feel that some fella in poltergeist garb is standing there, looking at you! I never felt my Guardian Angel was on my side. I hope he has abandoned me and is now working for the CIA. I'd like to think he was with Gordon Liddy at Watergate. Thinking about my Guardian Angel drives me right up the wall.

So, when I sit alone in a room, as Emerson says, I have to be very careful while I am waiting for God to enter "without ringing the bell" because it might very well turn out to be old Hawk-eye Guardian Angel again, still lurking around, waiting to watch my next foul deed!

Emerson's God did come to call one night in Dubuque, following a blizzard flight with some dead ducks. How I got together with those dead ducks is still incomprehensible to me. I know it couldn't have happened, but it did happen, and I have to live with it. I had started in New York. My plane was diverted to Kansas City! I placed a collect call to the man in Dubuque, telling him I could never make it for the appearance before his "packed house" to speak on alcoholism that evening. No planes to Dubuque! This fellow is a recovered alcoholic . . . and like all of us, he is doggedly determined. While they are drinking, most alcoholics are doggedly determined to die; while they are recovering, they are as doggedly determined to live, and sometimes they get very pushy about it. Within an hour this fellow had tracked down an obstetrician and his pilot buddy who were in flight from Nebraska to Dubuque in a small plane full of ducks they had just shot on a weekend of hunting. Oh, what the hell . . . I have to tell the whole truth . . . there was also a young woman. I don't know whose young woman she was, but I would hardly think she was built for hunting . . . not duck hunting anyhow. So this unholy *ménage à foie* was blissfully bumping its way homeward through the wintry, wasted skies of Missouri when they were radioed to turn about to the Kansas City Airport and pick up a stranded lady named me.

Off we went into the wild gray wander, flying blind all the way . . . baby doctor and pilot in front . . . alcoholic lady, sack of dead ducks, and "other woman" behind . . . behind the fellas in front, that is.

To die in a blizzard above Dubuque was nothing I had ever planned. Above the huge sack of dead ducks all I could see of the mysterious woman was a fake fur pompom on top of her orange woolen stocking cap . . . a pompom likely plucked direct from some poor rabbit's butt!

I have no use for people who hunt for what they call sport. I've always thought it was a cover-up for impotence. Men who shoot animals will never touch hand to this body, I can tell you. I surely wouldn't say that to my flying friends, however; not under the circumstances. Besides, if either of those men was going to touch a body, the pompom lady was surely closer to a possibility. She was young and quite pretty. I didn't like her very much. I decided, with the distance of the dead ducks between us, that she might be quite dumb. We had no communication during the flight. In the first place, we couldn't see each other over the sack of our bullet-ridden feathered friends, and the engine noises made speaking futile, but I figured, without knowing anything about her, that she must be dull-witted. I figure that about all pretty young women.

Dubuque was still there when we set down in a great white mass of snow and ice. That's one thing you can say about Dubuque. It's still there. I made my alcoholism speech and spent the night with the nuns at Clarke College.

I don't think my Guardian Angel was there that night in Dubuque. Maybe God sent him out for a pizza. I deeply love what happened that night. Surely it was just God and me.

It would be my last visit to my sweet and senile Sister Mary Leola Oliver, BVM. Her last years were lived out in Marian Hall, the nursing home on campus for the senior nuns; all the simple, narrow beds in all the severely stark rooms, all the wheelchairs, canes and walkers, all the grab-bars in the halls, all the devotedly caring, younger, sister-nurses in this place . . . a halfway house to heaven for women whose lives had been dedicated to God and His children . . . all these very old and ill "evergreen people" waiting for the morning they would not wake up; even a few confined on the top floor whose minds had left this earth forgetting to take their frail bodies in their penguin-type habits, slumped in rocking chairs or huddled in their beds. Behold the Handmaids of the Lord . . . I reverently thank each one of them for caring about me long ago. They knew me well and loved me in spite of it. Particularly Sister Mary Leola.

This last time she didn't recognize me. I had expected to stay at a hotel that night, but the nursing sisters had asked me to stay, and something made me want to . . . very much. My luggage had been lost . . . checked through from New York that morning, and all I had was a make-up case . . . no nightclothes . . . no robe. While they were fussing to make me comfortable—special towels, an extra blanket, etc.—they told me, cheerfully, that this humble bed, on which I would spend the night, had lost its previous occupant only yesterday. A ninety-year-old nun had breathed her last yesterday morning right here on this very bed. They patted the cotton spread in sisterly loving memory. They left me, then, for what I thought was the rest of the night.

I stood at the foot of the bed for a few minutes. It was not a comfortable feeling. The only chair in the room was a straight-backed armless chair that belonged to the maple desk. Spending the night in that chair wouldn't work. The floor was asphalt tile, the only rug was a tiny one next to the bed. There was, of course, no bathtub (the nurses had told me the shower rooms were down the hall, but sixteen years spent in schools with nuns positively prohibit even the *idea* of bathing in the same rooms they use). There was no place to sleep except on the bed, the bed of the newly dead.

I got out my toothbrush and face-cleaning junk and prepared my nocturnal toilette at the postage-stamp sink. The mirror above it was large enough for me to see both my eyes and teeth . . . but that's all. Vanity didn't have a prayer in this house of prayer.

Of course, I would have to sleep raw . . . no nightgown . . . and there I was . . . raw and erect . . . staring down at the bed when there was a knocking at the door. I could hardly open it as I was, so I put my coat on.

The dear whispering nursing nuns were excited. They had just had a wonderful idea. There were three of them, and they crowded into my tiny room and closed the door. Three fluttering little birds in long white skirts, and one coat-clutching naked person.

They had brought a tape recorder which was now placed smack in the center of the bed. It seems that the deceased sister was a great Chicagophile! And before she was bedridden, she would sing down in the therapy room as she wove her baskets or crocheted her afghans. Her favorite song was "Toddlin' Town . . ." a hymn to Chicago. She was teased about it, and she loved the attention. Sometimes, they said, she would sing it so loudly that visitors and tradespeople asked questions.

They told me, ruefully, that from the time she was stricken and ordered to bed . . . to this very bed . . . she never again sang "Toddlin' Town" until night before last. She had rung for a nurse, she was very weak, and she asked for a tape recorder. (Old people, when they are dying, ask for strange things. My uncle Thomas insisted on having his umbrella strapped to the foot of his bed.) The spunky old nun made them hold the microphone close to her mouth, and she gasped onto the tape a full chorus of her favorite song! The three young nuns in white wanted me to hear it.

The button marked "PLAY" was pushed. I held my coat about me, and we all stood there looking down at the ugly black box on the hundreds-of-times laundered coverlet. An eerie, wheezing, a capella voice oozed itself out of the wee speaker. In a wavering vibrato she was

singing to us . . . of Chicago, "that Toddlin' Town" . . . in tempo
. . . with a beat. She was an ancient imp gleefully reminding us of the
evils of her city. One of the nurse-nuns said: "Listen, can you hear it,
she's trying to clap her hands to keep the time. Can you hear that?"
The dying old chanteuse finished with a provocative flair as she
relished the word "Chicago" twice, and then as lustily as she could
she sang "My Home Town." There was a short silence on the tape.
We waited. She said, quite prettily: "Good-bye." And that was it.

The three nurses and I joined hands and bowed our heads over the
stilled box and the empty bed, and then they left me. I turned out the
lights, and at that moment, Emerson was right. I maneuvered my
naked body between the cold and tightly tucked sheets until I felt
what I imagined were the hollows made by my dead Chicago-loving
friend, and slowly the tears came . . . peacefully, warm and good. No
harm could come to me this night . . . I was surely not alone . . . in
Dubuque, Iowa . . . on a bluff above the Mississippi, in a building full
of fading holy women.

In a bed which had held the dead lay a silently weeping fugitive
wrapped in mystic communion with a shy visitor Emerson calls God. I
felt I was His beloved child in whom He was well pleased . . . for the
moment.

High Accuracy Instrumentation / High Speed (Table 1)

High Accuracy Instrumentation							High Speed					
Low Drift												
Op Amps					Preamps							
μA725C	μA725E	μA741E	208A	308A	μA726	μA727	μA715	μA748	μA776	μA777	301A	310
					$I_C = 10\,\mu A$ Temp. 0 to +85°C	Temp. −20 to +85°C	Feed-Forward	Programmable $I_{SET} = 500\,\mu A$	Feed-Forward	Feed-Forward		Voltage Follower
2.5	0.5	3.0	0.5	0.5	3.0	10	7.5	6.0	6.0	7.5	7.5	7.5
35	5.0	30	100	1.0	100	25	250	200	6.0	50	50	—
125	75	80	300	7.0	300	75	1500	500	10	250	250	7.0
250	1000	50	—	80	—	0.06	10	20	50	25	25	$.999 \times 10^{-3}$
±3.0	±3.0	±5.0	±5.0	±5.0	±5.0	±9.0	±6.0	±5.0	±1.2	±5.0	±5.0	±5.0
±22	±22	±22	±18	±20	±18	±18	±18	±18	±18	±20	±20	±18
1.0	1.0	1.0	1.0	1.0	20	1.0	65	1.0	1.2	1.0	1.0	20
—	—	0.6	0.3	0.3	—	—	18	0.5	15	0.5	0.5	30
—	—	0.6	0.6	0.6	—	—	100	6.0	15	6.0	15	—
—	—	0.6	—	—	—	—	38	2.0	15	2.0	5.0	—
±22	±22	±15	±15	±15	±30	±10	±15	±15	±15	±15	±15	±15
±22	±22	±30	±0.5	±0.5	±5.0	±15	±15	±30	±30	±30	±30	—
0.5	0.5	4.0	1.0	1.0	0.2	0.6	6.0	7.0	3.0	3.0	6.0	10
5.0	2.0	15	5.0	5.0	1.0	1.5						
X	X	X		X	X		X	X	X	X	X	X
X	X	X			X	X		X	X	X	X	X
		X			X							

High Accuracy Instrumentation / High Speed (Table 2)

High Accuracy Instrumentation						High Speed					
Low Drift											
Op Amps				Preamps							
μA725	μA725A	μA741A	108A	μA726	μA727	μA715	μA748	μA776	μA777	101A	110
				$I_C = 10\,\mu A$		Feed-Forward	Programmable $I_{SET} = 500\,\mu A$	Feed-Forward	Feed-Forward		Voltage Follower
1.0	0.5	3.0	0.5	2.5	10	5.0	5.0	5.0	2.0	2.0	4.0
20	5.0	30	0.2	50	15	250	200	3.0	10	10	—
100	75	80	2.0	150	40	750	500	7.5	75	75	3.0
1000	1000	50	80	—	0.06	15	50	50	50	50	$.999 \times 10^{-3}$
±3.0	±3.0	±5.0	—	±5.0	±9.0	±6.0	±5.0	±1.2	±5.0	±5.0	±5.0
±22	±22	±22	±20	±18	±18	±18	±22	±18	±20	±20	±18
1.0	1.0	1.0	1.0	20	1.0	65	1.0	1.2	1.0	1.0	20
—	—	0.6	0.3	—	—	18	0.5	15	0.5	0.5	30
—	—	0.6	0.6	—	—	100	6.0	15	6.0	6.0	—
—	—	0.6	—	—	—	38	2.0	15	2.0	2.0	—
±22	±22	±15	±15	±30	±10	±15	±15	±15	±15	±15	±15
±22	±22	±30	±0.5	±5.0	±15	±15	±30	±30	±30	±30	—
0.5	0.5	3.0	1.0	0.2	0.6	6.0	7.0	3.0	3.0	3.0	6.0
5.0	2.0	15	5.0	1.0	1.5						15
X	X	X		X		X	X	X	X	X	X
X	X	X	X	X	X	X	X	X	X	X	
		X		X							

Courtesy of Fairchild Semiconductor

COLLECTION OF
OP AMP TYPES
AND THEIR PARAMETERS

LINEAR OPERATIONAL AMPLIFIERS
$T_A = 25°C$

Device	Operating Temp. Range °C Min	Max	A_{VOL} Min K	R_i Min Ω	P_D mW	$|I_{io}|$ Max nA	I_b Max nA	CMV_i Min V	†Typ. Slew Rate SR V/µSec	V_o Min V	$|V_{io}|$ Max mV	Offset Adjust	Internal Compensation	Output Protection	Input Protection	JEDEC Package Type
709A	−55	+125	25	350K	108	50	200	±8	0.3	±12	1	no	no	no	no	TO-91, 99
709B	−55	+125	25	150K	165	200	500	±8	0.3	±12	5	no	no	no	no	TO-91, 99
709C	0	+70	15	50K	200	500	1500	±8	0.3	±12	10	no	no	no	no	TO-91, 99
739C(Dual)	0	+70	6.5	37K	420	1000	2000	±10	1.0	+12, −14	6	no	no	yes	yes	TO-116
741B	−55	+125	50	300K	85	200	500	±12	0.5	±12	5	yes	yes	yes	yes	TO-91, 99
741C	0	+70	20	150K	85	200	500	±12	0.5	±12	6	yes	yes	yes	yes	TO-91, 99
747B(Dual)	−55	+125	50	300K	85	200	500	±12	0.5	±12	5	yes	yes	yes	yes	TO-101, 1
747C(Dual)	0	+70	20	150K	85	200	500	±12	0.5	±12	6	yes	yes	yes	yes	TO-101, 1
748B	−55	+125	50	300K	85	200	500	±12	0.5	±12	5	yes	no	yes	yes	TO-99
748C	0	+70	20	150K	85	200	500	±12	0.5	±12	6	yes	no	yes	yes	TO-99
749B(Dual)	−55	+125	25	100K	220	400	750	±11	1.5	+12, −14.5	3	no	no	yes	yes	TO-116
749C(Dual)	0	+70	15	70K	330	500	1000	±11	1.5	+12, −14.5	6	no	no	yes	yes	TO-116
800B	−55	+125	10	250K	180	100	1000	±4	−	±6	50	no	no	no	no	TO-101
800D	−55	+125	10	100K	180	200	2000	±4	−	±12	−	no	no	no	no	TO-101
801B	−55	+125	10	250K	180	100	1000	±4	−	±12	50	no	no	no	no	TO-100
801D	−55	+125	10	100K	180	200	2000	±4	−	±12	−	no	no	no	no	TO-100
805B	−55	+125	30	500K	225	50	500	±8	2.5	±12	5	no	no	no	yes	TO-91, 99
805C	0	+100	10	100	225	100	1000	±8	2.5	±12	10	no	no	no	yes	TO-91, 99
806B	−55	+125	30	500	225	50	500	±8	2.5	±9	5	no	no	no	yes	TO-91, 99
806C	0	+100	10	100	225	100	1000	±8	2.5	±9	10	no	no	no	yes	TO-91, 99
807B	−55	+125	30	500	225	50	500	±8	2.5	±12	2.5	no	no	no	yes	TO-91, 99
808A	−55	+125	25	1M	225	15	50	±8	2.5	±12	5	no	no	no	yes	TO-91, 99
808B	−55	+125	25	1M	225	30	50	±8	2.5	±12	10	no	no	no	yes	TO-91, 99
809B	−55	+125	10	100	150	100	500	±10	−	±10	10	no	no	yes	yes	TO-99, 11
809C	0	+100	10	50	150	350	1000	±10	−	±10	10	no	no	yes	yes	TO-99, 11
810B(Dual)	−55	+125	10	100	150	100	500	±10	−	±10	10	no	no	yes	yes	TO-116
810C(Dual)	0	+100	10	50	150	350	1000	±10	−	±10	10	no	no	yes	yes	TO-116

†Unity Gain

LINEAR OPERATIONAL AMPLIFIERS
$T_A = 25°C$ (Cont.)

Device	Operating Temp. Range °C Min	Max	A_{VOL} Min K	R_i Min Ω	P_D mW	$|I_{io}|$ Max nA	I_b Max nA	CMV_i Min V	†Typ. Slew Rate SR V/μSec	V_o Min V	$|V_{io}|$ Max mV	Offset Adjust	Internal Compensation	Output Protection	Input Protection	JEDEC Package Type
15B	−55	+125°C	15	1M(typ)	210	250	750	±15	18	±10	±5	yes	yes	yes	yes	TO-100
'15C	0	+70°C	10	1M(typ)	300	1500	250	±15	18	±10	±7.5	yes	no	yes	yes	TO-100
'46B	−55	+125	100	25 M	90	5	30	±12.5	2.0	±12	±3	yes	no	yes	yes	TO-99
'46C	0	+70	50	15 M	75	15	50	±12	2.0	±12	±5	yes	no	yes	yes	TO-99
LM101A	−55	+125	50	1.5 M	120	10	25	±12	0.5	±12	±2	yes	no	yes	yes	TO-99
M101B	−55	+125	50	300 K	120	200	500	±12	0.5	±12	±5	yes	no	yes	yes	TO-99
LM201A	−25	+85	50	1.5 M	120	10	75	±12	0.5	±12	±2	yes	no	yes	yes	TO-99
LM201C	−25	+85	20	300 K	90	200	500	±12	0.5	±12	±7.5	yes	no	yes	yes	TO-99
LM301A	0	+70	25	500 K	120	50	250	±12	0.5	±12	±7.5	yes	no	no	yes	TO-99
LM307D	0	+70	25	500 K	120	50	250	±12	0.5	±12	±7.5	yes	no	no	yes	TO-99
'11B	−55	+125	10	100	150	100	500	±10	−	±10	10	no	no	yes	yes	TO-99, 116
'11C	0	+100	10	50	−	350	1000	±10	−	±10	10	no	no	yes	yes	TO-99, 116
'13C	0	+70	6	−	120	2000	5000	±5	−	−	4	no	no	yes	yes	TO-99, 116
'19B	−55	+125	5	50K	25	100	500	±4		±4	10	no	no	yes	yes	TO-99
'41B	−55	+125	50	300	85	200	500	±12	0.5	±12	5	no	no	yes	yes	TO-99
'41C	0	+100	20	150K	85	200	500	±12	0.5	±12	6	no	no	yes	yes	TO-99
344B	−55	+125	100	25 M	75	5	30	±12.5	2.0	±12	±3	yes	yes	yes	yes	TO-99
344C	0	+70	50	15 M	90	15	50	±12	2.0	±12	±5	yes	yes	yes	yes	TO-99
LM107B	−55	+125	50	1.5 M	120	10	75	±12	0.5	±12	±2	yes	yes	yes	yes	TO-99
LM207C	−25	+85	50	1.5 M	120	10	75	±12	0.5	±12	±2	yes	yes	yes	yes	TO-99
MC1437C(Dual)	0	+70	15	50K	200	500	1500	±8	0.3	±12	10	no	no	no	no	TO-116
MC1439C	0	+70	15	100	200	100	1000	±11	4.2	±10	7.5	no	no	yes	yes	TO-99, 116
MC1458C(Dual)	0	+70	20	150K	85	200	500	±12	0.5	±12	6	no	yes	yes	yes	TO-99, 116
MC1537B(Dual)	−55	+125	25	150K	165	200	500	±8	0.3	±12	5	no	no	no	no	TO-91, 99, 116
MC1539B	−55	+125	50	150	150	60	500	±11	4.2	±10	3	no	no	yes	yes	TO-99, 116
MC1558B(Dual)	−55	+125	50	300K	85	200	500	±12	0.5	±12	5	yes	yes	yes	yes	TO-101, 116

†Unity Gain

(Courtesy Teledyne Semiconductor)

SPECIFICATIONS
OF THE
709 OP AMP

	Parameter	Minimum	Typical	Maximum
A_{VOL}	Open loop voltage gain	15,000	45,000	
V_{io}	Input offset voltage		1 mV	7.5 mV
I_B	Input bias current		200 nA	1500 nA
I_{io}	Input offset current		50 nA	500 nA
R_o	Output resistance		150 Ω	
CMR (dB)	Common mode rejection	65 dB	90 dB	
R_i	Input resistance	50 kΩ	250 kΩ	

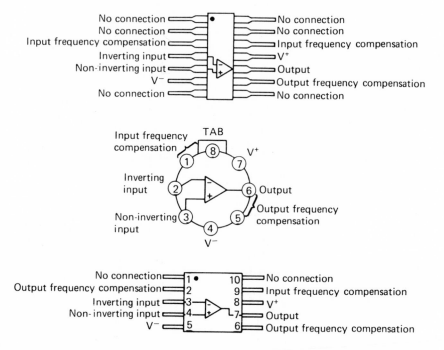

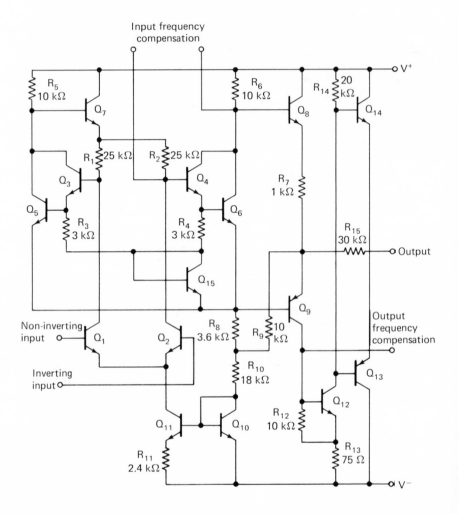

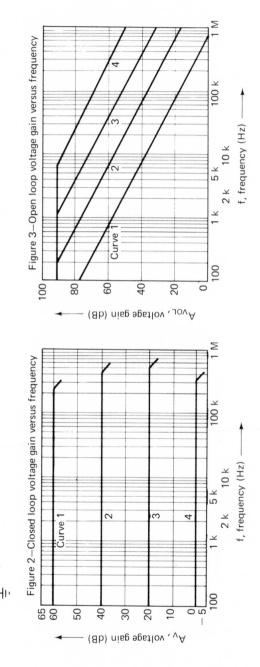

Figure 1

Fig. no.	Curve no.	Test conditions					
		$R_1 (\Omega)$	$R_2 (\Omega)$	$R_3 (\Omega)$	$C_1 (pF)$	$C_2 (pF)$
2	1	1 k	1 M	0	10	3
	2	10 k	1 M	1.5 k	100	3
	3	10 k	100 k	1.5 k	500	20
	4	10 k	10 k	1.5 k	5 k	200
3	1	0	∞	1.5 k	5 k	200
	2	0	∞	1.5 k	500	20
	3	0	∞	1.5 k	100	3
	4	0	∞	0	10	3

Figure 2—Closed loop voltage gain versus frequency

Figure 3—Open loop voltage gain versus frequency

SPECIFICATIONS
OF THE
741 OP AMP

	Parameters	Minimum	Typical	Maximum
A_{VOL}	Open loop voltage gain	50,000	200,000	
V_{io}	Input offset voltage		1 mV	6 mV
I_B	Input bias current		80 nA	500 nA
I_{io}	Input offset current		20 nA	200 nA
R_o	Output resistance		75 Ω	
CMR (dB)	Common mode rejection	70 dB	90 dB	
R_i	Input resistance	300 kΩ	2 MΩ	

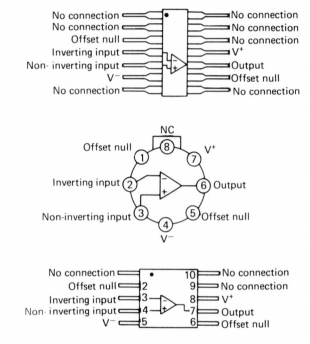

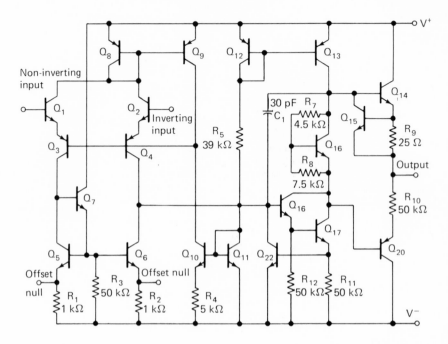

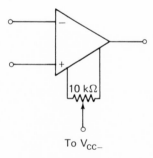

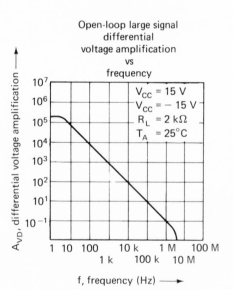

Open-loop large signal
differential
voltage amplification
vs
frequency

SPECIFICATIONS
OF THE
777 OP AMP

Electrical characteristics for 777 ($V_S = \pm 15$ V, $T_A = 25°C$, $C_C = 30$ pF unless otherwise specified)

Parameters		Conditions	Min.	Typ.	Max.	Units
Input offset voltage		$R_S \leqslant 50$ kΩ		0.5	2.0	mV
Input offset current				0.25	3.0	nA
Input bias current				8.0	25	nA
Input resistance			2.0	10.0		MΩ
Input capacitance				3.0		pF
Offset voltage adjustment range				± 25		mV
Large signal voltage gain		$R_L \geqslant 2$ kΩ, $V_{OUT} = \pm 10$ V	50,000	250,000		V/V
Output resistance				100		Ω
Output short-circuit current				± 25		mA
Supply current				1.9	2.8	mA
Power consumption				60	85	mW
Transient response (Voltage follower, gain of 1)	Risetime	$V_{IN} = 20$ mV, $C_C = 30$ pF, $R_L = 2$ kΩ, $C_L \leqslant 100$ pF		0.3		µs
	Overshoot			5.0		%
Slew rate (Voltage follower, gain of 1)		$R_L \geqslant 2$ kΩ		0.5		V/µs
Transient response (Voltage follower, gain of 10)	Risetime	$V_{IN} = 20$ mV, $C_C = 3.5$ pF, $R_L = 2$ kΩ, $C_L \leqslant 100$ pF		0.2		µs
	Overshoot			5.0		%
Slew rate (Voltage follower, gain of 10)		$R_L \geqslant 2$ kΩ, $C_C = 3.5$ pF		5.5		V/µs

- Low offset voltage and offset current
- Low offset voltage and current drift
- Low input bias current
- Low input noise voltage
- Large common-mode and differential voltage ranges

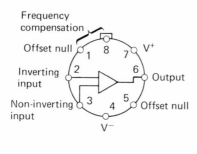

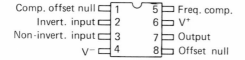

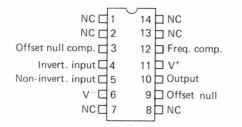

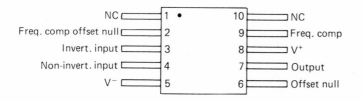

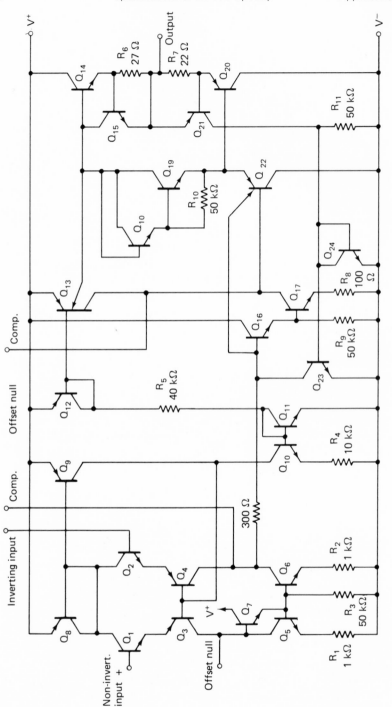

DERIVATION OF
EQUATION (4-4)

As shown in the circuit of Fig. A1, the bias current I_{B_1} flows through two

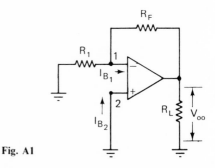

Fig. A1

paths, R_1 and R_F. This current sees essentially the resistors R_1 and R_F in parallel and causes a voltage drop across them, which is the voltage at the inverting input 1 to ground. This can be shown as

$$V_1 = \left(\frac{R_1 R_F}{R_1 + R_F}\right) I_{B_1}$$

The current I_{B_2} sees no resistance between the noninverting input 2 and ground, and therefore the voltage at this input is $V_2 = 0$ V to ground. Thus the differential input voltage caused by these currents is $V_1 - V_2 = V_1$. This voltage V_1 is amplified by the circuit's closed-loop gain, resulting in an output offset of

$$V_{oo} = A_v V_1 \cong -\frac{R_F}{R_1} V_1 = -\frac{R_F}{R_1}\left(\frac{R_1 R_F}{R_1 + R_F}\right) I_{B_1} = \frac{-R_F R_F}{R_1 + R_F}(I_{B_1})$$

283

Since R_F^2 is much larger than $R_1 + R_F$, the above simplifies to

$$V_{oo} \cong \frac{R_F^2}{R_F}(I_{B_1}) = R_F I_{B_1} \qquad (4\text{-}4)$$

where V_{oo} is positive if I_{B_1} flows into the Op Amp, as it does in most bipolar input Op Amps.

DERIVATION OF
EQUATION (4-7)

As shown in the circuit of Fig. A2, the bias current I_{B_1} flows through two

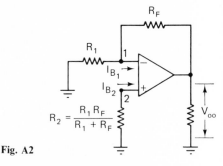

Fig. A2

paths, R_1 and R_F. This current sees essentially resistors R_1 and R_F in parallel and causes a voltage drop across them and at the input 1 with respect to ground, that is

$$V_1 = \left(\frac{R_1 R_F}{R_1 + R_F}\right) I_{B_1}$$

The current I_{B_2} flows through resistance R_2, causing input 2 to be off ground by

$$V_2 = R_2 I_{B_2} = \left(\frac{R_1 R_F}{R_1 + R_F}\right) I_{B_1}$$

The difference in these voltages, $V_1 - V_2$, is the differential input which is amplified by the circuit's closed-loop gain, that is,

$$V_{oo} = A_v(V_1 - V_2) = -\frac{R_F}{R_1}\left[\frac{R_1 R_F}{R_1 + R_F}(I_{B_1}) - \frac{R_1 R_F}{R_1 + R_F}(I_{B_2})\right]$$

$$= \frac{R_F^2}{R_1 + R_F}(I_{B_1} - I_{B_2})$$

Since R_F^2 is much larger than $R_1 + R_F$ and since $I_{B_1} - I_{B_2} = I_{io}$, then

$$V_{oo} \cong R_F I_{io} \qquad\qquad (4\text{-}7)$$

where V_{oo} is either positive or negative, depending on whether I_{B_1} is the larger or I_{B_2} is the larger of the two bias currents.

SELECTION OF
COUPLING CAPACITORS

The value of coupling capacitance C used between ac amplifier stages is determined by the required low frequency response and the dynamic output and input resistances of the stages being coupled. Generally, lower frequencies and smaller resistances require larger coupling capacitors.

If f_1 is the required low end of the bandwidth (that is, the low frequency at which the signal being coupled is 0.707 of its value at medium frequencies), then

$$C = \frac{1}{2\pi f_1(R_o + R_i)}$$

where

C is the capacitance between the two stages being coupled

R_o is the effective ac output resistance of the first stage

and

R_i is the effective ac input resistance of the second stage.

COLLECTION
OF OP AMP
CIRCUITS

All diagrams on pp. 289–306 are courtesy of the National Semi-conductor Corporation.

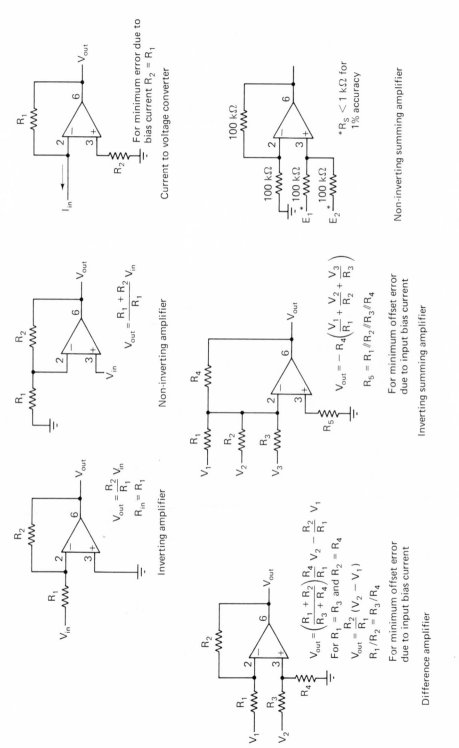

Current to voltage converter

For minimum error due to bias current $R_2 = R_1$

Non-inverting summing amplifier

$*R_S < 1\,k\Omega$ for 1% accuracy

Non-inverting amplifier

$$V_{out} = \frac{R_1 + R_2}{R_1}\, V_{in}$$

Inverting summing amplifier

$$V_{out} = -R_4\left(\frac{V_1}{R_1} + \frac{V_2}{R_2} + \frac{V_3}{R_3}\right) / R_4$$

$$R_5 = R_1 /\!/ R_2 /\!/ R_3 /\!/ R_4$$

For minimum offset error due to input bias current

Inverting amplifier

$$V_{out} = \frac{R_2}{R_1}\, V_{in}$$

$$R_{in} = R_1$$

Difference amplifier

$$V_{out} = \left(\frac{R_1 + R_2}{R_3 + R_4}\right)\frac{R_4}{R_1}\, V_2 - \frac{R_2}{R_1}\, V_1$$

For $R_1 = R_3$ and $R_2 = R_4$

$$V_{out} = \frac{R_2}{R_1}\,(V_2 - V_1)$$

$$R_1 / R_2 = R_3 / R_4$$

For minimum offset error due to input bias current

289

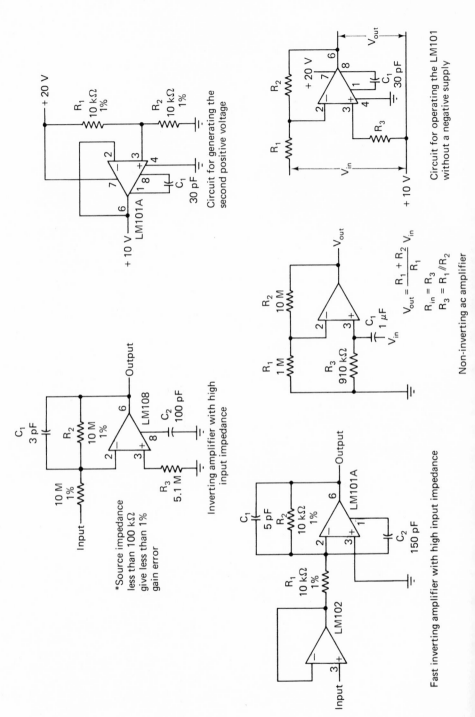

Circuit for generating the second positive voltage

Circuit for operating the LM101 without a negative supply

$$V_{out} = \frac{R_1 + R_2}{R_1} V_{in}$$

$R_{in} = R_3$
$R_3 = R_1 /\!/ R_2$

Non-inverting ac amplifier

Inverting amplifier with high input impedance

*Source impedance less than 100 kΩ give less than 1% gain error

Fast inverting amplifier with high input impedance

290

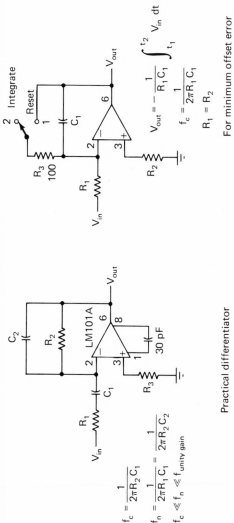

Integrate

Reset

V_{out}

C_1

6

1

2

3

+

−

R_3 100

R_1

R_2

V_{in}

$$V_{out} = -\frac{1}{R_1 C_1} \int_{t_1}^{t_2} V_{in}\, dt$$

$$f_c = \frac{1}{2\pi R_1 C_1}$$

$$R_1 = R_2$$

For minimum offset error
due to input bias current

Integrator

C_2

R_2

LM101A

6

8

2

3

+

−

1

30 pF

R_1

C_1

R_3

V_{in}

V_{out}

$$f_c = \frac{1}{2\pi R_2 C_1}$$

$$f_n = \frac{1}{2\pi R_1 C_1} = \frac{1}{2\pi R_2 C_2}$$

$$f_c \ll f_n \ll f_{unity\ gain}$$

Practical differentiator

V_{out}

R_2 100 kΩ

R_5 10 kΩ

6

2

3

+

−

R_1 100 kΩ

C_1 47 μF

V_{in} +5 V

R_4 100 kΩ

R_3 100 kΩ

D_1 6.2 V

D_2 6.2 V

Pulse width modulator

291

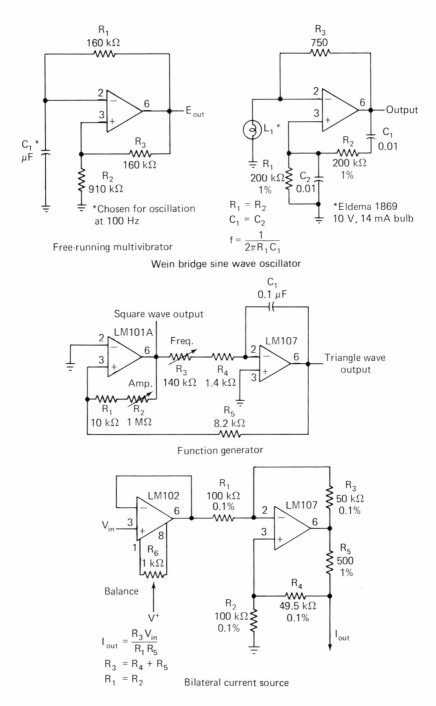

R_1
160 kΩ

2
3
6
E_{out}

C_1 *
μF

R_3
160 kΩ

R_2
910 kΩ

*Chosen for oscillation
at 100 Hz

Free-running multivibrator

R_3
750

2
3
6
Output

L_1 *

C_1
0.01

R_2
200 kΩ
1%

R_1
200 kΩ
1%

C_2
0.01

$R_1 = R_2$
$C_1 = C_2$

*Eldema 1869
10 V, 14 mA bulb

$$f = \frac{1}{2\pi R_1 C_1}$$

Wein bridge sine wave oscillator

Square wave output

LM101A

2
3
6

Freq.

R_3
140 kΩ

R_4
1.4 kΩ

Amp.

R_1
10 kΩ

R_2
1 MΩ

C_1
0.1 μF

LM107

2
3
6
Triangle wave
output

R_5
8.2 kΩ

Function generator

LM102

6

V_{in}
3
+
8
1
R_6
1 kΩ

Balance

V^+

R_1
100 kΩ
0.1%

2
LM107
6
3
+

R_3
50 kΩ
0.1%

R_5
500
1%

R_4
49.5 kΩ
0.1%

R_2
100 kΩ
0.1%

I_{out}

$$I_{out} = \frac{R_3 V_{in}}{R_1 R_5}$$

$R_3 = R_4 + R_5$
$R_1 = R_2$

Bilateral current source

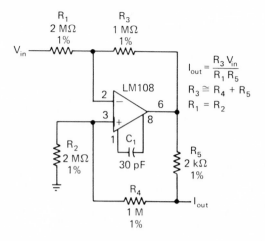

$$I_{out} = \frac{R_3 V_{in}}{R_1 R_5}$$

$$R_3 \cong R_4 + R_5$$

$$R_1 = R_2$$

Bilateral current source

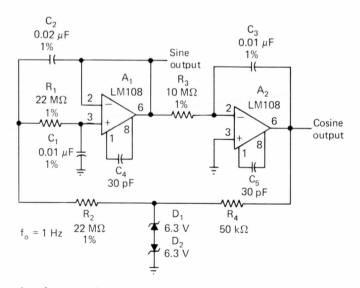

$f_o = 1\ Hz$

Low frequency sine wave generator with quadrature output

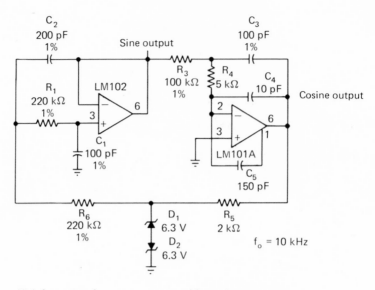

High frequency sine wave generator with quadrature output

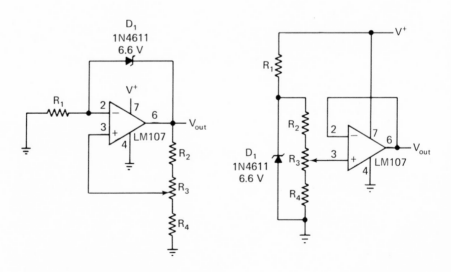

Positive voltage reference   Positive voltage reference

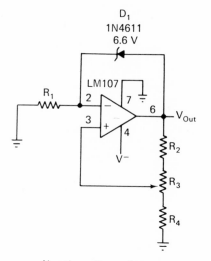

Negative voltage reference

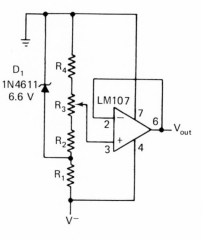

Negative voltage reference

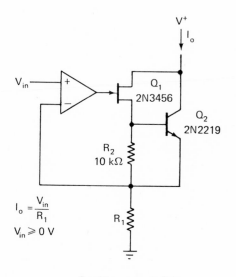

Precision current sink

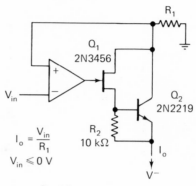

$$I_o = \frac{V_{in}}{R_1}$$

$$V_{in} \leq 0 \text{ V}$$

Precision current source

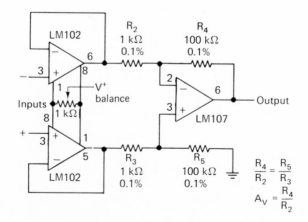

$$\frac{R_4}{R_2} = \frac{R_5}{R_3}$$

$$A_V = \frac{R_4}{R_2}$$

Differential-input instrumentation amplifier

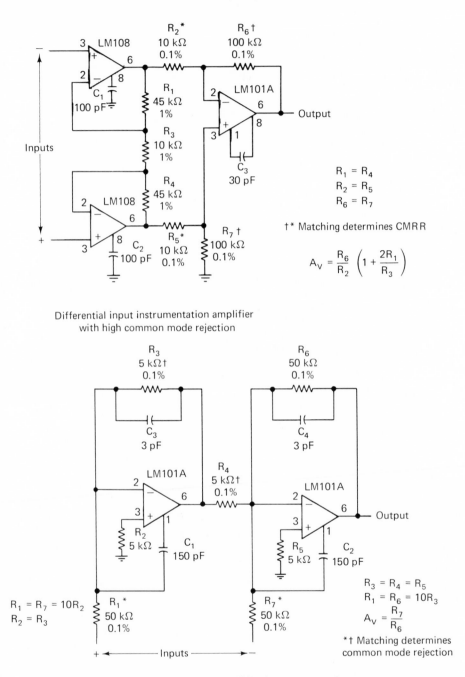

Differential input instrumentation amplifier
with high common mode rejection

$$A_V = \frac{R_6}{R_2}\left(1 + \frac{2R_1}{R_3}\right)$$

$R_1 = R_4$
$R_2 = R_5$
$R_6 = R_7$

†* Matching determines CMRR

$R_3 = R_4 = R_5$
$R_1 = R_6 = 10R_3$
$$A_V = \frac{R_7}{R_6}$$

*† Matching determines
common mode rejection

$R_1 = R_7 = 10R_2$
$R_2 = R_3$

Instrumentation amplifier with ± 100 volt common mode range

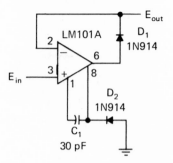

Precision diode

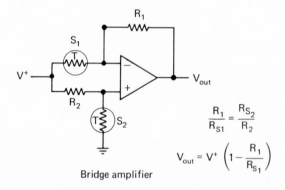

$$\frac{R_1}{R_{S1}} = \frac{R_{S_2}}{R_2}$$

$$V_{out} = V^+ \left(1 - \frac{R_1}{R_{S_1}}\right)$$

Bridge amplifier

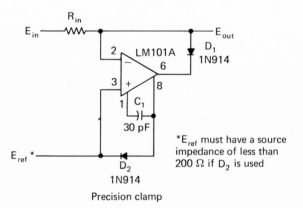

*E_{ref} must have a source impedance of less than 200 Ω if D_2 is used

Precision clamp

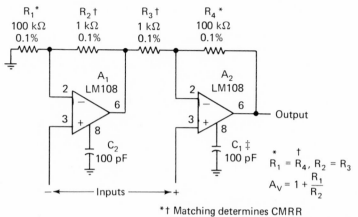

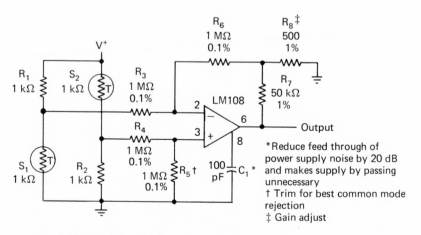

High input impedance instrumentation amplifier

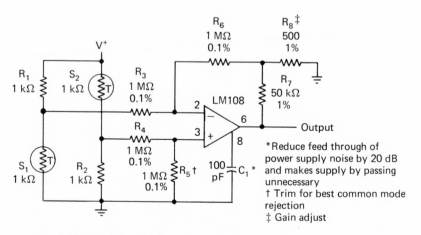

Bridge amplifier with low noise compensation

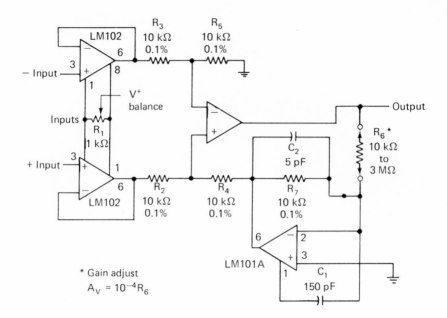

Variable gain, differential-input instrumentation amplifier

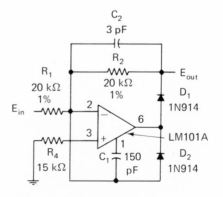

Fast half wave rectifier

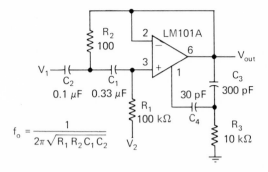

$$f_o = \frac{1}{2\pi \sqrt{R_1 R_2 C_1 C_2}}$$

Tuned circuit

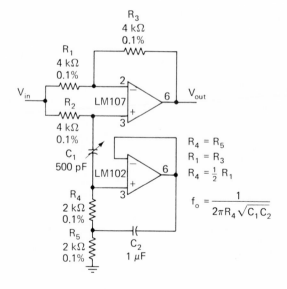

$R_4 = R_5$

$R_1 = R_3$

$R_4 = \frac{1}{2} R_1$

$$f_o = \frac{1}{2\pi R_4 \sqrt{C_1 C_2}}$$

Easily tuned notch filter

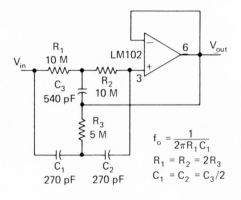

High Q notch filter

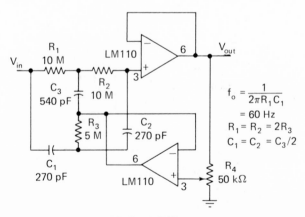

Adjustable Q notch filter

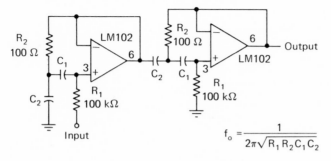

$$f_o = \frac{1}{2\pi\sqrt{R_1 R_2 C_1 C_2}}$$

Two-stage tuned circuit

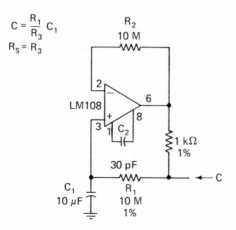

$$C = \frac{R_1}{R_3} C_1$$

$$R_S = R_3$$

Capacitance multiplier

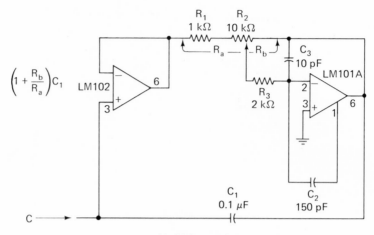

Variable capacitance multiplier

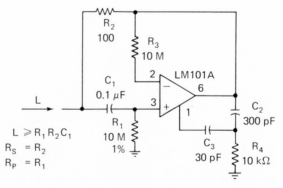

Simulated inductor

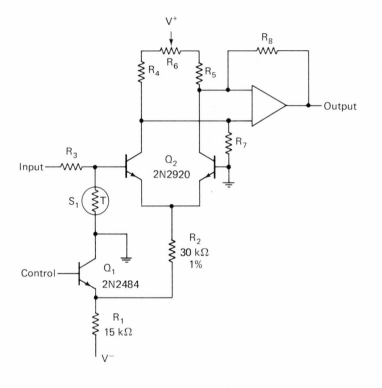

Voltage controlled gain circuit

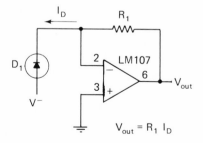

$$V_{out} = R_1 I_D$$

Photodiode amplifier

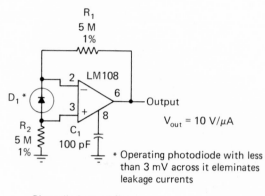

$V_{out} = 10 \text{ V}/\mu A$

* Operating photodiode with less than 3 mV across it eleminates leakage currents

Photodiode amplifier

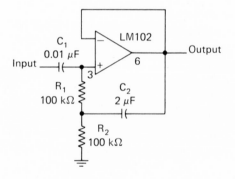

High input impedance ac follower

PACKAGE TYPES

Metal package
TO-99
8 pin

Ceramic package
TO-116
14 pin

TO-100 and TO-101
10 pin

Plastic package
TO-116
14 pin

Ceramic package
TO-91
10 pin

ANSWERS TO
ODD-NUMBERED
PROBLEMS

Chapter 1. 1. $I_B \cong 6.25\,\mu\text{A}$. 3. $V_{c_1} \cong V_{c_2} \cong 6.4\,\text{V}$. 5. $72 \leq V_{od}/V_{id} \leq 144$.
7. Increase the resistance between pin 3 and $-V_{EE}$ from 2.7 kΩ to a slightly larger
value or slightly decrease the resistance between pin 4 and $-V_{EE}$.

Chapter 3. 1. (b). 3. (e). 5. $A_v = 2$, V_o has waveform (a). 7. $A_v = 101$, V_o has
waveform (f). 9. As seen to the right of point x, the circuit of Fig. 3-17a has the more
constant input resistance. 11. About 20 mV dc. 13. About 3 V dc. 15. $R_{o(\text{eff})} =$
0.375 Ω. 17. $V_o = 400$ mV dc. 19. $A_{v(\text{min})} = 2$, $A_{v(\text{max})} = 202$. 21. Waveform V_o is
unclipped and 180° out of phase with the input with each of its peaks 150 times larger.
23. Waveform V_o is a sawtooth for the beginning alternations and is 180° out of phase
with the input. It is clipped at plus or minus 5.5 V at times t_4, t_5, t_6, t_7, etc. 25. The
output is in phase with the input and is unclipped on the first alternation with a peak
twice that of the input. The remaining alternations are clipped at about ± 3 V. 27. The
output is out of phase with the input and is not clipped on the first two alternations.
The remaining alternations are clipped at about ± 13 V.

Chapter 4. 1. -40. 3. -101. 5. Between 200 and 250 mV dc. 7. About 20 mV
dc. 9. Between 220 mV and 280 mV dc. 11. 990 Ω or about 1 kΩ. 13. About
20 mV dc. 15. Replace the 200 kΩ resistor with a smaller one or replace the 100 Ω
resistor with a larger resistance value. 17. 0.2 V. 19. 0.3 V. 21. Provides capability
to reduce (null) the output offset to zero. 23. About 6.2 V dc.

Chapter 5. 1. 80 dB. 3. (a) Output signal varies from 3 V to -2 V, (b) Output
noise is 1 V rms-60 Hz because there is no *CMRR* with this circuit which is not wired
in differential mode. 5. (a) 1.82 V, (b) -5 V to 5 V, (c) 20 μV rms-60 Hz. 7. $+15$ V
and -12 V. 9. 24 V. 11. 2.5 V and -2.5 V. 13. 4.8. 15. 0.2 V peak. 17. 600 to
5700. 19. 100. 21. -11. 23. $V_{CM} = 5.3$ V dc, $V_o = -4.4$ V dc.

Chapter 6. 1. 1 MHz. 3. $C_1 = 10$ pF, $R_1 = 0$, $C_2 = 3$ pF. 5. 1 MHz. 7. About
50 kHz. 9. $A_v = A_{VOL}$, BW less than 10 Hz. 11. -20 dB/decade or -6 dB/octave.

13. About 20 kHz. 15. $V_{cmo} = 0.2\,\mu V$ rms-60 Hz. 17. V_o is a sawtooth with 4V peak-to-peak amplitude. 19. $V_{no} \cong 50\,\mu V$ rms.

Chapter 7. 1. $\Delta V_{io} \cong \pm 40\,\mu V$, $\Delta V_{oo} \cong \pm 8\,mV$. 3. About $8\,\mu V$ rms. 5. $\Delta V_{oo} = 4.5\,mV$. 7. (a) about 500.2 mV. (b) about 500.3 mV. 9. (a) 97.5 ns. (b) 110 ns.

Chapter 8. 1. $A_v = 21$. 3. $A_v = 11$, $R \cong 1.8\,k\Omega$. 5. $A_v \cong 1$. 7. (a) 6.2 V, (b) 20. 9. 10.2 and 2.2 V, (b) $+4$ and -4 V. 11. (a) -2.5 V dc, (b) About 570 Ω. 13. (a) -0.8 V, (b) -4 V. 15. $y' = 1.6$ V, $y = -1.6$ V, $z = -0.4$ V. 17. $V_o \cong 6.6$ V, $R \cong 167\,\Omega$. 19. $V_o' \cong 11$ V, $V_{R_s} \cong 7.1$ V. 21. (a) About 15 W, (b) About 0.5 W. 23. $C_1 = 40\,nF$, $C_2 = 20\,nF$. 25. About 10 kHz.

Chapter 9. 1. Without the zener diodes, the output would be a sinusoid with 10 V peaks. With these zeners, the positive and negative alternations are clipped at about 6 V. 3. Without the diodes this circuit's output would be sinusoidal peaking at 11 V. With them, the positive alternations are clipped at approximately 4 V, but the negative alternations are not clipped. 5. Zener D_1 is forward biased when the output V_o attempts to swing negatively causing V_o to actually be about 0 V at such times. The positive alternations appear sinusoidal and are clipped at approximately 4 V. 7. 2000/1. 9. (a) $V_{o1} = -15$ V, $V_{o2} = 15$ V, $V_{o3} = 15$ V, (b) $V_{o1} = -15$ V, $V_{o2} = -15$ V, $V_{o3} = 15$ V, (c) $V_{oi} = V_{o2} = V_{o3} = -15$ V. 11. V_L is spiked (differentiated) with positive spikes appearing when V_s passes through zero into positive alternations and negative spikes appearing as V_s passes through zero into negative alternations.

Chapter 10. 1. $f = 250$ Hz. 3. 26 V. 5. The sawtooth output V_o' will have its positive and negative alternations clipped. 7. V_o' will be a nonsymmetrical sawtooth where half the alternations have a time period that is more than 20 times longer than the remaining alternations. 9. $C_1 = 4\,nF$, $C_2 = 2\,nF$, and $R_2 = 80\,k\Omega$. 11. $R_2 = 160\,k\Omega$, $C_1 = C_2 = 2\,nF$.

Chapter 11. 1. (a) 1.2 V, (b) 2.8 V. 3. Output is rectangular with positive alternations of 4.55 msec and 5.45 msec negative alternations. 5. 0.5 msec. 7. 0.75 V.

INDEX